The American Monetary System

William H. Wallace

The American Monetary System

An Insider's View of Financial Institutions, Markets and Monetary Policy

 Springer

William H. Wallace
Dallas, TX, USA

ISBN 978-3-319-02906-1   ISBN 978-3-319-02907-8 (eBook)
DOI 10.1007/978-3-319-02907-8
Springer Cham Heidelberg New York Dordrecht London

Library of Congress Control Number: 2013956361

Printed on acid-free paper

Springer is part of Springer Science+Business Media (www.springer.com)

To Amy, Doug and Bruce With Love and Gratitude

Acknowledgments

I would like to thank my good friend, Dr. Dede W. Casad, author and literary critic, who has encouraged me to prepare this book for publication. I am grateful to her for her persistence in seeing me through the project. Special thanks also go to my friend and colleague, Dr. Todd Jewell, Chairman of the Department of Economics at the University of North Texas, for his encouragement throughout the project. Finally, I am grateful to the many students at North Texas who used earlier versions of this book in my classes and have contributed immeasurably to corrections of fact and clarifications of concepts that I did not make clear initially.

Foreword

This book is a true tour de force – a readable, comprehensive description of the evolution of The American Monetary System since the founding of the nation. Very few would have the intellectual capacity, the talent, the training and the experience to put it all in perspective. But somehow Bill Wallace has done the job.

I worked with Bill closely when I was the Chairman of the Federal Reserve Board. Consequently, I was a principal beneficiary of his long experience, his well-balanced judgment, and his dedication to the Federal Reserve and its leadership.

His varied responsibilities over the decades at "the Fed" provided a superb vantage point from which he could observe and participate in rapid financial change, the associated turbulence, and the official response to all-too-frequent crises. What I was slow to recognize was his ability to write so clearly and simply, making this book not only a point of reference about the world of finance but a well-informed readable analysis of one important element of American economic and political life.

Bill Wallace was a model public servant, bringing his analytical skills together with a clear sense of the practical problems of monetary policy and financial regulation. He also loved to teach. It is the combination of those interests that make this book, with its subtitle An Insider's View of Financial Institutions, Markets and Monetary Policy, so relevant today.

The book is not a blow-by-blow description of the latest and largest crisis. It does something more important. It puts today's problems in the context of inevitable change – change that has recurrent market characteristics even as it has features unique to a world of computers and the internet, of instantaneous communication, and of "synthetic" securities and "derivatives" instruments.

Quite simply, it is a volume that deserves space on your book shelf.

Paul Volcker

Preface

Todays' financial system evokes many strong emotional reactions. Some people fear it because they can be hurt by it; others are exhilarated by it because of the perceived opportunity it brings to amass great wealth. Some throw up their hands and confess not to understand it at all. The system is considerably more complex than in years past – as new financial instruments have been introduced that are not well understood even by a number of people and institutions that invest in them. Numerous high-risk opportunities are available, and the number of people who unwittingly wander into such ventures seems to grow daily. Also, there is the realization that people's lives can be affected by the financial system without their overt participation in it. By taking no action at all, a person's pension can be eviscerated by a sudden decline in interest rates, or a rise in rates can increase the monthly payments on a mortgage, credit cards, or other debt.

An earlier version of this manuscript originated as a text that I used in teaching a senior level course in money and banking at the University of North Texas. But after some years of teaching that subject, and after 27 years with the Federal Reserve System and a variety of consulting assignments in banking, I was convinced that there is a need for a treatise for the uninitiated reader who simply wants to understand the system. It is my purpose to do exactly that. I hope to put some of the strong feelings that many people hold about the financial world into perspective.

To understand fully our monetary system as it now exists, we must look back to the beginning of the republic. Certain events stand out as milestones in our financial history that have had profound influences upon the direction in which the American financial system has developed. Those include our attempt to implement the policies of Alexander Hamilton, who believed in a strong central bank (or government bank) to handle the financial needs of the country, and the centralization of the public debt. These policies had the support of President Washington, but were strongly opposed by other influential leaders such as Jefferson and Madison.

The influence of our British forebears have had a strong influence on American thinking about financial affairs, such as our on-again, off-again relationship with the gold standard, which created for us as many problems as it did advantages, until it was finally abolished by President Nixon in 1971. Now, virtually the whole world operates on the basis of "fiat" currencies in which the value of a currency depends solely on peoples' faith in the government that issues it.

It was in the twentieth century, however, that most of the development occurred that has resulted in the financial system that we know today. Among these events were:

- The passage of the Federal Reserve Act in 1913, which established a central bank that has been an important factor in shaping the financial system of the United States for the past 100 years.
- The implementation of deposit insurance, along with certain other provisions of the Glass-Steagall Act of 1933, that greatly influenced banking practices for generations.
- The Bretton-Woods agreements, which laid the groundwork for the Eurodollar market, that, in turn, firmly established the Dollar as the world's reserve currency.
- The actions of the Federal Reserve System under Chairman Paul Volcker's leadership in the early 1980s that subdued inflation and, by example, influenced numerous other countries to bring inflation under control in order to become effective participants in the globalizing world economy.
- The forces of technological innovation, which have increased competition and globalization over the past four to five decades and revolutionized the way we do business in general. In particular, technology has impacted the financial industry by making financial services available to all people in a more efficient, less costly and more secure manner.

I shall discuss the interactions of financial institutions and markets in the U.S. economy today, and explain why each part of this financial structure is important in achieving stability and growth in the economy. The particular role of the central bank in implementing monetary policy to protect the nation's currency and to promote economic growth is stressed. Comparisons are made with other financially-mature countries in the world (basically the G-8: USA, UK, Canada, Japan, Germany, France, Italy and Russia).

We observe that the U.S. financial system is the envy of other nations – basically because it works effectively and efficiently. This is not to imply that the U.S. system is perfect in any sense of the word. It has its flaws, and it is riddled from time to time with corruption – as has been clear since the turn of the twenty-first century, when banks and other financial institutions have become involved in corrupt practices with firms like Enron, WorldCom, etc., and in deceitful practices such as misuse of customer funds and misrepresentation of investments to potential investors. These charges have produced heavy fines upon a number of our best-known financial institutions since the recent financial crisis.

Also, the system is prone to excesses and abuses, which can lead to financial crises, such as the recent sub-prime mortgage debacle that began in August 2007, and continues to drag the economy down 6 years later. Numerous other financial crises have occurred over the years which have become wake-up calls, or learning experiences, that have led to reforms in practices as well as regulations. We shall look at several of these crises to see why they occurred and the impact that they had on the economy at large, and on the credibility of the financial system.

How the Congress and the regulators attempt to deal with financial crises is discussed, and why they have had only limited to moderate success in doing so. In this context, we examine the Dodd-Frank Act, passed by Congress in 2010 for regulatory reform, and the ongoing process of implementing the changes it mandates. I hope that readers will form opinions of their own on how effective those changes are likely to be in the longer term.

Basically, however, the fact remains that the U.S. financial system works well and continues to be emulated by numerous other countries. Therefore, it would be correct to say that the study of the U.S. financial system is tantamount to the study of the world's financial system – not that all countries do everything the same way. Differences do exist, but the trend is that major countries are coming closer together in financial practices as well as in laws and regulations. As nations learn from each other's experiences, systems become more alike. Common practices are more necessary today because of the contagion effect that technological change has produced, which causes problems that develop in one part of the world to be quickly transmitted around the globe – for example, the recent mortgage crisis that began in the USA, and the European crisis that originated in Greece.

Overall, my objective is that previously uninitiated readers will gain a broad understanding of how the financial system works, why it is important to the economy as a whole, and what its strengths and weaknesses are. Also, readers should gain an understanding of what the Federal Reserve, other regulators and other central banks are doing, and will be in a position to critique their actions and say with some depth of understanding why they agree or disagree with them.

Contents

Part II Banking: Asset and Liability Management; Banking Supervision and Regulation

Charts, Graphs and Tables

Part I
Historical Perspectives on Money, Financial Institutions and Markets

Chapter 1
What Gives Money Its Value?
From Gold to Paper

The monetary system of the United States evolved from an international gold standard. This standard, in its pure form, existed in the United States only briefly – roughly 1879 to 1914. However, some modified form of the gold standard – that is, a fractional gold bullion standard – remained in the United States until 1971. Since then, no metallic backing of American currency of any kind has existed. So, we were on and off and on and off again, for about 100 years.

Why didn't the nation stay on the gold standard if, as many believed, it was such a good thing? It wasn't the gold standard itself, which was the problem, so much as it was the way it was administered. In addition, several external forces, such as wars and depressions, also kept it from being able to operate effectively.

In recent years, the increase in the market price of gold, to a peak of about $1,865 per troy ounce in 2011, was an indication that people were buying it as a hedge against expected future inflation, reflecting a deterioration of confidence in the US Dollar. How good is it for that purpose?

Facts indicate that gold clearly has some drawbacks as an investment. Unlike bonds or stocks, gold earns an investor nothing. It pays no interest or dividends. At a time when most investments – including stocks and bonds – exist only in electronic form, gold is a real, tangible asset that has to be stored and safeguarded. Gold's value as an investment depends on how likely its price is to increase in the future, because any return on an investment in gold is entirely in the form of capital gains. Over the past 30 years, research has shown that gold's record as a hedge against inflation is not encouraging [1].

Metallic Money

Metallic money prevailed around the world for centuries. A variety of metals were used at one time or another, including gold, but also including silver and copper. Sweden, for example, had a copper standard in the early 17th century and, later in the 18th century, a bimetallic silver-copper standard. Other European

W.H. Wallace, *The American Monetary System: An Insider's View of Financial Institutions, Markets and Monetary Policy*, DOI 10.1007/978-3-319-02907-8_1, © Springer International Publishing Switzerland 2013

countries and the United States tried bimetallic systems – combining gold and silver or silver and copper, etc.

A bimetallic system was more difficult to manage, however, because an official price (a mint price) was set for each metal used. This established the ratio of values between the metals. For example, 15½ to 1 was a commonly accepted ratio in numerous countries, where the official price of an ounce of gold was 15½ times the official price of an ounce of silver. But market prices of the metals could vary, above or below official prices, which often happened. If the market price of silver declined, say to 16 to 1, but the official ratio remained fixed, a person with an ounce of gold could buy 16 ounces of silver.

Then, as expected, owners of gold would buy silver, have it coined, and would use the silver coins instead of gold. Thus, if these market prices prevailed, silver would ultimately replace gold as the monetary metal. This phenomenon was known as "Gresham's Law," where the "bad" money, the cheaper silver, drives out the "good" money, the more expensive gold. The process of arbitrage takes over, and arbitrageurs will act on even the slightest difference in market prices.

In the final analysis, there were no happy solutions with metallic money. The smallest gold coin practical for everyday use was still too valuable for many transactions. Therefore, gold had to be used with silver or, as some countries discovered, with tokens that were coined out of a cheap material and given an arbitrary value as a fraction of the smallest gold coin. But tokens were easier to counterfeit and, likewise, did not provide a satisfactory solution.

One has to be careful in defining what is meant by the "gold standard." Bear in mind that in referring to *metallic* money, we mean systems in which the metal itself – stamped into coins by either public or private mints – was the circulating medium of exchange, or money. The market value of the metal imbedded in the coins was usually equivalent to the face value of the coin, except, of course, for tokens. Today's references to the gold standard usually connote a paper monetary system which is *backed* by gold – not the use of the metal itself as the medium of exchange. In any event, it is surprising that the old metallic systems lasted as long as they did, in the Italian money centers in medieval times in particular, in view of the fact that they were so unsatisfactory and cumbersome in normal commerce.

It is useful to pause and think of the stark contrast between then and now. Think of the vast quantities of these heavy metals that had to be transported by ship from one country to another to settle international transactions or by rail and stagecoach to make domestic payments.

Today, one can go online with a bank and transfer money – literally at the speed of light – and with instant finality of settlement, that is, no float.[1] That is, there is no

---

[1] Float is delay in the settlement of transactions, which results in double counting of the transaction amount. For example, under the old paper check system, if I deposit a check in my bank and the bank gives me credit for the amount in my account before the check is received by the bank on which it was drawn and charged to the drawer's account, there is float in the amount of that transaction. It was not until 2004, with the Check 21 Act, that Congress eliminated the requirement that checks be returned to the bank on which they were drawn. Now, electronic images are transmitted among banks to settle the transactions, and checks do not physically move beyond the bank of first deposit. This eliminated the float.

wait for transactions to clear and no need to move anything physical such as paper to settle transactions. Settlement is achieved by the electronic transfer of balances on the books of banks. Risk is virtually eliminated, accuracy is improved, and business is vastly simplified.

The Emergence of Paper Money

By the beginning of the 19th century, nations had begun to experiment with paper money, most of which was fiat currency, unbacked, and issued by government edict, or fiat. Even though there was considerable doubt and skepticism about the legitimacy of paper money, the fact was that, as the volume of trade grew, both domestically and internationally, the older, metallic systems became less and less satisfactory. Paper-based systems of commerce were becoming more common. By the early 18th century, England had introduced various kinds of paper financial instruments – bonds, notes, shares of stock, warehouse receipts for deposits of gold and silver, etc. [2].

This was the beginning of the period of "merchant banking." Merchants were the first bankers; they made loans with their surplus funds and provided safekeeping (deposit) services. In the process they issued warehouse receipts, which could be traded – like checks today – as evidence of ownership of the real thing of value, gold or silver. This is the same as our current definition of a bank – any institution that both accepts deposits and makes loans.

During this period, Britain clearly emerged as the world's financial center, supplanting Italy and other continental European centers. Thus began what was known as the "Lombard Street era."[2]

US Banks and Their Involvement with Paper Currency

In 1791, near the beginning of the United States, there were four commercial banks in the country. The first was the Bank of North America, founded in 1782 in Philadelphia, and one each in Boston, New York, and Baltimore. During this period, US financial history became more interesting.

The new US constitution, in Article I, Section 8, Paragraph 5, gave Congress the exclusive power to "coin money and regulate the value thereof" [4, p. 95]. We now simply interpret this phrase to mean the power to issue money – in whatever form. Remember that when the Constitution was written in 1787, virtually the only form

---

[2] See Walter Bagehot [3]. This book, which has become a classic, has been rediscovered in the early 21st century, as Bagehot's observations about the financial system of his day, taken from his perspective as a banker and editor of *The Economist*, presages numerous conditions that prevail today in the fields of banking and monetary policy.

of money in use in this country was either gold or silver coins. The only alternative was "continental currency," which had been authorized by the Continental Congress as fiat currency. It served adequately during the Revolution, but its lack of a backing of value meant that it became worthless and was soon phased out of existence. Of course, many Americans, both before and after the Revolution, continued to use British currency, which was well accepted everywhere.

The Constitution also prohibited – in Article I, Section 10 – the states from issuing currency [4]. Therefore, the "note-issue function," as it came to be called, was constitutionally established as a monopoly power of the federal government.

At that time, however, banks – all chartered by states – could issue currency notes (bank notes), which were the specific obligations of the banks that issued them, not of the government. Thus, the constitutional prohibition did not apply to such notes. Aside from any British money still in circulation, all paper currency circulating in the United States in the early 19th century was either fiat currency issued by the federal government or bank notes issued by state banks.

Some state banks issued notes with metallic backing, promising to redeem their bank notes on demand in silver or gold. Others issued notes without backing, putting their own reputations at stake. Many banks honored these obligations and redeemed their notes at par on demand. Others did not. As a result, a large proportion of the bank notes issued were discounted or redeemed for only a fraction of their face value. This inconsistency led to confusion and a lack of confidence in money and in banks and is one of the principal reasons the financial history of the United States in the early 19th century was so chaotic.

Attempts to Establish a Central Bank

This period also saw two failed attempts in the United States to establish a central bank – first, the Bank of the United States, 1791–1811, and the Second Bank of the United States, 1816–1836. The first of these banks was proposed by Alexander Hamilton, the first Secretary of the Treasury, who believed the nation needed a central bank to handle trade settlements with other countries, to consolidate the debt of the colonies, to handle future debt, and, in general, to be the government's banker.[3] Ron Chernow, biographer of Hamilton, notes that he "…was setting in place the building blocks for a powerful state: public credit, an efficient tax system, a customs service, and now a strong central bank" [5, pp. 334–355].

---

[3] Many will see in this discussion an ironic comparison between the issues that early Americans struggled with in the 1790s and those facing members of the European Monetary Union in the 21st century. In recent times, Europe's attempts to establish a fiscal union that would consolidate the debt of member countries in order to ease the challenges associated with solving the Greek crisis and the potential crises of others such as Italy and Spain, are reminiscent of the issues presented by Alexander Hamilton in his arguments for the Bank of the United States.

The idea of a government bank was vehemently opposed by Thomas Jefferson, then Secretary of State, who believed it to be unconstitutional for the federal government to establish a bank.[4] He was joined in his opposition by John Adams and James Madison. For Jefferson, banks were "...devices to fleece the poor, suppress farmers, and induce a taste for luxury that would subvert republican simplicity" [5]. Adams believed that a banking system was "...a confidence trick by which the rich exploited the poor," and he dismissed bankers as swindlers and thieves [5]. President Washington sided with Hamilton, however, and the bank was chartered – organized as a private bank with private shareholders, but authorized to handle the government's business. Virtually all central banks of other countries in existence at that time were also organized as private banks.

Under allegations of profiteering by private individuals on government business and other charges of corruption, Congress allowed the bank's 20-year charter to expire in 1811.

A second try was made with the Second Bank of the United States in 1816, now under the administration of President Madison, who had initially opposed the first Bank, but subsequently changed his mind. The war of 1812 with Great Britain had convinced Madison of the need to have improved control over the nation's finances. Soon after the Second Bank was established, its directors appointed Nicholas Biddle, a member of a prominent banking family of Philadelphia, as its President.

The Second Bank, also organized under a 20-year charter, operated successfully for a few years, until Mr. Biddle locked horns with President Andrew Jackson, who took office in 1829. Again, charges of profiteering and corruption arose, and this time, Jackson, a populist who thought all banks were evil, vetoed Congress's attempt to recharter it. The President then had the Treasury withdraw all federal money from the bank and redeposit it in other private banks around the country. This assured the demise of the bank. Jackson's veto message to the Congress has become a classic in populist literature [6, p. 210].

These events profoundly influenced the way our financial system developed, and they contributed to the chaos that characterized our monetary history in the 19th century. The United States went from 1836 to 1913 without a central bank.

By the first decade of the 20th century, because of the persistent and frequent financial crises (or panics) that occurred, it had become obvious to all, including the populists, that a central bank was needed to control the volatility of the economy and to protect the nation's currency – or, in other words, to control inflation. A detailed discussion of the creation of the nation's present central bank, the Federal Reserve System, will be developed in subsequent chapters.

---

[4] All references to central banks in this book refer to today's generally accepted definition of a central bank, owned and operated by and for the government for the purposes of economic stabilization and protection of the currency. In earlier times, most central banks were established as private banks, with authorization to do certain functions for the government as ancillary activities. Since World War II, this has ceased to be the case, and all central banks now are agencies of their respective national governments.

The National Banking Act (Greenback Act) of 1863

In 1863, in the midst of the Civil War and in a desperate effort to finance the war, Congress passed the National Banking Act ("Greenback Act"). This authorized the issue of greenbacks – paper currency – up to $50 million, not redeemable in gold or silver, but based only on faith in the US Treasury. Again, these were fiat currencies, labeled "US Notes" and sometimes referred to as "Treasury Notes."

This Act also authorized the chartering of "national banks" and established the Office of the Comptroller of the Currency within the Treasury Department to issue the national charters. This act mandated, and its provisions still require, that banks so chartered carry the word "national" in their title, either as such or by the abbreviation NA, for national association.

Finally, the Act authorized the national banks to issue National Bank Notes, which again were obligations of the banks – not of the government. These note issues were required to be backed 100 % by holdings of US Treasury securities, in the form of bonds, notes, or bills.

At the same time, in a rather bold move, Congress placed a 10 % tax on the face value of notes issued by state-chartered banks, eventually driving state bank notes out of circulation. It is fairly clear that, by this act, Congress intended to drive state banks entirely out of existence. It didn't work. States resisted, although many state banks converted to national charters and became national banks at the time [7, pp. 18–19].

These moves were the beginning of the "dual banking system" in the United States, under which banks can be chartered either by federal or state governments, and this anomaly still exists today. Later, we shall discuss the dual banking phenomenon further, along with some other peculiarities of state banking laws such as restrictions on branching. These factors have contributed to the large number of banks in the United States, which, by comparison to most other countries, is far in excess of the number needed to handle the nation's banking requirements.

Although the National Banking Act brought improvements by enhancing public confidence in the currencies in circulation, it didn't fully solve the problem. The value of the currency was still volatile, inflation was rampant, and financial panics – which began as currency shortages – occurred throughout the remainder of the 19th century and into the early 20th century. (For a time line of these developments, see page 9).

Gradual Movement to a Pure Gold Standard

Great Britain led the way to a pure gold standard with the Bank Charter Act of 1844. Under this system, paper money is issued in a fixed ratio to the value of gold held by the nation involved. In theory, the fixed relationship can be set at any given level – that is, 1/1, 5/1, 10/1, and 20/1 – but it must remain fixed in order to instill credibility in the system. One not uncommon problem during the gold standard era was that countries that got into financial trouble perverted the gold standard by arbitrarily varying the gold reserve ratio.

Historical time line of the development of the banking industry in the United States

1781	The Bank of North America is chartered by the Congress of the Confederation as the first US bank
1787	US Constitution is drafted, authorizing the Congress to issue currency (Article I, Section 8, Paragraph 5) and prohibiting states from issuing currency (Article I, Section 10, Paragraph 1)
1791	The Bank of the United States is chartered by Congress, as private bank, with authority to act as bank for the federal government
1811	Bank of the United States' charter expires
1816	The Second Bank of the United States is chartered by Congress, with similar powers as the first bank
1832	President Andrew Jackson vetoes bill to recharter the Second Bank. He also withdraws federal government funds from the bank and distributes it among other banks in the country
1836	The charter of the Second Bank expires
1863	The National Banking Act (Greenback Act) of 1863 establishes national banks and creates the Office of the Comptroller of the Currency in the Treasury Department to issue national charters and to supervise national banks
1913	The Federal Reserve Act establishes the Federal Reserve System as the nation's central bank
1927	The McFadden Act prohibits banks from branching across state lines and places national and state banks under the same rules regarding branching
1933	The Banking Act of 1933 (Glass-Steagall Act) creates the Federal Deposit Insurance Corporation and separates banking from the securities industry
1935	The Banking Act of 1935 creates the Federal Open Market Committee (FOMC)
1946	The Employment Act of 1946 mandates the Federal Reserve to be responsible for full employment, economic growth, stable prices, and a stable exchange rate
1956	The Bank Holding Company Act and the Douglas Amendment (to the McFadden Act) clarify the status of bank holding companies and give the Federal Reserve regulatory responsibility over bank holding companies
1977	The Federal Reserve Act is amended to establish the "dual mandate" of stable prices and full employment for Federal Reserve policy
1980	The Monetary Control Act imposes uniform reserve requirements on all depository institutions and places them under Federal Reserve regulation and raises deposit insurance to $100,000 per account
1982	Depository Institutions Act (Garn-St Germain Act) gives thrift institutions expanded powers in commercial and consumer lending
1989	Financial Institutions Reform, Recovery, and Enforcement Act (FIRREA) provides funds to resolve S&L failures and creates the Resolution Trust Company to resolve insolvent thrifts and creates the Office of Thrift Supervision to supervise thrifts
1991	Federal Deposit Insurance Improvement Act (FDICIA) recapitalizes the FDIC, places limits on the too-big-to-fail policy, requires the FDIC to establish risk-based premiums, and authorizes the Federal Reserve to supervise foreign banks in the United States
1994	Riegle-Neal Interstate Banking and Branching Efficiency Act removes all prohibitions on interstate banking and authorizes branching across state lines
1999	Gramm-Leach-Bliley Act repeals parts of Glass-Steagall to remove the separation of the banking and securities industries
2002	Sarbanes-Oxley Act requires certification by CEO and CFO of financial statements and the independence of audit committees
2010	Wall Street Reform and Consumer Protection Act (Dodd-Frank Act) permanently increases deposit insurance coverage to $250,000 per account, imposes increased regulation of the financial industry, expands the powers of the Federal Reserve, eliminates too-big-to-fail, increases bank capital requirements, and imposes the Volcker rule against proprietary trading by banks and numerous other provisions. As of late 2013, the Act is still in the process of being implemented (discussed further in Chap. 9)

The industrial revolution of the 19th century brought pressure to develop financial systems to help support economic growth. By the 1870s, other industrializing countries gravitated to the gold standard following the example set by Britain, which was recognized as the financial leader of the world at the time. These countries included Germany, Denmark, Norway, Sweden, and, finally, the United States in 1879.

When nations fixed their gold reserve ratios, this, in effect, resulted in a fixed exchange rate system – for example, in the pre-World War I era, 1 ounce of gold was set at $20 per troy ounce; in Britain it was set at 4 Pounds sterling, thus automatically setting a fixed exchange rate between the Dollar and the Pound at $5 to £1. All countries on the gold standard were therefore locked into similar fixed exchange rates with each other.

This system had the advantage of encouraging international trade by eliminating the uncertainty associated with fluctuating exchange rates. The industrialized world stayed on the gold standard until the beginning of World War I in 1914.

The Politics of Gold Versus Silver

At the same time, there was much political controversy in the United States regarding the gold standard. The leader of the populist movement was William Jennings Bryan, senator from Nebraska, and three-time candidate for President. He spoke for the agrarian sector of the economy – farmers and small businesses – mainly Western and Southern interests. These were the "soft money" advocates, who wanted to base US money on silver. They believed in keeping the trade value of the Dollar low to facilitate exports, 75 % of which were agricultural products in the late 19th century. Thus, they strongly opposed the gold standard. Most students of American history remember the speech that Bryan gave at the Democratic Convention in 1896, where he said "You shall not press down upon the brow of labor this crown of thorns; you shall not crucify mankind upon a cross of gold." Indeed, the election of 1896 was the only presidential election in American history in which the nation's money supply came to occupy a central focus [8, pp. 276–279].

The Eastern manufacturing interests, the "hard money" advocates, pressed for the gold standard. They wanted the trade value of the Dollar high to facilitate foreign investment in the United States, which was badly needed to finance industrial expansion, particularly the building of railroads.

Gold standard advocates argued that a monetary system based purely on gold would have two major advantages: (1) It would bring price stability, thus keeping inflation down by preventing central banks and governments from expanding the money supply without mining more gold. (2) It would be self-regulating. That is, outflows of gold to make international payments resulting from trade deficits would cause the value of the nation's currency to decline. This would boost exports and bring about offsetting inflows of gold, causing the value of the currency to rise again.

Opponents of the gold standard, on the other hand, argued that it would not provide sufficient flexibility in the supply of money–elastic currency, as it was then called. Thus, the money supply could not be expanded adequately to support a growing economy. The gold standard advocates, in effect, won this battle at that time, although, as we shall see, their victory was fleeting, as the gold standard was destined not to last.

As the nation moved into the 20th century, the United States continued to produce silver certificates, which were firmly backed by silver, and US Notes (or Treasury Notes) that were fiat currency, authorized by the National Banking Act of 1863. We also had National Bank Notes that were obligations of the banks issuing them and which were backed by US Treasury securities. After the Federal Reserve System was established as the nation's central bank, most currency was gradually converted to Federal Reserve Notes. These became obligations of the Federal Reserve System, as opposed to either the Treasury or individual banks, as the other notes in circulation were.

The Creation of the Federal Reserve System as the Central Bank of the United States

The financial panics of 1893 and 1907 were two of the worst that the United States had experienced in the previous 100 years. They were, in effect, recessions brought about by currency shortages, and they demonstrated the main objection that critics of the gold standard had voiced over and over again. These shortages meant that, because of the restrictions that the gold standard placed on the money supply, it could not be expanded adequately to meet the needs of the economy. There was a lack of an elastic currency.[5] People of all political persuasions were finally convinced that a central bank was needed that could create an elastic currency and provide liquidity to banks when they became strapped for funds.

Many draft bills were sent to Congress proposing a central bank. One of the most prominent of these was advanced by Republican Senator Nelson Aldrich of Rhode Island, the grandfather of Nelson Aldrich Rockefeller, later governor of New York and Vice President of the United States. His plan for a central bank was patterned after the Bank of England, but with 15 regional branches called National Reserve Associations and under the control of private bankers. It is likely that this plan would have been enacted had the election of 1912 not intervened. Republican President William Howard Taft ran for reelection, but due to the entrance of former President Theodore Roosevelt as a third-party candidate, the election was handed to Democrat Woodrow Wilson.

---

[5] Robert F. Bruner and Sean D. Carr [9]. There is further discussion of the Panic of 1907, beginning below on page 136. This episode had a catalytic effect in spurring Congress toward the passage of the Federal Reserve Act and the establishment of a central bank.

Wilson was sympathetic with populist views and favored a plan authored primarily by Congressman Carter Glass of Virginia. This plan became the Glass-Owen bill, named for Congressman Glass and Senator Robert Latham Owen of Oklahoma. The President supported this plan, as did Secretary of State William Jennings Bryan, and this ultimately became the Federal Reserve Act, passed on December 23, 1913. This plan proposed a decentralized central bank structured in such a way as to keep control of the central bank out of the hands of the banking industry and especially out of the control of the Eastern financial interests represented by the New York money-center banks.[6]

There will be further discussion of the structure and functions of the Federal Reserve System in Chap. 11, which is specifically devoted to monetary policy. The focus of our discussion at this stage is on those issues which led to its passage. It is sufficient to note that as of 1914, the United States had finally established a central bank which could successfully create an elastic money supply and could assure the liquidity of the banking system through the process of lending to banks by discounting customer paper that those banks held from their own customers. This new system worked as planned in those early years [10].

The Federal Reserve began operations in November 1914, the year World War I began in Europe, but well before the United States entered in 1917. The impact of that war on the financial situation of the world at large could not possibly have been anticipated at the time, and it significantly changed the world in many ways. Most nations abandoned the gold standard during World War I because its restrictions prevented them from raising the necessary funds to finance the war. Once a single nation abandoned the gold standard, virtually all had to do so because, to work effectively, it had to be an internationally based system.

The Federal Reserve declared its support for the gold standard in the early years of its operation and fully intended to continue to do so. But, as we shall see, it became virtually impossible to return to the prewar financial structure.

The Broader Definition of Money

To understand the importance of money in any economic system, we must consider what the functions of money are – that is, what do people expect money to do for them?

First, money is a *unit of exchange*. All prices of goods or services are typically expressed in units of money – Dollars, Euros, Yen, Rubles, Yuan, Pounds, etc. People are therefore accustomed to thinking of the value of goods or services in terms of the amount of money it takes to acquire them.

Of course, it is technically possible to have an economic system without money, but all commerce would have to be conducted by barter. Such a system in modern

---

[6] Allan H. Meltzer [10]. See especially Chaps. 1, 2, and 3.

times would be unthinkable because of the need to express prices of items in terms of all the other items that could be traded for it. For example, for N commodities, it would be necessary to have $N(N-1)/2$ prices, expressing each item in terms of the number of units of each other item that could be used to purchase it. However, it is surprising that one can still find instances of barter in use around the world. I can remember, for example, working in Russia in the 1990s, shortly after the fall of the Soviet Union, when the Russian economy was very unstable and the value of the ruble was quite volatile. Cigarettes, vodka, barrels of oil, Pepsi-Colas, etc. became frequent substitutes for money. Thus, the unit of exchange feature of money is an extremely useful function, often taken for granted.

The second function of money is that of a *store of value*. This feature was more commonly practiced in the metallic money days when the actual piece of metal had an intrinsic value that bore some equivalency to its face value. In modern times, people do not usually relish holding actual cash and certainly not for its intrinsic value, because it is only paper. Instead, people will tend to put whatever money they have into some instrument that will earn a rate of return – a bond or stock, a savings account or certificate of deposit (CD), or some collectible that is expected to increase in value: jewels, antique autos, artwork, or, today, perhaps Bitcoins. Thus, while the principal disadvantage of holding money is the foregone earnings on one's wealth, another potential disadvantage is the loss of value of money through inflation. Add to this the advantage that people in most advanced economies now have, of knowing that they can access their money quickly by withdrawing it from a bank account or liquidating their investment instruments, which takes no time at all in today's efficient markets. All these have put to rest the notion of the need for money as a store of value.

The third, and most important, function of money is that of a *medium of exchange*, that is, to enable transactions. People therefore tend to hold money because of the prospective need to use it for some purpose – to spend it, to invest it, to speculate with it, or perhaps, just to have a reserve in case of an emergency. John Maynard Keynes described these motives for holding money as the transaction need, the precautionary need, and the speculative need. He summed these up in what he defined as the "Liquidity Preference" of people or the need to hoard money [11]. Schumpeter shows that the recognition that people's desire to hold money relates to the rate of interest goes back to the work of Henry Thornton in the late 18th century [12].

Ideas about money have evolved considerably, as the nature of what people regard as money has changed. By the latter part of the 19th century, the widespread acceptance of bank drafts (checks) as money had become commonplace. The efficiency of the check payment system has advanced to the point that checks, also referred to as deposit currency, have become a major part of the money supply. The Federal Reserve System, over the years, has put in place and enforced regulations requiring banks to pay checks drawn on them at par or face value. For many years, some banks took a discount off the face value of checks, leaving the payee short-changed. This practice is illegal today – in accordance with Federal Reserve Regulation J, but it lasted until the late 1960s. In addition, the Fed, also in Reg. J, placed strict limits on the time that a check deposited in a bank may be held before credit is passed to the payee.[7] Thus, the check has become an almost perfect substitute for currency. Although there is a somewhat greater level of risk due to nonpayment, insufficient funds, closure of accounts, etc., these events are rare compared to the total value of checks written. The section "Payment System Risk" in Chap. 10 discusses further enhancements in payment systems that have reduced reliance on paper.

The effect of the growth of check payments (and today, the use of debit cards) and their general acceptability means that checkable deposits in banks are money in the same sense that currency and coin are money. Therefore, checkable deposits must be counted as part of the total money supply, and the checks and debit cards are simply tools for transferring money from one holder to another.

The Fed keeps and publishes data on the money supply and on its rate of growth, and as a result, its definitions of the money supply are the ones commonly used. There are essentially three statistics that are most often used in this connection: M1, M2, and the Monetary Base. M1 is the most liquid measure of money that is immediately available for spending. It includes currency and coin in circulation, checkable deposits in banks, and traveler's checks outstanding. A broader definition, M2, is M1 plus small denomination time deposits (under $100,000), savings deposits, money market deposit accounts, and money market mutual funds. These are items that can be quickly converted to cash.

As of February 28, 2013, M1 was $2.5 trillion, where currency in circulation was $1.1 trillion – or 44 % of it. But over two-thirds of US currency outstanding, or around $759 billion on the February 28, 2013 date, is outside the United States, owned by foreigners, and is therefore unavailable for domestic use. Taking this into account, checkable deposits comprise about 86 % of the M1 money supply available domestically [13]. For the same date, M2 was $10.4 trillion.

When the Fed, as well as most financial analysts, speaks of money for monetary policy purposes, it means the *total* money supply. The Fed itself uses M2 for most analytical purposes as it is perceived to be the most reliable statistic.

Another statistic for measuring the money supply is the Monetary Base, which is currency in circulation plus total reserves of the banking system. This number was $2.6 trillion on May 16, 2012. Total reserves of the banking system in this definition mean total funds in the system available to lend; for an individual bank, this means the bank's own vault cash plus its deposits with other banks, including its deposits with the Federal Reserve Banks.

M1 and the Monetary Base are simply two ways of looking at the same concept; M1 is based on the liability side of the balance sheet of the US banking system, whereas the Monetary Base is calculated from the asset side. Therefore, under normal conditions, and over time, M1 and the Base tend to be relatively close together in amount. These three measures of the money supply are referred to in the financial press as the "monetary aggregates."

---

[7] It is common parlance in the financial world today, and in the financial press, to refer to the Federal Reserve System as "the Fed." This book follows that convention.

The growth of credit cards and the increased use of ATMs have reduced the use of both checks and cash. Also, debit cards – which are exact electronic substitutes for checks – have grown in use in recent years to equal that of currency and coin in transactions in the US economy as of 2011. Checks are now declining in use in America at the rate of about 4 % a year, after reaching a peak in 2002 of about 60 billion checks written per year.

Total payments of all types grow as the economy grows. The decline in checks as a component of total payments is offset by the rapid growth of electronic means of payment, including credit cards, debit cards, other electronic money cards, preauthorized payments through online bank systems, and other electronic payment systems, such as PayPal, which now boasts over 100 million users. The result has been that overall, in 2012, Americans held about 610 million cards and owed a total of roughly $850 billion on them, leading some observers to speculate that the end of the use of money is in prospect [14].

In the final analysis, however, remember that it is the checkable deposit component of the money supply that makes all these newer systems work. They are all based upon bank deposits and are processed and cleared through the banking system.

These various definitions of the money supply further illustrate the complications associated with the gold standard. Bear in mind that the gold standard was developed at a time when the concept of money was limited to that of the circulating medium itself, metal or paper instruments backed by that metal. To apply the gold standard today to the total money supply would require deciding which of the monetary aggregates to use and establishing a gold reserve ratio applicable to that measure. This would be virtually impossible to implement or manage in our modern culture.

The Demise of the Gold Standard

Officially, the gold standard was terminated in Europe and in the United States at the outset of World War I. European countries abandoned it because, under its restrictions, they could not obtain sufficient funds to finance the war. The result was that deficit spending began among European governments. England and others borrowed from the United States, and America became a creditor nation for the first time. This brought about the beginning of a shift of the financial center of the world from London's Lombard Street to New York's Wall Street.

Of all the countries on the gold standard, Britain was arguably the most dedicated to it, but after World War I, Britain attempted to go back on it. The United States followed Britain and made an attempt to reestablish it, but the Great Depression intervened, and most countries had to abandon it again. Many economic historians, including Ben Bernanke, the current chair of the Federal Reserve Board, believe that the existence of the gold standard at the outset of the Depression increased the severity of the Depression and kept countries from expanding liquidity when they most needed it [15].

In the United States, the Gold Reserve Act was passed in 1934, which did away with private ownership of gold for monetary use. This was America's first real move away from the gold standard, but not the last. Holders of gold, including all banks and the Federal Reserve Banks, were asked to turn in their holdings of gold for monetary purposes and were compensated for it at the then official price of $20.67 per troy ounce.

Following this move, the US government officially devalued the Dollar by raising the price of gold to $35.00 per ounce. Such a devaluation is regarded as an extreme policy move and one that would not be used except in emergency circumstances, which were perceived to exist at that time. A devaluation is an unpopular move with a nation's trading partners because it makes it more difficult for them to sell their goods to the country which has devalued. The advantage to the United States, of course, was that by lowering the value of the Dollar, American goods were cheaper to foreigners, and US exports were boosted. This is one way for a nation to grow its way out of a recession and was the principal reason it was enacted.

After the Gold Reserve Act, the United States adopted a 40 % gold reserve ratio for the currency, which was later reduced to 25 %. That meant we would keep in our vaults at Fort Knox an amount of gold, which, valued at the official price, would equal at least 25 % of the value of the currency outstanding, still based only on currency, not on M1, the Monetary Base, or any other measure of the total money supply.

Most people perceived that the Gold Reserve Act took us off the gold standard, although it did not completely do so. Even though people no longer used gold for transactions, the country was still on a "fractional gold reserve" system. Some referred to this as a "gold bullion" standard, that is, the gold that the Treasury held was not minted, but simply kept in bullion form in gold bars.

Lessons of the 1930s

The United States learned a lot about economics in the 1930s. The nation did not have the institutional structure that it has today which allows it to deal with economic crises. Indeed, some might say that, in light of the economic calamity of the period 2007–2012, the nation still doesn't have an adequate regulatory system in place. Congress has partially rectified this deficiency with the passage of the "Wall Street and Consumer Protection Act" (the Dodd-Frank bill) in July 2010. Details of this Act will be discussed in Chap. 9.

It is true that the nation does have better fiscal and monetary policy tools than it had in the 1930s, and it has the protection of the FDIC (Federal Deposit Insurance Corporation), which can keep the banking system functioning, even in the face of a crisis. Many banks, which were not capital insolvent, closed in the 1930s. They closed because of a lack of liquidity, which is not, or should not be, an occasion for closure today. *Liquidity insolvency* is an inability to pay current obligations and an inability to borrow to pay them. *Capital insolvency*, however, means a bank's liabilities exceed its assets, and under US banking laws, the institution must be closed.

At the beginning of the Depression, many runs on banks occurred – depositors lining up to withdraw their funds from banks. There was no way to stop this panic-type situation, which began in most cases simply as a liquidity insolvency, but often led to a capital insolvency and, ultimately, a bank failure.

While banks in the 1930s could borrow from the Fed if they had adequate collateral, many ran out of collateral, and their sources of funds dried up. Therefore, Congress established the FDIC, with the enactment of the Glass-Steagall Act of 1933 (the Banking Act of 1933), and this restored depositors' confidence in the banking system and minimized the impact of bank runs. When federal deposit insurance began, it covered deposits to a limit of $2,500 per account. Over the years it was increased to $100,000 per account and, in 2008, as a result of the serious economic decline, was raised to $250,000 per account, and under the terms of the Dodd-Frank bill in 2010, this amount has been permanently set as the insurance limit. There will be further discussion of deposit insurance in Chap. 3.

Also, in the 1930s, nations and their banks learned ways of getting around the use of gold in international settlements. The United States, Britain, and France demonstrated through a tripartite agreement in 1936 that they could settle transactions among each other without the transfer of gold. They simply settled by the transfer of balances on the books of banks, exactly the same way we do it today through either checks or bank drafts or, most likely, through electronic transfers. The same can be done by extensions of credit, where settlement is not necessarily made on each and every transaction, but is done on a "net settlement" basis at the end of a period of time through electronic funds transfers. Ironically, it took the rest of the world a number of years to catch up to (and to trust) this process of settlement [10, pp. 538–545]. Nevertheless, this practice was the beginning of putting to rest the myth of the gold standard as a necessary ingredient in international trade.

Even some central banks, which have held gold for generations, have recognized that gold is not important and have begun to sell it to obtain the profit, such as the Reserve Bank of Australia. When market values are sometimes over 40 times higher than the official prices on the books, there is a great incentive to sell. For example, the US Treasury shows on its balance sheet an $11 billion asset, which is its holdings of gold at an official price of $42.22 per ounce. This gold, if valued at the peak market price reached in 2011, would be worth over $485 billion. While the Treasury holds the gold and reports its value on its own balance sheet, it then issues "gold certificates" in the same amount to the Federal Reserve System. Thus, the Fed's balance sheet shows an asset entitled "Gold Certificate Account" in the amount of $11 billion [16].

References

1. Hubbard RG, O'Brien AP (2012) Money, banking, and the financial system. Prentice-Hall, Boston, pp 432–433
2. Thornton H (1802) An inquiry into the nature and effects of the paper credit of Great Britain. Reprinted by AM Kelley, New York, NY, 1962

3. Bagehot W (1873) Lombard street: a description of the money market. Reprinted by Richard D. Irwin, Inc., Homewood IL, 1962, with new introduction by Frank C. Genovese
4. Corwin ES (1978) The Constitution and what it means today, 1978 edn, Fifth Printing. Revised by H. W. Chase and C. R. Ducat. Princeton, Princeton University Press, p 95
5. Chernow R (2005) Alexander Hamilton. The Penguin Press, New York, pp 344–355
6. Meacham J (2008) American lion: Andrew Jackson in the White House. Random House, New York, p 210
7. Friedman M, Schwartz AJ (1963) A monetary history of the United States, 1867–1960. Princeton University Press, Princeton, pp 18–19
8. Bernstein PL (2000) The power of gold: the history of an obsession. Wiley, New York, pp 276–279
9. Bruner RF, Carr SD (2007) The Panic of 1907. Wiley, New York
10. Meltzer AH (2003) A history of the Federal Reserve, volume I: 1913–1951. (With a foreword by Alan Greenspan). The University of Chicago Press, Chicago
11. Keynes JM (1936) The general theory of employment, interest and money. Harcourt, Brace and Co, New York, Chap. 13
12. Schumpeter JA (1959) History of economic analysis. Oxford University Press, New York, p 720
13. Board of Governors of the Federal Reserve System, Statistical Release H.6. Money stock measures. 21 March 2013
14. Wolman D (2012) The end of money: counterfeiters, preachers, techies, dreamers – and the coming cashless society. DaCapo Press, Boston, Introduction and Chap. 4
15. Bernanke BS (2000) Essays on the Great Depression. Princeton University Press, Princeton
16. Board of Governors of the Federal Reserve System, Statistical Release H.4.1. Factors affecting reserve balances. 24 May 2012

Chapter 2
What Is Driving the Financial World Today?

World War II and Its Aftermath: The Bretton Woods Agreements

We survived the 1930s only to find that different kinds of economic problems waited for us in the 1940s. World War II devastated the economies of nations all over the world. In 1944, after it had become clear that the Allied powers would win, representatives of 44 free nations, not including Germany and Japan, gathered at the invitation of the United States to a conference in Bretton Woods, New Hampshire, to discuss and plan for the world economy after the war.[1]

There was a concern that the world would lapse back into a serious recession of the pre-World War II variety and/or that it would experience rampant inflation, which had afflicted Europe after World War I. Most nations wanted to prevent either occurrence. The conference achieved three major results: it established the International Monetary Fund (IMF); it formed the International Bank for Reconstruction and Development (IBRD), now commonly referred to as The World Bank; and it established a fixed exchange rate system among the major countries of the world.

After the war, the IMF was capitalized by its member countries, the original attendees at the conference, in addition to numerous others who were invited to join after the war, including Germany and Japan. Its function was defined to help stabilize currencies of its members. It continues to play that role today, and while most would say it has handled its mission well, it has generated controversy from time to time over certain policies that it requires of countries that it helps, in that it has often imposed counterproductive austerity measures on those nations. In 2009, the G-20 Conference reached agreement to expand the IMF's capital and to enlarge its role. (Note: the G-20 is the G-8 plus Argentina, Australia, Brazil, China, the European Union, India, Indonesia, Korea, Mexico, Saudi Arabia, South Africa, and Turkey. The EU is counted as one member, even though four of its members are separate members of the G-20).

---

[1] For an interesting and detailed account of the discussions at Bretton Woods, see Benn Steil [1].

W.H. Wallace, *The American Monetary System: An Insider's View of Financial Institutions, Markets and Monetary Policy*, DOI 10.1007/978-3-319-02907-8_2, © Springer International Publishing Switzerland 2013

The World Bank was established to be a development bank, as its official name implies. Its initial mandate was to help countries rebuild their infrastructures destroyed during the war. It did that job very well and now primarily helps developing countries in establishing and strengthening their economies. Unlike the IMF, the World Bank does not generally use its own capital in funding its projects, but goes into the capital markets to issue bonds or notes to raise its operating funds.

The third major outcome of the Bretton Woods Conference, and perhaps the most important in terms of the impact that it had on the world at the time, and the longer-term implications of it, was an agreement among countries to establish a fixed exchange rate system, applicable to all participating countries and those that would later join. Under this plan, each country agreed to set its exchange rate relative to the US Dollar, and the Dollar in turn would be fixed to gold, at an official price of $35 per ounce. Again, gold came back into the picture for international settlement purposes.

The US Dollar was the only stable currency of any significance at the end of World War II. So, in effect, the rest of the world leaned on the Dollar to stabilize currencies all over the globe. Japan and Germany, which had been initially left out of this process, joined in, and it is ironic that they later became the second and third largest economies in the world, respectively.

The Bretton Woods agreements worked as expected, and the transition back to peacetime was relatively smooth. There was much work to be done, however, in rebuilding the institutions and infrastructures of the defeated nations. The Allied powers, recognizing the mistakes made at the end of World War I in trying to extract large reparations from the defeated countries, realized this time that they had to help their former enemies rebuild their economies.

Even in the United States, the decision to do this was surrounded by great controversy; there were those who wanted to see the Axis powers broken up and thus weakened to the extent that they would never again be strong enough to become a threat to peace, most especially Germany, which had provoked wars three times within 100 years.

In the aftermath of the war, there was initially a Dollar shortage around the world as Dollars were in great demand by virtually every other country. Later, however, with the initiation of the Marshall Plan and other foreign assistance programs that were begun by the United States, Dollars began to flow out of the country in great abundance. The eventual result of this turn of events was a Dollar glut, as foreigners held larger and larger quantities of Dollars. The United States became worried that these large Dollar holdings outside the country would drain our existing gold supplies, as we were still committed under the Bretton Woods agreements to redeem anyone else's currencies for gold, if requested.

In addition, it was becoming increasingly clear by the late 1950s and the early 1960s that the Dollar alone could not support the stabilization effort for all the world's currencies. By the 1960s, our obligations to foreign holders of Dollars exceeded our gold reserves. Fortunately, an unexpected result occurred. Foreigners were satisfied to hold Dollars rather than gold, so that the crisis the United States anticipated never happened. This has continued to be the case even until today.

It was obvious, however, that we would have to abandon the Bretton Woods agreements. Paul Volcker, then Under-Secretary of the Treasury, later Chair of the Federal Reserve, was handed the assignment of negotiating with nations around the world the conversion from fixed to floating exchange rates. These negotiations, in effect, put in place and made operational the systems of international exchange and payments that most nations now use. It took until 1973 to complete the transition [2]. Under this new system, all currencies were to be priced continually by the market, and economic imbalances would generate corrective pressure on exchange rates [3]. In other words, each country's currency became subject to supply and demand conditions in the currency markets, and exchange rates would move to whatever level those conditions took them. Most major nations have converted to floating exchange rates, and it is now generally agreed that this is a superior system to that of fixed exchange rates in that it eases the adjustment process when countries face financial crises.[2]

The process of extricating ourselves from the Bretton Woods agreements provided President Richard Nixon the opportunity, on August 15, 1971, to issue an executive order *totally* eliminating gold as backing for the currency. That was a great relief to the Fed, which had the task of monitoring the 25 % reserve ratio daily. This event became known as "The Nixon Shock," and it finally and completely took the United States off the gold standard. Since this action, the nation's monetary system has been 100 % paper based. Now, the Fed maintains a supply of Treasury securities in an amount at least equal to the currency outstanding.

In this discussion of the transition away from gold, let us not lose sight of what gives money its value in the first place. First, money has value only if it is universally accepted for the face value it represents, and second, what gives it such integrity and makes it accepted is faith in the credit of the entity that backs it. In America's case, that is the US government.

The Birth of the Eurodollar

An unexpected legacy resulted from the 25-year period in which we operated under the Bretton Woods agreements, and during which time the entire world relied upon the US Dollar for reserve currency and stabilization. Large deposits of Dollars had built up in banks around the world, and foreigners were using these Dollars, borrowing and lending them, investing them and using them for ventures where there were not enough other currencies to support such uses. The Bretton Woods agreement to use

---

[2] The Southeast Asian Financial Crisis of 1997–1998 illustrated this fact quite clearly. The affected countries had remained on exchange rates that were fixed in that they were tied to other currencies such as the Dollar and the Yen. This made it more difficult for them to deal with the financial crisis that occurred because the market was unable to adjust their currencies on a gradual basis to ease the impact of the very substantial withdrawals of capital from the countries when the crisis hit. More discussion of this is in Chap. 9.

the Dollar as the reserve currency for virtually the rest of the world established the fundamental structure of what became the Eurodollar market. It set the stage for the Dollar to become the principal reserve currency for the entire world, as it still is today.

This agreement was the beginning of the use of Eurodollars. The term means Dollar-denominated deposits in foreign banks or foreign branches of American banks. While the prefix suggests correctly that this market began in Europe, it has become worldwide. So, today, it simply means Dollar deposits outside the United States. American officials originally thought they had created a monster because of the enormous mass of Dollars floating around outside the United States, not subject to the control or regulation of US monetary authorities. The Fed worried that a reflow of these Dollars back into the United States would create a horrendous, if not uncontrollable inflation problem.

This has been a needless concern so far, however, because foreigners continue to demand Dollars for use outside the United States. One major user of the Eurodollar market was the Soviet Union. It wanted Dollars to rebuild its infrastructure, but it did not want to come to American banks to get them, on the fear that, for political reasons, the United States might freeze its assets. They got what they wanted through the Eurodollar market. This market has become enormously useful to many countries because it allows access by foreigners to a currency other than their own, a boon to countries whose own currencies are weak or in limited supply.

There have been endeavors – for example, the Euro-tunnel, Euro-Disney, Norwegian hydroelectric systems, the privatization of previously state-owned industries in former iron-curtain countries – where an inadequate supply of money in the home countries prohibited the projects from proceeding. The managers of those projects turned to the Eurodollar market where the supply of funds available was more than adequate. Smith and Walter have noted that such projects would have been indigestible if offered only in the currencies of the home countries of the companies [3, p. 317].

Estimates of the size of the Eurodollar market vary because of the scarcity of reliable statistics. It has grown from a modest $20 billion in 1964 to a multitrillion level today. There is general agreement, however, that it is the largest source of capital in the world today, including over 90 % of all international loans. In any event, the Eurodollar market is now a permanent feature of the world's financial system.

A common source of confusion to keep in mind is that Eurodollars are Dollars – not Euros. The Euro prefix adds to this confusion. There are other financial instruments, for example, that carry this prefix: Euro-bonds are Dollar-denominated bonds issued outside the United States; Euro-equities are Dollar-denominated equities issued outside the United States. There is also Euro-commercial paper. Further, other currencies other than the Dollar are subject to the same treatment – for example, Euro-Yen are Yen-denominated deposits in banks outside Japan.

The potential confusion continues. As the European Monetary Union (the Euro-zone) has recently begun to issue a bond, which is the collective obligation of all members of the Euro-zone, what will it be called? Will it be a Euro-bond? Wait! There already is a Euro-bond! Some have attempted to sidestep the issue by referring to it as a "Euro-zone bond." The answer is yet to be determined because the market for these issues is brand new.

Regardless of the confusing nomenclature, the Eurodollar market will certainly continue as one of the major financial markets of the world, and the impact that it has had to date on worldwide finance has been profound. For example, the increased dependence on the Eurodollar market over recent decades has virtually spelled the end of capital controls around the world. The widespread availability of Dollars in banks all over the world, and the ability to move those Dollars electronically, make it much more difficult to enforce capital controls. Although, until around the 1960s, restrictions on capital flows among countries were commonplace, they are now essentially gone, and the world financial system is now characterized by free movement of capital everywhere. The one remaining major exception is China, and it too is moving toward the removal of such restrictions, albeit ever so slowly [3, p. 20].

The US Dollar as the World's Reserve Currency

The Dollar continues to be the world's primary reserve currency, meaning that foreigners wish to hold it, either in cash or in the form of financial instruments denominated in Dollars, such as Eurodollar deposits, Euro-bonds, Euro-equities, or US Treasury debt. It has been previously noted that over two-thirds of the $1.1 trillion in US currency outstanding is outside the United States.[3] That, when added to the Eurodollar market and other Dollar-denominated debts, means that the US Dollar is in wide use all over the world.

This phenomenon is attributable to the long-term stability of the Dollar and that it is virtually risk-free compared to other assets. This is due to the "safe-haven" argument that money is safer in the United States than in most other places and also to the fact that the US Treasury has never defaulted on its debt. Even in the face of the 2007–2012 financial crisis, in which some questions about the viability of the Dollar have arisen, the Dollar has strengthened, and the world has witnessed a massive flight to the Dollar rather than away from it, as some had predicted.

One issue that economists and world market observers ponder today is whether the Euro–now circulating officially in 19 countries in Europe, and soon to be circulating in perhaps another dozen or so, as new countries are phased into the Euro-zone–might ultimately supplant the Dollar, at least partially, as a worldwide reserve currency. So far, this has not happened.[4]

Moreover, the turmoil in Europe that began in 2010 with the Greek financial crisis, and extending to Italy and Spain, and potentially to others, has seriously eroded the credibility of the Euro as a possible successor to the Dollar on the global stage. Contrary to what many expected, not only did the Euro not save Greece, but Greece almost sank the Euro.

---

[3] See Federal Reserve System balance sheet, pages 184–185.
[4] See table, "Membership in the European Union," pages 104–105.

Even these crises may pass, and the Euro will return again as a strong world currency, but that cannot be taken as a foregone conclusion. A factor in this competition will be how well the European Central Bank manages the stability of the Euro, vis-a-vis how well the Federal Reserve System manages the Dollar. These issues will be discussed further in Chaps. 11 and 12 on monetary policy.

The Forces of Change: Technology, Competition, and Globalization

Thus far in our discussion, we have completed an overview of how the US financial system developed into what it is today. Let's turn our attention now to some of the major forces at work in the world's economy currently and how these trends are helping to shape the financial industry and its markets and institutions.

There are essentially three major forces at work, which have influenced and helped to form the financial system of the United States and the world as we know them today. First is *technological innovation* – particularly in the field of information technology. This trend has shaped the way business is done today and has enormously increased productivity. Second is *competition*, which has become more intense as a result of technological change. Third is the force of *globalization*, which has followed the interaction of technology and competition and has further increased the intensity of competitive forces.

Free trade agreements and the creation of free trade zones have expanded business activity all around the world. Globalization has become a controversial and even an emotional term. Today, we must look at how these trends affect not only the distribution and cost of goods and services, but also the people. For example, in 2006, over 27 % of all trade throughout the world was trade between countries. Strictly internal or domestic trade was the remaining 73 %. The definition of foreign trade has changed with the formation of the European Union because trade among its members is now defined as domestic.

On a global basis, foreign direct investment has quadrupled since 1986, and portfolio investment has grown by a multiple of eight during the same time frame. These numbers illustrate the overall effect that some of the institutional and structural changes that we discussed earlier have had and are continuing to have on the global economy.

Because of technology, it is easier and more efficient today to move goods and services around the world, and the same is equally true of money (capital). Capital controls have been virtually eliminated, as noted earlier, and the trend toward free movement of capital has become global in scope. It is easier and faster to communicate and to make payments globally – literally at the speed of light through electronic networks. This has reduced or eliminated goods shortages and bottlenecks. Because of instant information, the old inventory cycle, which caused volatility in the overall economy, has virtually been superseded by "just-in-time production."

The enhancement of competition has made it more difficult for firms to raise prices arbitrarily. Thus, inflation is better controlled. The result has been expanded economies, increased employment, and enhanced standards of living. These are the positive results, and in a macro sense they are indisputably true.

But there has also been a downside to this process of change. Benefits of the trends are not equally shared. Some disruption has inevitably occurred, as jobs have moved from one country to another. And, as whole functions of a business's operations are outsourced, there is greater risk of political uncertainties when nations become increasingly dependent upon operations housed in other countries. As an example, the sharp decline in goods production in the United States has become both a political and an economic issue. Many feel, with some justification, that there needs to be a sense of balance between goods and services so that a nation can be self-sustaining in adverse circumstances. We have seen great resistance arise in the United States, for example, against the planned takeover of a major energy company by CNOOC, a Chinese company. Also, a proposal by Dubai interests to take over and manage all US ports was similarly resisted. Both of these takeover attempts failed because American citizens saw these moves as increasing their dependence on foreign interests in key areas of industry. One might ask, "Is this xenophobia, or is it simply a practical concern about the need to be in control of one's own destiny?"

Therefore, change engenders both positive and negative reactions – to wit, rioting in recent years at global meetings of the G-8 in Seattle, Quebec, Genoa, Prague, Edinburgh, etc. There have been protests against globalization. Why? I have argued that protesting globalization is akin to standing on the seashore and protesting the tide coming in and going out. That is about how much control we have over the process. Yet, the concern remains: to some, globalization is "…the march of international capitalism – a force of oppression, exploitation and injustice." To others, it is the inevitable result of new technology, competition, and free trade; it is the rising tide which raises all boats, and it leads to the integration of economies through trade and financial flows. This book will not solve this issue. The reader must pick the right answer!

For the present, it is necessary to take the existence of globalization as a given. It is unfortunately the case, however, that often the political rhetoric overshadows the facts. Studies have shown that the US economy has gained more from insourcing than it has lost from outsourcing. This is a macro view and does not help or comfort those who have lost their jobs at the local factory. However, job training and educational policies aimed at helping workers who are displaced by trade or technology would be a wiser course than protesting the inevitable [4].

Free Trade and the Free Movement of Capital

There are two related, but separable, issues involved in globalization. One is free trade itself, which most would agree is good, in terms of efficient production, cheaper goods and services, higher standards of living, etc. The other is free movement of capital, which has two faces – a positive one in that it enables foreign investment, free trade, and the spread of employment, income, and growth globally, and a negative one, which can be disruptive of markets, jobs, etc., when it involves sudden withdrawals of capital, as in Southeast Asia in 1997–1998.

The second of these issues, the free movement of capital, is one in which banks have had a role. It is a more complex issue and has been brought about by the fact that the world economy has evolved, only in recent years, into a virtually free market for capital. In prior years, even as late as the 1960s, it was common for nations to place restrictions on the movement of capital in or out of their countries. But today the growth of technology, the globalization of banks, and the widespread use of Eurodollars have made it more difficult to enforce restrictions on capital movements, even where they still exist.

The CIA World Factbook for 2010 notes that the nation-state, as a bedrock economic-political institution, is steadily losing control over international flows of people, goods, funds, and technology [5]. Banks have been both perpetrators and victims of problems caused by volatile capital movements. Fed Chairman Bernanke has stated, "The challenge for policy makers is to ensure that the benefits of global economic integration are sufficiently widely shared – by helping displaced workers get the necessary training to take advantage of new opportunities – that a consensus for welfare-enhancing change can be obtained" [4].

The Quickened Pace of Change in the Financial World

It should be clear from the discussion thus far that not all of the issues that bear upon the financial sector of the economy are economic in nature. A number of them are political and/or cultural issues. However, banks and other financial institutions must operate within an economic environment and within a system of markets of some kind. How that environment is shaped and how those markets function determine whether banks can operate successfully – that is, be profitable, sustain changes in their economic environment, and continue to function. Banks, generally, have not been the leaders in the process of change; they have reacted to change. But unless banks adapt quickly to the needs of their constituents, who are global or multinational corporations, firms, individuals, etc., they are left in the dust.

Future chapters will illustrate how drastically the environment of banking has changed and how the industry has had to struggle to keep up. Developments in the financial industry in recent years have almost made the traditional concept of a bank obsolete. With *virtual* banks, for example, no longer is there a need for a physical bank to do banking business. Moreover, even if one lives in the most remote location in the country, one can still get into the financial markets in the major financial centers to buy or sell financial assets, to lend or to borrow, in New York, London, Frankfurt, or Tokyo, as easily as if one were on Wall Street or were dealing with Chase, Bank of America, or Deutsche Bank, as long as there is a telephone line and access to the Internet.

Never has the pace of change been faster or more profound in its impact; we are shooting at a moving target. How has this process of change manifested itself in the last couple of decades? Competition is bringing about a worldwide convergence of practices and laws and regulations. Changes in financial practices *lead* changes in laws and regulations, for better or for worse. One country after another has adapted to changes, led primarily by the United States and to a lesser degree by the European Union. Japan has so far resisted significant change. Economic historian Michael Lind has noted that there is a lag, sometimes as long as several decades between technology-driven change in America's economy and society and the adaptation to that change by America's political and legal institutions [6].

An example of this phenomenon was the merger of CitiCorp and Travelers Insurance to form CitiGroup in 1998. Laws in existence at that time did not permit this merger. Combinations of banks and insurance companies were prohibited by the Glass-Steagall Act of 1933. Yet, the firms went ahead and announced the merger on the assumption that Congress would amend the law. They did. Now, there are some regrets and a number of people have argued for a return to Glass-Steagall, but whether good or bad, this was an example of laws and regulations changing to accommodate actual practice.

Technological change was the driving force that made that merger happen and has continued to be the main force that drives competition in this industry. In the ability to move funds electronically and instantly achieve finality of settlement, in making information – interest rates, exchange rates, prices – instantly available, business managers, money managers, bankers, traders, speculators, money launderers, and all who profit from information, now know the opportunities open to them at any moment in time, worldwide, for good or bad.

Technology now permits markets to move to 24-h real-time operations, and time zones no longer matter. As technology has removed the necessity for the physical presence of a bank, NASDAQ has demonstrated the same concept with respect to markets. It operates entirely on an electronic network and has no trading floor, as the NYSE does. These market-based examples will expand in the years ahead as major exchanges convert from heavy dependence on physical facilities to major reliance on electronics. Anyone can do banking, trading, or speculating from anywhere; operating systems are or will be transparent to users, and as noted, all that's needed is Internet access.

Therefore, we are witness to a "paradigm change," in which it is recognized that antiquated laws, regulations, and customs cannot prohibit people from taking advantage of the technologies available to them. Consider, for example, how the Chinese have fought and basically lost their battles against the Internet and Google in particular. The overriding desire of people for knowledge seems repeatedly to overcome political resistance to it.

Today's Financial Institutions: The Emergence of Shadow Banking

Today's financial institutions fall into two broad categories – depository financial institutions and nonbank financial institutions. See the list below.

Depository financial institutions (DFIs):

- Commercial banks
- Thrift institutions (savings and loan associations, mutual savings banks, credit unions)
- Industrial loan companies

Nonbank financial institutions:

- Investment banks
- Brokers and dealers in securities
- Insurance companies
- Merchant banks
- Trust companies
- Foreign exchange dealers
- Specialized dealers in financial instruments such as derivatives, and mortgage-backed and asset-backed securities
- Fund managers – mutual funds, money market mutual funds, hedge funds, private equity funds, and other private money funds

The group of nonbank institutions is called the "Shadow Banking System." They are not banks – that is, they do not both take deposits and make loans. But they engage in financial functions and thus compete with the banking system. The financial crisis of 2007–2012 nearly wiped out many of these institutions, and proposals have been made to eliminate thrift institutions and industrial loan companies. Investment banks were also seriously hurt in the early stages of the crisis, and the major ones that remain still have financial difficulties. AIG, the large insurance company which overindulged in credit default swaps, also declared bankruptcy. There will be more details on these issues in Chaps. 7 and 8.

References

1. Steil B (2013) The battle of Bretton Woods: John Maynard Keynes, Harry Dexter White, and the making of a new world order. Princeton University Press, Princeton
2. Volcker PA (1992) Changing fortunes. Times Books, New York
3. Smith RC, Walter I (2003) Global banking, 2nd edn. Oxford University Press, New York, p 20
4. Bernanke BS. (2007) Testimony before the Joint Economic Committee of Congress. http://www.federalreserve.gov/boarddocs/speeches/2004
5. U.S. Central Intelligence Agency (2010) World Factbook, U.S. Central Intelligence Agency, Washington, DC
6. Lind M (2012) Land of promise: an economic history of the United States. Harper Collins, New York, p 9

Part II
Banking: Asset and Liability Management; Banking Supervision and Regulation

Chapter 3
How Are Banks Funded?

Intermediation

The principal function of the banking *system* is to facilitate the process of intermediation – that is, to convert the savings of society into productive investments, by obtaining deposits and making loans. Note that the emphasis is on system, as opposed to the individual bank, because a single bank cannot accomplish this task, but the system as a whole can do so and does. This is the reason that banks are referred to as financial intermediaries – the banking system brings together savers and investors.

Therefore, we define a bank as an entity which both accepts deposits and makes loans. If it does both functions, it is a bank, whether it calls itself one or not, and is subject to regulation as a bank. If it does not do both, it is not a bank, but it can be a nonbank financial institution and, thus, a member of the Shadow Banking industry as defined in the previous chapter. There has been a substantial growth of the number and types of nonbank financial institutions in recent years.

Why is a bank unique among business enterprises? It has a special responsibility to depositors unlike that which any other business entity has to its funding sources. Even though it uses depositors' funds to make loans and investments, it is obligated not to place those funds at excessive risk. This is a *fiduciary* responsibility or a relationship of trust. But, at best, it is a judgment call. What is excessive?

We have seen much that is excessive during the financial crisis of 2007–2012. Therefore, we know it when we see it, but it is difficult to define and particularly difficult when it comes to specifying those activities of banks that should or should not be regarded as permissible. For example, the Dodd-Frank bill, passed in July 2010, approved the "Volcker Rule," which prohibits banks from engaging in proprietary trading or speculative trading involving their depositors' funds. Arguments are still raging, at the time of this writing, as to how to define what such trading is, as opposed to normal "market-making" trading, which banks would typically pursue in order to put depositors' funds to use to earn a return at non-excessive risk levels. There will be further discussion of this dilemma in Chap. 9, but it illustrates the

W.H. Wallace, *The American Monetary System: An Insider's View of Financial Institutions, Markets and Monetary Policy*, DOI 10.1007/978-3-319-02907-8_3,
© Springer International Publishing Switzerland 2013

degree of sensitivity, both within the banking industry and among its regulators, as to a proper understanding of the fiduciary role of banks.

Another requirement that sets banks apart from other businesses is that they are required by their regulators to submit quarterly balance sheets and income statements referred to as "call reports," and these are released to the public through local newspapers and online. A bank must produce its call report upon request from customers. Thus, financial reports of banks have a wider audience and involve greater sensitivity than those of many other kinds of business entities.

In addition, a bank must have a government-issued banking charter to engage in banking business – issued either by a state government or by the federal government though the Treasury's Office of the Comptroller of the Currency. Therefore, banks, as we use the term broadly, include all depository financial institutions, shown on the list on page 28. This encompasses everything from small, community-oriented, consumer banks to multitrillion-dollar conglomerates financing global corporations.

An economy could not operate effectively without the functions of a banking system. Michael Lewis, author of *The Big Short*, notes, "When banking stops, credit stops; when credit stops, trade stops; when trade stops, well…" [1]. The implication is that the result is recession, economic paralysis, or something worse.

As noted, from the perspective of the economy, it is the banking system that is important as opposed to individual banking institutions. While the aggregation of institutions obviously comprises the system, it is how well the system as a whole performs that is important to the economy. For a banking system to be effective, banks must be willing and able to extend credit to businesses and individuals. This is one reason that there is concern about individual banks becoming so large as to be able to monopolize, or even impair, the operation of the system as a whole.

Because of the special status that banks have in the US economy, the American government provides them a "safety net." First, their deposits are insured by the FDIC, a federal agency since 1933. Of course, banks pay for that insurance through a premium assessed on their deposits, but, nevertheless, the insurance is guaranteed by the full faith and credit of the US government.

The second aspect of the safety net is that banks can borrow from the central bank – the Federal Reserve – which is tantamount to borrowing from the US government. Again, the institution must have the required collateral. Such loans are never unsecured, and the lack of collateral can at times be a problem – such as in the case of the 2008 failure of Lehman Brothers, one of the largest US investment banks, which in its final days had no acceptable collateral left to offer.

The third and less well-known aspect of the safety net is that banks have access to the Fed's electronic funds transfer network, Fedwire, for the instantaneous and final settlement of large-dollar transactions. (More discussion of this is in Chap. 10 on payment system risk).

No institutions other than banks are granted these privileges.[1] The reason for this special treatment is the importance of the banking system to the economy as a whole.

---

[1] The reader should be aware that, with respect to most categorical statements like this one, there are occasional very rare exceptions that can occur in extreme financial emergencies. Examples of this will be discussed later in the chapter.

The Balance Sheet of a Bank

Liabilities and capital represent the sources of funds to a bank or any business enterprise, and assets represent the uses of those funds. There are some key differences, however, between the financial statements of banks and those of other business entities, such as manufacturing companies, service companies, and retail establishments.

These differences reflect the unique nature of banks. Many banks in earlier years were organized as partnerships rather than corporations, and that continued to be the case with investment banks until very recently. Investment banks are discussed further in Chap. 8. See the simple example below of the balance sheet of a bank in comparison to that of any company.

Any company		Bank	
Assets	Liabilities	Cash	Deposits
	Net worth	Investments	Other debt
	(or capital)	Loans	Capital

Financial statements of banks are in a continuing state of transition, reflecting numerous fundamental changes that have taken place in the industry over the years – especially since the 1980s. The reader will see why this is happening as we get into the changes that banks are making in their operations, both the sources of funds that they rely upon and the uses they make of those funds.

Consolidated balance sheet: all US commercial banks May 1, 2012

	Amount ($ billions)	Percentage
Reserves and cash items	1,629	12.8
Securities	2,605	20.4
Loans	7,044	55.3
Other assets	1,467	11.5
Total assets	12,745	100.0
Deposits – checkable	963	7.6
Deposits – nontransaction	7,710	60.5
Borrowings and other liabilities	2,602	20.4
Total liabilities	11,275	88.5
Capital	1,470	11.5
Total liabilities and capital	12,745	100.0

A comparison of these numbers with those of earlier years would indicate that because of the serious financial crisis and recession that hit the US economy between the years 2007 and 2012, banks adjusted their balance sheets by increasing capital. Also increases were noted in reserves and cash items and decreases occurred in borrowings and other liabilities because of banks' growing fear of debt. Numerous banks failed during this period because of their overly risky activities prior to the crisis. At the same time, overall deposits changed very little. The effect of these changes has been a shift by banks to a more conservative financial posture [2].

The liability and capital side of a bank's balance sheet shows the degree of dependence of the institution on specific types of funding sources. And it reflects the stability and creditworthiness of the institution or the lack thereof.

The asset side portrays the use of funds. It shows what the bank does with its money – its own capital as well as its depositors' funds. It reflects the degree of either conservatism or aggressiveness of a bank's management and, in a sense, indicates the level of service to the public. For example, the higher the percentage of loans relative to investments in securities reveals that a bank is serving the economic needs of its community, whereas the higher the percentage of investments as opposed to loans indicates a more conservative approach. The proper balance between these competing approaches would be determined by the overall economic condition of the bank's market and its community.

It must be remembered also that the asset side of the balance sheet shows the earnings potential of the bank, since it is the assets which generate the earnings. And it also represents the risks to which the bank is exposed since the quality of a bank's assets defines its risks.

Financial Holding Companies

A bank may be a member of a financial holding company, formerly referred to as bank holding companies. A holding company, in a general sense, is simply a corporation that owns one or more other corporations or companies. Therefore, a bank holding company would be one that owns one or more banks, and a financial holding company is one that owns one or more banks and/or other kinds of financial institutions – bank or nonbank.

In the earliest days of US banking, banks did business in one or more states – wherever they could obtain state permission to operate – and as long as they held properly issued banking charters. Notwithstanding the influence of Hamilton, who favored large, strong, and nationally oriented institutions, the American banking industry, from its early days, has tended to follow the Jeffersonian model of small, independent and locally oriented institutions, in most cases limited to a single state [3]. This issue was put to rest in 1927 when Congress passed the McFadden Act, which prohibited banks from branching across state lines. Some, which had already done so, were grandfathered. The prohibition applied to both national and state banks.

As a result of McFadden, bank holding companies (BHCs) began to be formed which either organized de novo (new) banks in one or more states or took over existing banks in other states. This technique enabled banks to effectively achieve the objective of branching – even using the same bank name – but which were legally separately incorporated units under the holding company umbrella. Therefore, banks were able to continue their expansion and growth into national markets despite the prohibitions against branching. After allowing the banking system to operate for almost 30 years under this hybrid situation, Congress passed the Bank

Holding Company Act in 1956, which officially acknowledged the existence of BHCs, put them under the regulatory control of the Federal Reserve, and required Federal Reserve Board approval for the establishment of a bank holding company. One purpose of this act was to assure that BHCs did not own any subsidiaries other than banks or activities "closely related to banking." The logic behind this limitation was the perception that involvement in other nonbanking activities would pose a risk to the soundness of the bank itself.

This legislation also included an amendment to the McFadden Act – known as the Douglas Amendment – which prohibited BHCs from acquiring banks across state lines unless specifically approved by the banking authorities of that state. The Federal Reserve Board continued to approve the formation of numerous BHCs but rigidly upheld the restriction to closely related activities. In 1999, Congress acted again to pass the Gramm-Leach-Bliley Act (GLB Act), which not only repealed various provisions of Glass-Steagall that kept banks from engaging in investment-related activities but also changed the definition of BHCs to financial holding companies (FHCs), and permitted them to own nonbanking subsidiaries, such as investment banks, brokerages, securities dealers, hedge funds, and insurance companies. GLB requires that an FHC derive at least 85 % of its income from financial-related activities. Regulatory authority over FHCs continues to be vested in the Federal Reserve Board.

Today, most large banks are members of FHCs. This increasingly has meant that a financial analysis of the overall financial institution requires a review not only of the bank's balance sheet but the balance sheet of the holding company as well.

Deposit Sources of Funds: Checkable

Historically, the principal source of funds for banks has been deposits. The term "core deposits" is often used to refer to the most stable and dependable component of deposits – that is, deposits derived from businesses and consumers in the bank's given market area. This is the essence of retail banking, in that a bank's depositors are most likely also to be borrowers of funds from the bank – for business loans, home loans, and consumer loans.

Core deposits consist of checkable deposits of private individuals and businesses, time and savings deposits, money market deposit accounts (MMDAs), and public entity deposits – that is, deposits of federal, state, and local governments; school districts; and public authorities.

Banks usually try to maximize core deposits for reasons of stability and to serve their respective market areas. Core deposits, with the exception of MMDAs, require reserves – that is, a percentage of deposits, which must be kept on deposit in a "reserve account" with the Federal Reserve Bank serving the community. Banks are allowed to count cash held in their vaults as part of that required reserve. Core deposits are also usually insured. Deposit insurance is not required of banks, but virtually no bank dealing with the public today would be without it.

One other aspect of core deposits is that they may include the deposits of other banks. In the parlance of the financial press, banks that hold deposits for other banks are referred to as "correspondent banks." Interbank deposits are as old as banking itself and are held for a variety of reasons – to establish a relationship with another bank on which a bank might wish to depend for an additional source of funding if a need should suddenly develop, or for services that the correspondent bank may be able to provide. A bank that places funds on deposit with another bank is called a "respondent bank."

Banks may hold checkable deposits for individuals and businesses that are interest-bearing accounts or non-interest-bearing accounts. For many years, banks were prohibited from paying interest on checkable deposits of any kind, under Federal Reserve Regulation Q. The theory behind this regulation was to prevent the intense competition in which some banks engaged in order to acquire deposits. The rate of return banks could pay was thus removed as an element of competition, and banks had to resort to other trivial ways of attracting accounts, such as the presentation of toasters for opening a new account. This prohibition was removed after several years with respect to consumer deposits, but it remained in place for business deposits until 2012.

One technique that banks latched onto to compete for business deposits, especially large corporate deposits on which the bank could earn substantial returns, was to offer cash management services. For example, banks could offer sweep accounts to help corporate cash managers better control and manage their flows of funds. The cash manager of a large nationwide retail establishment could ask the bank to sweep all the funds from its accounts all over the country, on an overnight basis, into a central account in the location of the corporate headquarters. The bank could easily handle this task by electronic funds transfers (EFTs). This allowed the cash manager to know at the opening of business each day the amount of cash the company had available for use that day or to invest in some financial instrument that would generate earnings for the company. The efficiency with which banks handled this activity was an important element of competition in their quests to obtain profitable corporate deposits.

Under cash management services, banks could also offer investment account services in which a corporate depositor could rely on the bank to make decisions for the depositor and to place any excess funds into earning financial instruments on behalf of the depositor. One additional service banks could provide for corporate depositors was to offer repurchase agreements (Repos). Under this arrangement, the bank could sweep the end-of-day balance from the corporate customer's checkable account into an overnight repurchase agreement – the technical name of which is "Securities Sold Under Agreement to Repurchase" – in which the bank simply earmarks some of its financial instruments (usually bonds) that it is holding in its investment account and transfers their ownership on an overnight basis to the corporate customer, allowing that customer to earn the interest on those bonds for that overnight period. Then, at the opening of business the next day, the bank transfers them back to its own portfolio and places the funds back into the non-interest-bearing deposit account of the customer. This is a way of legitimately sidestepping Regulation Q and allowing the corporate customer to earn some return on an otherwise non-interest-bearing account. We shall discuss repurchase agreements later in the context of other uses they have in the financial system.

Therefore, cash management services have become a big source of business for banks and have allowed them to compete effectively for corporate deposits. Depending upon the size of the account that a corporate customer keeps with a bank, the bank may or may not charge a fee for such services. In fact, many banks have become so adept at offering financial services to customers that fee income has become a growing source of bank earnings, in some cases rivaling interest income, which the bank earns on its loan portfolio.

As part of the Dodd-Frank bill of 2010, Congress removed the Fed's authority to restrict the payment of interest by banks on any kind of deposit account. Thus, the Fed repealed Regulation Q and began to pay interest on business demand deposits on July 21, 2012. It remains to be seen just how much this change will affect the kinds and quality of services that banks provide to businesses, since now banks can openly compete in terms of interest rates on business accounts.

Deposit Sources of Funds: Other than Checkable

Other types of deposits held by banks include a variety of time and savings deposits. These accounts have certain limits on the checkable nature of the funds. Traditional savings accounts and small denomination certificates of deposit (CDs) are an important source of funds, especially for consumer-oriented banks or retail banks. These accounts usually pay relatively small rates of interest compared to rates available on other instruments available in the market. During the early years of the 21st century, market interest rates have been markedly lower than historical patterns shown in earlier years. One reason for this has been the downturn in the economy beginning in 2007 and continuing through 2012. In this period, rates have been held lower by monetary policy in an effort to revive the economy. Thus, savers, in periods such as this, suffer from reduced earnings on savings, and this has affected those dependent on fixed-income securities, which include many retirement incomes.

These types of accounts usually lock in savings for a certain period of time and involve penalties for early withdrawals. A distinction is made between small CDs, issued in denominations of less than $100,000, and larger CDs – sometimes referred to as "jumbo CDs." For reasons that will be explained later in this chapter, jumbo CDs are not thought of as deposit sources of funds for banks, but rather as "market sources" of funding, and a totally separate market exists for them.

Finally, one other type of deposit – that of money market deposit accounts (MMDAs) – is offered by banks and has become popular with consumers in recent decades. These accounts had an unusual beginning in the sense that they were first issued by brokerage firms, where an investor was allowed to keep cash, which usually resulted from the sale of securities. Customers found it convenient to keep cash in these accounts for purposes of reinvestment in securities, and for this, the brokerage firm would pay a competitive rate of return to encourage the customer to leave the money on deposit with them. Banks became envious of this development because it seemed to them that brokerage firms were invading banks' territory by offering what amounted to savings accounts. Thus, under pressure from banks, Congress finally allowed banks to offer the same kinds of accounts.

Therefore, MMDAs are interest bearing like regular savings accounts but also offer limited checking privileges, such as six withdrawals per month, three of which can be by check.[2] Banks are also required to place the funds deposited in these accounts in short-term financial instruments – referred to, as we shall see later, as money market instruments – such as Treasury bills, commercial paper, and other items of a maturity of 1 year or less. The customer earns an average of the rates of return on those items in the market.

Savings accounts and MMDAs in the US banking system today do not require reserves as checkable accounts do. Reserve requirements were removed from such accounts in 1991 by the Fed in order to encourage savings in the economy, under the rationale that the lower cost to the bank to offer the accounts would encourage them to pay higher returns to savers.

Reserve Requirements

Most central banks around the world require a certain percent of deposits to be held on reserve – as a deposit in a "reserve account" with the central bank.

Currently, the Fed requires of US banks the following percentages:

– For total checkable deposits less than $12.4 million, 0 %
– For amounts over $12.4 million but less than $79.5 million, 3 %
– For amounts over $79.5 million, 10 %[3]

Given the heavy concentration of deposits in the largest banks in the United States, these requirements amount to almost 10 % of all deposits in the entire banking system. This results from the fact that deposits in the smallest banks in the country are such a minuscule portion of the total.

In the early years of the Fed, Congress retained the authority to set reserve requirements, and it did not delegate this power to the Fed until 1935. Thus, today the Fed has the authority to change reserve requirements within certain ranges established by Congress and articulated in the Fed's Regulation D [3].

---

[2] The reason for limiting the checking privileges was to distinguish MMDAs from regular deposits with unlimited checking privileges, which would require reserves.

[3] Board of Governors of the Federal Reserve System, Reserve Requirements, October 26, 2011. The Fed issues a press release updating reserve requirements in October of each year to be effective at the beginning of the following calendar year. It modifies the amounts defining each of the three categories on the basis of the percentage of annual growth or decline in total checkable deposits in the US banking system – for example, if total deposits in the United States grow by 5 %, the $79.5 million and the 12.4 million will be raised by 5 %.

The reader will recognize that the ability to change reserve requirements is a powerful tool of monetary policy. For example, to raise reserve requirements reduces the funds that banks have available to make loans, and to decrease them would increase funds that banks could lend. The required reserves that banks must keep with the Fed represent sterile money that cannot be used for any other purpose by the banking system, and, until very recently, banks earned nothing on the reserves they were required to keep with the Fed. Congress approved a change in this policy in 2008, at the depth of the most recent recession, to provide some degree of relief to banks. The banking industry had lobbied for this change for generations before Congress finally granted it.

The changing of reserve requirements is a seldom used tool of the US monetary policy. The last time a change was made was in April 1992, when the economy was recovering from the recession of 1990–1992. At that time, the highest reserve level was lowered from 12 % to the present 10 %.

The Fed also has the authority to impose reserve requirements on Eurodollar deposits if necessary for either monetary policy or other regulatory reasons. These would be Dollar-denominated deposits borrowed from foreign banks and brought back into the United States for deposit in an American bank. Although the Fed has never used this authority, it requested it to protect against the possible inflationary impact of a significant reflow of Dollars into the United States from foreign sources – which, incidentally, has never happened.

Some central banks in other nations allow their banks to hold government securities – for example, bonds issued by the nation's government – as required reserves. While this has been proposed a number of times in the United States, it has never been allowed. Volatility of the bond market is an argument against such a proposal because the values of the bonds would vary and undercut the reliability of having a fixed percentage reserve against deposits. In a consulting assignment with the Ministry of Finance in Ukraine in 2010, I faced a similar proposal and advised the Ministry against adopting it for the reasons stated. Notwithstanding my views on the matter, the ministry continues to allow Ukrainian banks to hold Ukrainian government bonds as required reserves. Ukrainian banks were unenthusiastic about buying their government's bonds. They preferred the US Treasury bonds or those of more stable European countries, such as Germany or Switzerland. But the acceptance of Ukrainian bonds as required reserves is, in effect, a way of forcing them to sell.

Deposit Insurance

The adoption of deposit insurance in 1933 has probably done more to stabilize the American banking industry than any other measure that Congress has passed, at least since the beginning of the Great Depression. Starting out at $2,500 per account, it steadily grew in coverage over the years to $40,000.

In 1980, Congress passed the Monetary Control Act, which, among numerous other provisions, raised the insurance limit to $100,000 per account. Many critics at that time thought this change was unwise because it was widely believed that the higher limit would cause banks to become more risky in their investment and lending decisions.

The 1980 change, as expected, did make banks more risky and increased the "moral hazard" associated with banking.[4] Even so, the FDIC believed the $100,000 limit needed to be further increased and they proposed in 2002 and again in 2005 to raise the limit to $130,000. On both occasions, the Fed opposed the change because of its view of the increased risk that had resulted from the 1980 change. Congress turned down both proposals.

The banking crisis of 2007–2012, however, threatened the continued existence of many banks, and a number of them failed. Deposits were being withdrawn because depositors' trust in banks had declined rapidly. To ease this crisis situation, the FDIC, with the concurrence of the Congress, and without any objection from the Fed, changed the deposit limits in 2008 to $250,000 per account. In addition, it offered insurance for "other debt" of banks, and these moves quickly restored the confidence of depositors and other creditors of banks – that is, bondholders. The FDIC, then under the leadership of Sheila Bair, indicated, in effect, that it would do whatever it had to do to save the American banking system [4]. These changes were introduced as temporary, and the intent of the FDIC was to roll them back to the $100,000 level in 5 years – in 2013. The Dodd-Frank bill of 2010, however, made the new limits permanent. The FDIC did remove the coverage of other debt, however, in 2009, after things had settled down somewhat, and it was thought to be no longer needed.

Non-Deposit Sources of Funds

There are numerous other ways for banks to fund their operations aside from deposits. These are most often referred to as "market sources," because they are dependent on the financial markets. These sources generally do not have insurance – again with one exception – and require no reserves. Greater emphasis on this type of funding is typical of wholesale banking.

Some financial institutions in recent years have tended to shift away from the traditional model of retail banking, in which banks seek deposits from their respective market areas and attempt to use those funds to make loans to businesses and consumers in their areas. This model emphasizes numerous branches and, in general, a structure that is conducive to providing the conveniences that attract businesses and consumers. Wholesale banking, on the other hand, is a model in which banks

---

[4] The term, "moral hazard," in a banking context, has come to mean the tendency of banks to take greater risk with depositors' money because they know they are protected by the federal government (i.e., the FDIC), which will cover their losses by protecting the depositors in case the banks make wrong decisions. We have seen the truth of this during the banking crisis of 2007–2012.

eschew branches, discourage small accounts, and do not offer many conveniences that individuals would expect. Instead, they rely upon market sources of funding that do not involve individual depositors, and while they may accept deposits from large depositors, they are not interested in small accounts. On the asset side, these banks do not seek to make consumer or small business loans, but concentrate instead on large projects, such as major real estate developments and other commercial ventures. The motivation is to increase profits and to lower the costs that are typically associated with retail banking.

The move from retail to wholesale banking was most noticeable in the 1980s as both commercial banks and thrift institutions – such as savings and loan associations (S&Ls) – saw greater opportunities in the wholesale arena. Thrifts, in particular, were especially eager to break the mold in which they had been entrapped for generations by law and regulation, which limited them to housing and other consumer-related lending. These institutions found themselves in situations – in the climate of rising interest rates in the late 1970s and the early 1980s – in which they were having to pay more for funds through the deposit channel and were stuck with long-term loans – for example, mortgages – that carried low interest rates on the earnings side. They were, in other words, in a long-term loss predicament. Congress relieved them from this dilemma with the passage of the Garn-St Germain Act in 1982, which allowed them to branch into virtually any other areas of banking that they wished. While some were successful at this transition, others were not prepared and failed as a result. The S&L financial crisis followed, and many banks were in the same boat.

One of the consequences of this transition was that non-deposit sources of funds rose to greater importance in managing the liabilities of wholesale banks. Among these sources are (1) use of repurchase agreements, (2) use of the Federal Funds market, (3) Eurodollar borrowings, (4) borrowing from the central bank, (5) increased use of jumbo CDs, and (6) interbank borrowings. These sources are explained in greater detail in the text that follows.

One characteristic of market sources of funds, as opposed to deposits, is that they can be much more volatile in nature. Generally, however, funds can be obtained very quickly through these sources, because both national and international markets exist for them. Rates are known at any time around the clock and are published daily in the financial press. (See the Table of Money Rates on pages 42–43).

Another feature of these financial markets, which is critical to their successful operation, is that they are highly liquid. A "liquid market," in this context, means that extremely large volumes of activity flow through a given market on a daily basis, and there is virtually never a situation in which a buyer cannot find a seller or a seller cannot find a buyer. Exchanges and/or brokers and dealers exist so that investors and borrowers can always complete their desired transactions within the course of a business day, in whatever financial instrument they are interested.

Each of the market sources of funding discussed above has unique advantages – and sometimes disadvantages. We shall now consider these pros and cons and how and why each of them is used.

Money rates (From *The Wall Street Journal*, May 31, 2012)

Inflation (April)	
U.S. consumer price index	
All items	230.085
Core	229.303
International rates (latest)	
Prime rates	
U.S.	3.25 %
Canada	3.00 %
Euro zone	1.00 %
Japan	1.48 %
Switzerland	0.52 %
Britain	0.50 %
Australia	1.75 %
Overnight repurchase	
U.S.	0.26 %
U.K. (BBA)	0.46 %
Euro zone	0.15 %
U.S. Government rates	
Discount	0.75 %
Federal funds	
Effective rate	0.17 %
High	0.38 %
Low	0.10 %
Treasury bill auction	
4 weeks	0.06 %
13 weeks	0.09 %
26 weeks	0.14 %
Secondary market	
Freddie Mac	
30-yr mortgage yields	
30 days	3.08 %
60 days	3.12 %
Fannie Mae	
30-yr mortgage yields	
30 days	3.20 %
60 days	3.24 %
Bankers acceptances	
30 days	0.23 %
60 days	0.20 %
90 days	0.28 %
Other short-term rates	
Call money (latest)	2.00 %
Commercial paper	
30 days	0.14 %
31–59 days	0.10 %
60–89 days	0.14 %
210–270 days	0.33 %

(continued)

Euro commercial paper	
30 days	0.22 %
3 months	0.26 %
6 months	0.48 %
London interbank (Libor) rate	
1 month	0.24 %
3 months	0.47 %
6 months	0.74 %
1 year	1.07 %
Euro Libor rate	
1 month	0.33 %
3 months	0.60 %
6 months	0.90 %
1 year	1.23 %
Euro interbank (Euribor) rate	
1 month	0.39 %
3 months	0.67 %
6 months	0.95 %
1 year	1.23 %
Eurodollars	
1 month	0.12 %
3 months	0.20 %
6 months	0.45 %
Weekly survey	
Freddie Mac	
30-year fixed	3.75 %
15-year fixed	2.97 %
5-year ARM	2.84 %
1-year ARM	2.75 %

Note: US Prime, effective December 16, 2008; Discount rate, effective February 19, 2010. Call money rate is on loans to brokers on stock exchange collateral. Libor is British Bankers Assn. average of rates on interbank loans of Dollars in London market

Repurchase Agreements

As noted, repurchase agreements are technically labeled "Securities Sold Under Agreement to Repurchase" and referred to in the financial press as "repos." They involve the selling of an asset by the bank – for example, bonds – to a customer or other investor on an overnight or other short-term basis with the understanding that it will be repurchased the next day or at the end of the loan period, not exceeding two weeks. Banks use them in two ways: (1) as an outside funding source for the bank derived from short-term investors and (2) as overnight internal shifts of funds from non-interest-bearing business deposits to repos in order to pay interest to commercial depositors, as discussed earlier.

The first type of repo is simply sold to an investor as an overnight – or up to two weeks – source of funds to the bank. Banks successfully offer this service to investors who are attracted by the repo rates. Rates are published (see table on pages 42–43) and are highly competitive – even negotiable if the investor is large enough. Note in the table that the overnight repo rate in the United States as of May 31, 2012, was 0.26 %. That is an annualized rate of 26/100 of 1 % – or, as generally stated in the financial press, 26 basis points – where one basis point is equal to 1/100 of 1 %. This is a very low rate by historical standards, but it reflects the generally low rates of interest throughout the short-term financial markets at that time, which, in turn, reflects the continued easing of monetary policy to combat the recession affecting the US economy.

The securities, or bonds, in question are owned and held by the bank and usually do not change hands. They represent earmarked collateral that the bank pledges to the investor, so that if the bank failed within the duration of the repo, the investor would collect the bonds. This avenue of funding is not limited to banks; any institution holding the necessary securities as collateral can issue repos, and many do – for example, investment banks, hedge funds, and insurance companies. Technically, this market is wide-open to anyone who holds collateral and wants to raise short-term funds, as well as to any investors who want to earn a rate of return on their funds.

There has been a substantial increase in the use of repos as funding sources by banks in the past few years – as some other funding sources have dried up during the recession. While the use of repos is a legitimate and safe method for raising funds as well as for investment, their increased use has brought attention to them in recent years as never before because of certain abuses that have been revealed.

For instance, there has been recent criticism of certain large banks by regulators and by the financial press – for example, Bank of America, Citigroup, and Deutsche Bank – for "window dressing" their call reports by eliminating repos on the call report date to avoid reporting them and then building them back up significantly after the report is published. This practice reduces the bank's debt as reported on the call report, which fictitiously raises its credit standing with potential investors [5].

Banks can be purchasers of repos, in addition to issuers when they wish to use the technique to place their own surplus funds. Such items would appear on the asset side of the bank's balance sheet as "Securities Bought Under Agreements to Re-sell," called "reverse repos."

Federal Fund Purchases

This source of funds involves the process of a bank's borrowing, usually referred to as buying, the excess balances that another bank holds in its reserve account at the Federal Reserve – that is, excess reserves. Large banks, which typically use funds more efficiently, are most often buyers of Federal Funds. Small banks are typically sellers or lenders. The Federal Funds market developed over time as a means of earning a return on excess reserves or allowing banks in need of additional reserves to find them efficiently.

Technology has made the Federal Funds market feasible. Transactions are executed by electronic transfers of funds from one bank's account in the Fed to the account of another bank. Federal Funds brokers exist to assist banks in locating and placing excess balances and in finding balances for those who are deficient.

The name Federal Funds is often misleading because the funds bought or sold are *not* government funds; they are owned by the banks in whose accounts they reside – just as your account in a retail commercial bank is not the bank's money, but yours. The Fed itself has no operational role in Federal Funds transactions; that is, the funds simply pass through its Fedwire network.

For purposes of accounting, the process of keeping required reserves is known as a "lagged reserve system." There is a reserve computation period and a reserve maintenance period. The computation period begins on a Tuesday and ends on a Monday two weeks later. Required reserves are calculated on the basis of end-of-day balances of checkable deposits for the 14 days of that period, with Saturdays and Sundays being counted the same as the preceding Fridays, and bank holidays, the same as the preceding business day.

The maintenance period is lagged by one month from the computation; it begins on the corresponding Thursday one month after the end of the computation period and runs through the Wednesday two weeks after that. Thus, banks must maintain daily balances with the Fed that will average for the 14-day maintenance period an amount equal to or greater than the required reserve.

Despite this lagged system, and the simplicity of the process, banks still sometimes have difficulty meeting their requirements since the average for the 14-day maintenance period isn't finally calculated until the close of business on that final Wednesday. Large banks, with millions of transactions a day flowing through their reserve accounts, in a volatile transaction climate, can have difficulty hitting the requirement exactly. More cautious banks will hedge by holding larger excess reserves, but many banks do not wish to forego any profit on their funds by holding more reserves than are needed.

As a result, banks are allowed to carry forward for one maintenance period an excess or deficiency up to 4 % of their required reserves. If, after taking any carry-forward into account, the bank is still deficient, it is penalized at the primary discount rate plus 200 basis points. (This rate will be explained later in this chapter.)

If a bank continues to fail to hold the required reserves, it will receive a visit from a Fed official. I can remember being sent on such missions, to sit down with the CEO or CFO of the bank and explain to that person how to calculate the bank's required reserves. This is embarrassing to both the bank and the Fed official.

Purchases and sales of Federal Funds are almost always overnight, but banks may enter into agreements with other banks on "term Fed Funds" that range from a few days to a year. Longer-term Federal Funds borrowings have become more common during the recent financial crisis as banks' funding needs have become more critical.

The Federal Funds market is a very important source of funding for banks, and as we shall see later in this chapter, it has become an alternative to borrowing from the central bank. Technology, as noted, has made this market much easier and more efficient to use by banks over the years, and it has become one of the most popular and most important of all financial markets.

At the time the US central bank was established in 1913, it was thought that borrowings from the Federal Reserve would be the most important source of funding for banks. But the Federal Funds market was not foreseen. Nor could the efficiency with which it operates have been imagined since electronic transfers of funds did not emerge for many years. There are still important differences, as we shall see, among countries in the extent to which banks rely on interbank borrowing as a source of funding, *vis-a-vis* borrowing from the central bank.

The Federal Funds rate is a published rate. (See Table of Money Rates on pages 42–43.) The rate that is published – while it is not labeled as such in the table – is the "market" Federal Funds rate. The other rate that must be considered in this context is the "target" rate, which is set by the Federal Reserve as a matter of monetary policy, which we shall discuss further in Chap. 12. The market rate is determined by the forces of supply and demand in the short-term money market. The Federal Reserve will then conduct its monetary policy operations in such a way as to try to move the market rate into line with the target rate, which it has set. It can do this by increasing or decreasing the supply of funds in the market or by increasing demand in that market to cause the market rate to move accordingly. Again, this process is explained in detail in Chap. 12.

Note that the market rate for Federal Funds in the table on pages 42–43 is 17 basis points – very close to the rate on overnight repos, discussed earlier, of 26 basis points and also close to the 1-month Eurodollar rate of 12 basis points. This phenomenon illustrates an important feature of financial markets – that is, that these markets are competitive with each other in that they are all markets for short-term funds. Thus, rates will tend to cluster fairly close together among markets representing similar maturities among the financial instruments involved.

The Federal Funds rate is a highly sensitive market rate. It indicates, as other similar rates do, the degree of tightness or ease in the short-term market for funds. Some say it reflects the "pulse" of the market.

The Federal Funds rate has one other feature of importance to economic analysts – that is, its movements over time reflect the path of operations that the Fed is conducting in monetary policy. As we shall see in Chap. 12, the Fed does not control the market rate directly, but it influences it by its operations in the open market. The Federal Funds rate rises as the central bank sells securities in the open market, which reduces overall funds available to banks, and makes money and credit conditions tighter. As the central bank buys securities in the market – as it did during the period of "quantitative easing" for most of 2011 and 2012 – the money supply in the economy is expanded, interest rates decline, and money and credit conditions are eased. One can easily see, therefore, why this market is so important to the central bank in its conduct of monetary policy and why the rate is so closely watched as an indicator of monetary policy.

Eurodollar Borrowings

From a global perspective, most central banks permit interbank borrowing and lending using accounts with the central bank, but the practice began in the United States.

It is also quite common for banks to arrange to borrow from or lend to each other outside the Federal Funds market itself. For example, the use of Eurodollars for this purpose, especially in countries outside the United States, has been a rapidly growing source of funding, and as noted earlier, the US banks can borrow Dollar-denominated balances from foreign banks if they choose to do so. These are Eurodollar borrowings. The choice as to the source obviously depends on the relative rates involved. Thus, we tend to think of the Federal Funds market as being essentially domestic and the Eurodollar market as being international in scope.

Chapter 2 discussed the origin and growth of the Eurodollar market. As noted there, Eurodollars are Dollar-denominated deposits in foreign banks or foreign branches of the US banks. Though Eurodollars began in Britain, the name today doesn't necessarily imply Europe – it simply means outside the United States. Hence, Euroyen would be Yen-denominated deposits in banks outside Japan – they could be in the United States, South America, Africa, or anywhere. This terminology often causes some confusion with the Euro, the European currency, so it is important to remember the distinction. Eurodollars are not Euros; they are Dollars. Euros are Euros.

Any deposits of Dollars placed in banks outside the United States, and which remain denominated in Dollars, become Eurodollars, regardless of who places them there – Americans, foreigners, or anyone else. These are usually held in the form of time deposits. Similarly, US banks, businesses, and individuals can borrow Dollars from banks outside the United States, just as foreigners do. Such borrowings, say by an American bank, would be labeled "Eurodollar borrowings" and would be shown as such on the liability side of the borrowing bank's balance sheet.

These transactions carry a market rate – sometimes stated in a range, where the lower is the "bid rate" posted by seekers of Dollars, and the upper is the "offer rate" posted by banks offering Dollars. As noted above, the borrower will likely choose on the basis of the relative rates involved. In this connection, it should be noted that the origin of the Eurodollar market coincided roughly with the introduction of the Libor rate (the London Interbank Offer Rate). This is the rate that emerged – again resulting from the forces of supply and demand in the market for Dollar balances – among banks in London. For many years it has been the prominent interbank lending rate among banks for Dollar-denominated loans on a worldwide basis. It has been adopted for many other uses since its beginning and is now a common reference rate for commercial loans of all kinds. It has become the most common rate for floating-rate loans where banks will state their actual lending rate as Libor plus or minus a certain number of basis points, so as to make it consistent with current market conditions, at any given time or place. (There will be more on the Libor rate in Chap. 8).

Large Certificates of Deposit

As noted earlier, a distinction is made between small and large certificates of deposit as sources of funds to banks. Small CDs are treated as deposits, which, of course, they are. Large-denomination – or jumbo – CDs, while they are actually deposits, are treated as market sources of funds. The principal reason for this distinction is that there is a separate market for jumbo CDs. One can buy or sell these instruments in a secondary market at any time – that is, the investor is not locked in to a fixed term, as with small CDs. Therefore, prices and interest rates on them vary from day to day, as in other financial markets. There are CD brokers who help to make this market function by arranging CD sales for banks that are looking for funds and for directing investors to banks which have them for sale. Jumbo CDs are issued in denominations of $100,000 or more, an outgrowth of the fact that the FDIC insurance limit was set at this amount from 1980 until 2008, when it was raised to $250,000 to help restore confidence in banks during the financial crisis. This higher level of insurance, which was made permanent under the Dodd-Frank bill of 2010, means that jumbo CDs are now insured to that amount. However, the market still draws the line of distinction between small and large CDs at the $100,000 level. This is the only one of the market-based sources that is insured, which increases its attractiveness to investors.

Because of the volatility of this market, jumbo CDs are often referred to in the financial press as "brokered CDs" or, by the less complimentary term, "hot money." What has made this market popular among banks is that it is easily accessible – because of the existence of brokers and the ability to move funds electronically – so that banks can quickly raise funds through this channel. Rates are published daily, and the market is global in scope. A bank that is in dire need of liquidity can negotiate for funds in this market by offering a rate slightly above the published rate. A difference in rates of only a few basis points will move money around very easily among banks. I remember instances during periods of financial crises when the Fed and other regulators watched for the existence of disproportionately large amounts of brokered CDs among a bank's liabilities as a potential indicator of trouble – for example, an impending liquidity crisis. Thus, movements of funds by sharp money managers are often watched by bank regulators to identify trouble spots.

Borrowing from the Central Bank

Another source of funds, which, with very rare exceptions, is exclusively available to banks, is borrowing from the Federal Reserve through the "discount window," and the rate charged is the "discount rate."

The lending process is closely administered, but the way the practice is managed varies among central banks around the world. The United States and Japanese practices provide an interesting contrast. For example, daily average borrowing from the Federal Reserve by the US banks – under normal conditions, say, prior to 2007 – would range from as little as $50 million to as high as $150 million, a minuscule amount compared to the size of the $12.7 trillion US banking industry. In Japan, however, during a comparable, normal period, borrowing by Japanese banks from the Bank of Japan would be around $18–20 billion in Dollar equivalent – that is, 400 times as much as in a considerably smaller banking system. Why does this disparity exist? It boils down to a difference in philosophy between the two central banks and the availability of alternative funding sources to American banks.

If we look at borrowing of the US banks through the Federal Funds market for the same period, we would see that it ranges on a daily average basis from about $100–150 billion. This suggests that American banks have typically used the Federal Funds market rather than resorting to borrowing from the central bank. The opposite was true in Japan, and the Japanese experience was more typical of other central banks around the world in this regard than that of the Federal Reserve.

This pattern of lending by the Federal Reserve is also in sharp contrast to its early policies. When the Fed began operations in 1914, other funding sources – especially market sources – did not exist as they do today. Therefore, banks turned to the Fed for loans to solve their recurring liquidity problems, and the Fed expected them to do so. Indeed, this was one of the principal reasons for establishing the central bank at that time – to create an elastic currency by lending to banks to meet their liquidity needs. It was later, principally in the latter half of the 20th century, after the Federal Funds market began to develop and mature, that the Federal Reserve adopted a philosophy of "lender of last resort" and encouraged banks to use market sources of funding before turning to the Fed. Under this strict philosophy, banks were not allowed to profit from a positive spread between the Federal Funds rate and the discount rate – that is, to borrow from the Fed and, at the same time, lend funds through the Federal Funds market.

Therefore, many bankers saw a stigma attached to borrowing from the central bank. Bankers viewed borrowing from the Fed as an admission that they had not managed their funds properly and came to believe that reliance on market sources was better than reliance on the "government," which the discount window was seen to be. This hard-nosed and highly restrictive philosophy remained in place until after the turn of the 21st century.

It should be noted that even from the very beginning of central bank lending, there has been some controversy and debate as to what constitutes an appropriate use of the discount window. As with many of its early policies, the Federal Reserve was influenced by the practices of the Bank of England, which was, and still is, the oldest central bank in continuous operation in the world, dating from 1694, and is affectionately called, "The Old Lady of Threadneedle Street." The Bank of England had long held to a policy called the "real bills doctrine." Under this philosophy the belief was that central bank loans should be extended only to banks that held collateral based on the production of real goods and services – that is, business firms, farmers, and miners. This logic excluded loans to banks that held collateral based on any speculative activity – such as the purchase of bonds, stocks, or any securities subject to market fluctuation. The underlying rationale was that central bank loans under this doctrine would never be inflationary because they ultimately supported only real production. The Fed in its early days adhered to the real bills doctrine but later abandoned it because it could not be proved that loans for other purposes would necessarily be inflationary.

In those early years of central banking in the United States, the discount window was the only tool of monetary policy available to the Fed. The ability to change reserve requirements, mentioned earlier, was not given to the Fed until the mid-1930s, and the other major tool, open market operations, had not been discovered.

Changes in Lending Policies and the Term Auction Facility

This highly restrictive tradition was changed drastically in January 2003. At that time, the Fed announced a new "market-oriented" discount window. Under the new policy, the discount rate was renamed the "Primary Discount Rate." The Fed stated in its press release announcing the change that the discount window would be an improved means of injecting new money into the economy. It was thought that this would eliminate the stigma of borrowing from the central bank that still strongly lingered in the minds of many bankers. Also, it was expected that the new policy would be particularly beneficial in periods of economic slump or financial crisis. The timing of this move was uncanny! Little did anyone know what a major calamity was about to strike the US economy 4 years later. This new policy was of great benefit in dealing with that crisis.

Under the market-oriented discount policy, the Federal Reserve announced that "qualified banks" would be given access to the discount window, and as long as they had the collateral, they would be able to borrow freely, with no questions asked. Qualified banks were defined as those with CAMELS ratings of 1, 2, or 3.[5] At the time of this policy change in 2003, most US banks were in sound financial condition and would have been qualified.

The primary discount rate was set initially under the new policy at the Federal Funds target rate plus 100 basis points. And until August 17, 2007, it was moved, either up or down, in lock-step with changes in the target Federal Funds rate to keep the 100 basis point spread. Therefore, for the first four years after the change, not much happened in the volume of discount window borrowing because the spread between the two rates continued to provide a disincentive for banks to use the discount window.

In August 2007, the Fed's initial move in response to the impending crisis was to encourage banks to borrow by lowering the primary discount rate 50 basis points and leaving the Federal Funds target rate unchanged. This was at least a modest improvement in the incentive for banks to borrow, but the cost of funds through the discount window was still 50 basis points higher than through the Federal Funds market.

The Fed did, however, take other actions that were incentives to borrow. It extended the borrowing period for the discount window from overnight credit only to as much as 30 days. This was followed by successive moves over the next several months – from September 18, 2007, to December 16, 2008 – to lower the discount rate from a high of 6.25 % at the outset of the crisis to its lowest level ever of 0.50 %, a decline of 575 basis points. Over the same time period, the Fed also lowered the Federal Funds target rate from a high of 5.25 % to a range of 0–0.25 %. Thus, at the end of the year, 2008, which was near the lowest point of the recession, the spread between

---

[5] The CAMELS rating, which will be explained in more detail in Chap. 6, is an evaluation assigned to banks by their regulators, where the acronym stands for Capital, Assets, Management, Earnings, Liquidity, and Sensitivity to market risk. A bank is given a grade on each of these attributes and then averaged for the bank as a whole, ranging from 1, which is the highest, to 5, which is the lowest.

the discount and target Federal Funds rates stood at 25 basis points. These sharp declines in rates over a relatively short period of 15 months were motivated by dire predictions that the US economy was about to enter another Great Depression akin to that of the 1930s.

It is arguable whether the Fed saw the financial crisis coming; some within the Fed had warned about it several years earlier. But, then Chairman Alan Greenspan did not take these warnings seriously, and therefore, the Fed passed up an opportunity to have taken some actions – for example, forcing cutbacks in mortgage lending and enforcing higher lending standards for banks – which might have averted some of the worst aspects of the oncoming crash in financial markets and among financial institutions. This was an oversight for which the Fed has been justifiably criticized in the aftermath of the debacle and has seriously damaged its credibility for the future.

The rate reductions that the Fed enacted did have an impact upon the banking system, as banks were sitting on hundreds of billions of Dollars worth of defaulted loans and were in serious need of liquidity in order to keep operating. On November 21, 2007, near the beginning of the downturn, the US banks were borrowing $58 million; as of March 25, 2009, near the trough of the recession, borrowing had reached $61.3 billion, an increase of over 1,000 times.

Noting, however, that the stigma about the use of the discount window still existed for many bankers, the Fed tried another approach to get banks to borrow and to stimulate the economy. They announced in December 2007, the establishment of the Term Auction Facility (TAF). The increases in borrowing through the discount window were further amplified by borrowing through the TAF.

This was a separate lending arrangement whereby any depository financial institution qualified to borrow at the primary discount rate could bid for funds at auction. This, in effect, released the Fed's lending process from the discount rate; banks bid the rate they were willing to pay. An announcement of the amount to be auctioned was made prior to each scheduled auction – the first of which was held on December 17, 2007, for $20 billion for a 28-day term. The auctions were deemed successful, as the amounts bid were substantially in excess of the amounts offered, frequently by two to three times as much. The Fed continued the process, reaching an average level of borrowing of about $500 billion per month, usually for terms of 28–30 days, throughout the years 2008 and 2009. The rates paid by the borrowers, referred to as the "stop-out" rates, consistently averaged some 20–30 basis points below the primary discount rate. As of March 25, 2009, the date used in the above comparison, the level of credit outstanding through the TAF stood at $468.6 billion.

It was the Fed's intention to continue the TAF until they were satisfied that the liquidity needs of the financial markets – particularly the mortgage market – had been met. Consequently, they decided in late 2009 to terminate the facility as of March 31, 2010, which they did. At that same time, the Fed raised the primary discount rate to 75 basis points, which was its level on June 1, 2012. (See Table of Money Rates, pages 42–43).

The 2003 policy change also set a higher "secondary" rate, which is available for banks in questionable financial condition that borrow under conditions resembling the old lender-of-last-resort philosophy. The secondary rate is set at 50 basis points above the primary rate. Also, there is a seasonal credit program that is available to banks that have recurring intra-year seasonal fluctuations in their funding needs, such as those in agricultural or seasonal resort communities. The Fed, however, has attached so much administrative red tape into the process of qualifying for this seasonal borrowing privilege that many banks shun it entirely.

In addition to these lending programs – all of which we would consider more or less routine – there is an "Emergency" credit provision, for which no rate is published, provided by Section 13(3) of the Federal Reserve Act. This is the "rare exception" referred to above where it was noted that the privilege of borrowing from the Federal Reserve is exclusively available to banks. Section 13(3) allows the central bank to extend credit to nonbanks, or even to nonfinancial enterprises, under "unusual and exigent circumstances." Over the years, this reference in the law has been open to wide interpretation, but the Federal Reserve usually interprets it to mean national emergencies or extremely serious systemic risk situations. In addition, the use of this section requires the approval of five of the seven members of the Board of Governors. It is not unusual to find that there are two vacancies on the board – which has been the case for two years during the recent financial crisis – which means that the use of this section required the unanimous approval of all existing members.

Section 13(3) has been used during the economic crisis of 2007–2012, as we shall see. In earlier years, however, when its potential use has been considered, the Fed has often found other ways to accomplish the purpose of supplying credit without having to use this section.

The use of moral suasion – which is a polite way of saying "arm-twisting" – has been used in cases where the Fed has been able to pull together a consortium of banks and prevail upon them to supply credit to the needy entity, which sidesteps the necessity of the Fed having to supply it directly. In such cases, the Fed usually assures the cooperating banks that it will come to their rescue with discount window loans if the loans they are being asked to extend should result in liquidity problems for them.

One of the early examples of the use of this type of credit came about by the impending bankruptcies of Chrysler Corporation and Penn Central Railroad in 1970. The failure of these two large corporations would have had serious consequences on the economy, which was already weak at that time. There was no question that their difficulties represented a systemic risk – that is, a risk of the disruption or perhaps the breakdown of the financial system as a whole. These companies were faced with the need to roll over huge quantities of commercial paper to stay in business, but the commercial paper market had turned them away, and they could not otherwise arrange the credit. This was during an era in which the Fed still rigidly controlled rates that banks could pay on deposits and CDs under Regulation Q. When this crisis arose, the Fed removed the ceiling rate on large CDs, and money started flowing into banks. And through moral suasion, the Fed persuaded these banks to lend to Chrysler and Penn Central. Within a short time frame, the problem cleared up, and the crisis was over. Thus, the Fed avoided the necessity of using Section 13(3).

Another similar situation arose in 1975, in which this author, then Staff Director at the Board of Governors, was involved. This was the threatened financial failure of New York City. I was assigned to help arrange a meeting between Fed Chairman Arthur Burns and the Mayor of New York City, Abraham Beame, who was also to be accompanied by the Governor of New York, Hugh Carey. This meeting was held at the Board's offices in Washington, at which the Mayor and the Governor appealed to Chairman Burns to use Section 13(3) to help the city. Burns refused, as he thought that the central bank's extension of credit directly to the city would open Pandora's Box. After this meeting, the Governor and the Mayor went to see President Gerald Ford at the White House and appealed to him. Ford also refused, and the headline in *The New York Times* the next morning read: "Ford to New York: Drop Dead."

This story had a happy ending after all because Burns, a New Yorker himself, was not unsympathetic to the needs of the city. He then prevailed upon the city to issue a new special class of bonds and promised that he would try to get banks to buy them. Thus, again through moral suasion, he persuaded a large consortium of banks, primarily New York banks, to purchase the new series of bonds. This tactic worked very well; the city got its liquidity and was able to correct its problems and pay off its bonds. The banks knew that they had the backing of the Fed if they ran into liquidity problems by buying the city's bonds. As we know, the city survived. Again, this sidestepped the use of Section 13(3).

The situation had changed a great deal, however, at the time of the crisis of 2007–2012. The US banking system was in better financial condition in the 1970s than it was during the most recent crisis. Therefore, when two of the big-three automakers turned to the federal government for help in the period, 2008–2009, the banking system – already flat on its back and facing numerous failures of its own – was in no position to help. Again, the question arose about the use of Section 13(3). As it turned out, it was not used because the US Treasury, itself, with the concurrence of the President and the noninterference of the Congress, extended credit to the automakers by purchasing their stock.

Many Americans were uncomfortable with the idea that the federal government had become the largest shareholder of General Motors. The old adage, coined by GM CEO Charles Wilson in the 1950s, "What's good for General Motors is good for America," was heard again and again. People screamed, "Socialism!!!" but it saved millions of jobs. In any event, the process worked, and the automakers who took advantage of this line of credit are now out of bankruptcy and have substantially redeemed their stock.

Other situations emerged that confronted the Fed and the Treasury with similar challenges. The potential failure of the five largest investment banks in the country was threatened by their growing financial problems. Since they were nonbanks, these institutions were not eligible to access the Fed's discount window. Bear Stearns was the first to go, but, because it was taken over by JPMorgan/ Chase, which is a bank, discount window credit could be and was extended to it through the bank. The second was Merrill Lynch, but again, by virtue of its being taken over by Bank of America, Fed credit could be extended via the bank. The third was Lehman Brothers, which could not find a merger partner, either in the

United States or abroad. Moreover, it had virtually no collateral left of sufficient value to support even a Section 13(3) loan, and it was therefore allowed to fail. The ripple effect of that failure is still felt in the US financial system. Finally, the remaining two that were headed for failure – Morgan Stanley and Goldman Sachs, converted their charters to banks, which gave them access to the Fed's discount window.

The remaining institutional crisis that could not be resolved by merger or any other conventional means was that of American International Group (AIG), then the largest insurance company in the world. AIG became overly extended in the field of credit default swaps, which are a kind of insurance policy, issued usually to banks, to insure against losses on their loan portfolios. In view of the fact that bank loan portfolios throughout the banking system consisted of very heavy concentrations of mortgage loans, and that these loans were going into default at an unprecedented rate, the market for credit default swaps mushroomed. A secondary market developed in these instruments, and investors were buying them who had no vested interest in the loans upon which they were based. These investors saw, or thought they saw, opportunities to collect vast sums of money when these loans ultimately failed and had to be written off. The insurers – for example, AIG – would pay. What was not counted upon was that AIG, and some other issuers, had significantly overextended themselves on the coverage they had insured against. When AIG finally failed, it had a half-trillion Dollars of these instruments on its books, and its reserves were woefully inadequate to even begin to pay off its obligations. Thus, Section 13(3) came into the picture, and AIG was ultimately extended central bank credit of $182 billion to keep it afloat. Again, systemic risk was the driving concern.

These crises brought Section 13(3) to the public's attention. Most people had never heard of it before. Regulators and Congress are still working on solutions to the problems raised by the recent financial crisis, and one lingering question is, "What should be the limits of the Federal Reserve's authority in such crises?" There has always been a kind of unwritten understanding that the central bank should be able to step into a situation and to take necessary action when it perceives that the financial system of the country is in danger. However, during this recent crisis, there were many who believed that the Federal Reserve went too far in the bailout process. These critics argued that the effect of the failure of large institutions would not be as dire as the Fed would have the public believe. Thus, they believed that the Congress and regulators should let institutions fail and live with the consequences of whatever collateral damage might occur. Sheila Bair agreed with this argument. She argued, "People intuitively *know* that bailouts are wrong and that our banking system was mismanaged and badly regulated" [4, p. 14].

Lawyer and Consultant Vern McKinley, with whom I have worked on consultancies with central banks in Kenya and Ukraine, has noted that Congress and the regulators engage in a reflex action, "…to do something by using public funds in a pointless attempt to make the short-term circumstances less volatile. The best approach is to simply shutter the failing institution in question, no matter how large or complex" [6, p. 313].

To some extent, Congress addressed the uncertainty about the Fed's role in the economy in the Dodd-Frank bill of 2010. It created the Financial Stability Oversight Council – made up of 10 representatives of federal financial regulatory agencies and headed by the Secretary of the Treasury. This council can authorize the Federal Reserve to regulate and subject to prudential standards, nonbank financial institutions if the council believes they are endangering financial stability. And the Fed can use this authority to force such institutions to divest any of their holdings if the Fed determines that a threat to stability exists [6, p. 282]. Also, in Dodd-Frank, Congress modified Section 13(3) to require that it not be considered applicable to an individual institution, but, instead, must apply to all institutions in similar circumstances. In the words of the law, this is defined as "broad-based eligibility." For example, if it were to be applicable to a situation like AIG in the future, it must also be applicable to all insurance companies having the same problems with credit default swaps, as AIG did. It further requires that 13(3) be applied only to solvent institutions, so that if an institution is deemed to be already insolvent, that institution must be closed and not be extended credit through 13(3). These changes narrow the applicability somewhat but do not change the essential thrust of the section [6].

In summary, we have discussed many aspects of the lending function of the central bank and described how this function has changed markedly over the 100-year-existence of the Federal Reserve System – ranging from an open access credit facility in the early days for all institutions having collateral, to a narrow, rigidly administered "lender-of-last-resort" policy, and then returning to an open-market-oriented facility providing access without any restrictions other than that the institution be "qualified," as described above, and have the necessary collateral.

This last change of lending policy was badly needed in the first decade of the 21st century in light of the seriousness of the financial crisis that ensued. This brought the discount window back into the picture as an active tool of monetary policy from a period of almost complete dormancy that had lasted several decades.

Other Bank Debt

One final note regarding non-deposit sources of funds for banks pertains to other bank debt. Long-term debt, for example, in the form of bonds or notes, can be issued by banks as they are by other kinds of business enterprises. Debt maturing after five years or longer can be counted as part of a bank's capital under SEC rules. Whether such debt is feasible for banks depends upon their bond ratings in the credit markets that are assigned by the bond rating agencies – for example, Moody's, Standard and Poors, and Fitch. There will be more to say on these rating agencies when we discuss the bond market in more detail in Chap. 8. Beginning in 2008, because of the existing financial crisis, the FDIC decided to extend insurance coverage, which is normally restricted to deposits, to other bank debt. Again, this was done to restore investor confidence in the banking system. The FDIC withdrew this coverage in September 2009, under the assumption that it was no longer necessary.

The use of long-term debt is also common among financial holding companies (formerly bank holding companies) to raise funds either for the subsidiary bank or for other subsidiaries of the holding company. Thus, the holding company can be an important source of funding for the bank, either by adding to the bank's capital through the purchase of its stock or by lending directly to the bank.

Off-Balance-Sheet Items

Off-balance-sheet items are not technically liabilities of the bank, such as the other items we have covered in this chapter, but are contingent liabilities or obligations that the bank might have in the future. Accounting rules require that potential obligations be included as footnotes in a bank's balance sheet. These would include standby letters of credit, unused credit lines, and certain derivative contracts that could involve costs to the bank. Often, bank customers may have to call upon the bank to make good on these credit commitments when other sources of credit dry up, as in periods of financial crisis.

Some banks – particularly the larger, more aggressive ones – may carry off-balance-sheet items far in excess of total assets. These typically are unused credit card lines, unused loan commitments, and standby letters of credit. Banks can comfortably leverage in this manner because they know from experience that the total of such amounts would virtually never have to be met.

Consider an example of a derivative contract as a potential liability or an off-balance-sheet item for a bank. An American producer ships goods to England; the contract calls for payment in six months of £50 million. Let's say that the exchange rate at the time the contract is entered into is £1 = $1.60. Therefore, the contract is worth $80 million, which is the amount the shipper would expect to collect. What if the Pound declines to $1.53? The contract is worth $76.5 million – a loss of $3.5 million. The shipper worries that this might happen and purchases an option to sell £50 million at today's exchange rate of $1.60. The option costs the shipper $50,000.

If the Pound does decline to $1.53, the shipper's position is protected. The net is $79,950,000. If the Pound does not decline, or goes up, the shipper lets the option lapse and has made money on the exchange rate.

But who is the other party to this contract? That person is the "counterparty" in the terminology of the derivatives market. The counterparty could be any investor willing to take the risk; it might be a bank or other financial institution. It might be the shipper's own bank, which provides this risk protection. It is easy to see that if the counterparty prices the risk appropriately, the contract could be quite lucrative – for example, the $50,000 fee. Many banks are in the business of selling derivative contracts, or selling protection against someone else's risk for a fee. This type of business activity has grown phenomenally for banks in the last two decades – to the chagrin of many of them who have guessed wrong on the degree of risk exposure.

Thus, there is a contingent liability to the bank in this example. Realistically, its estimated loss is $3.5 million – or whatever is a reasonable estimate of the risk exposure. But the entire £50 million is not at risk; this total value of the contract is referred to as the "notional value." Therefore, the bank should show in the footnotes to its balance sheet an off-balance-sheet liability of $3.5 million. The bank (or whoever the counterparty is) would probably put a "floor" at this level, indicating the maximum portion of the loss it is willing to take for the given fee.

Other examples of potential risk seem to be invented every day. Within recent years, for example, we have seen the development of Structured Investment Vehicles (SIVs). A number of these entities, which are subsidiaries of banks and other financial institutions, hold subprime mortgages or other risky assets and have acquired them by issuing debt. Only the net investment in the SIV is shown on the bank's balance sheet, and this deceives investors who do not know that the SIV masks the risk of massive losses if its assets go bad.

To illustrate, assume that the SIV is set up with $10 million investment in its capital by the parent bank. The SIV can then go into the market and issue debt of its own – say $100 million – which it uses to purchase risky mortgages from banks. Suppose the mortgages go into default and have to be written down to 20 % of their face value. The SIV, with only $10 million in capital, is now $70 million into capital insolvency and must be closed. This means it would have to be consolidated into the parent bank's balance sheet, and the parent would have to absorb the $70 million loss as well as the loss of its $10 million investment in the SIV. This happened in December 2007, when Citigroup had to absorb a $41 billion write-off of its losses on its SIVs. Off-balance-sheet items shown in the footnotes of a bank's balance sheet should show this exposure to risk.

References

1. Lewis M (2010) The big short. W.W. Norton, New York
2. Board of Governors of the Federal Reserve System, Statistical Release H.8, Assets and liabilities of commercial banks in the United States. 25 May 2012.
3. Lind M (2012) Land of promise: an economic history of the United States. Harper Collins, New York, Chap. 1
4. Bair S (2013) Bull by the horns. The Free Press, New York
5. Eaglesham J, Baer J (2010) SEC to target bank 'Window Dressing'. Financial Times, London, 17 Sept 2010
6. McKinley V (2011) Financing failure: a century of bailouts. The Independent Institute, Oakland, p 313

Chapter 4
How Do Banks Use Their Funds? The Asset Side of the Balance Sheet

We have discussed virtually all funding sources for banks and bank holding companies – except the capital accounts, to which we shall return in Chap. 5. But first, we are interested in examining the kinds of assets that banks would typically hold, focusing on the earning assets – investments and loans.

Secondary markets exist for all bank assets. Therefore, a bank may choose to keep an asset until it matures and is paid off, or may sell it if it sees an opportunity for profit, or perceives some other reason to get the asset off its books. In Chap. 7 we shall examine the markets for all kinds of financial instruments on which banks and other investors depend.

There are many ways to look at the nature of assets – earning or non-earning assets, liquid and nonliquid assets, or assets as reserves. By reserves, we mean funds that an individual bank, or the banking system as a whole, has available for use to make loans or other investments in order to produce earnings. An individual bank's reserves would be the funds it holds in its reserve account with the Fed, plus its vault cash, as well as any short-term investments that it can quickly convert to cash.

Earning assets, as noted above, are essentially loans and investments, while non-earning assets may consist of any portion of cash in the vault that is not counted as required reserves, items in the process of collection – or float – and premises of the bank and its equipment. For obvious reasons, banks attempt to minimize non-earning assets, even to the extent in many cases of not owning their buildings and equipment, but leasing them instead. Many bankers resist the idea of having any non-earning assets shown on their balance sheets for window-dressing purposes.

Liquid assets are either cash or those items that can be very quickly converted to cash. This distinction has less significance today than it did in the past years because of the efficiency of markets, which can liquidate nonliquid assets very quickly – although sometimes at a loss or a penalty. Nevertheless, there is generally a trade-off between liquidity and earnings because the assets that have the greater earning potential generally are those that are less liquid – that is, loans and longer-term investments.

W.H. Wallace, *The American Monetary System: An Insider's View of Financial Institutions, Markets and Monetary Policy*, DOI 10.1007/978-3-319-02907-8_4, © Springer International Publishing Switzerland 2013

Bank Reserves and the Fractional Reserve System

Returning for a moment to the discussion of required reserves, we have noted earlier that the central bank requires a percentage of checkable deposits to be held in the bank's reserve account with the Fed and that this is fixed by regulation D. Vault cash can be counted as a portion of required reserves; the rest is deposited with the Fed.

Until recently, these reserves in the US banking system were non-earning assets, as the Fed did not pay interest on them. However, under pressure from the banking industry, Congress changed this policy as part of the financial bailout package of October 2008 (the TARP program) to require that interest be paid on both required and excess reserves held with the Fed, including any vault cash counted as required reserves. Rates initially were set at the target Federal Funds rate −10 basis points for required reserves and at the same −75 basis points for excess reserves. Because of the recession that followed after this change was made, the Fed reset this rate to make it equal to the target Federal Funds rate – or the upper level of its range – at 25 basis points.

This change of policy will likely have a bearing on monetary policy in the future because, in setting the rate it will pay, the Fed has a new tool for controlling market interest rates. Raising the rate would draw funds from the banking system into the Fed, thus demonetizing those funds – that is, decreasing the money supply. Conversely, lowering the rate would give banks an incentive to draw down excess reserves with the Fed, placing the money back into the banking system – that is, increasing the money supply. These moves, respectively, would represent either a reduction or an increase in the supply of money and credit available to the economy at large and thus become instruments of monetary policy.

Our system, similar to that of many other countries, is a fractional reserve system. The "multiple expansion of bank deposits" rests upon this system. A reserve requirement of 10 % means a potential expansion of deposits of ten times any initial deposit of *new* money into the system – that is, 1/(reserve requirement ratio) = deposit multiplier. New money – for example, funds from outside the country or originating as central bank credit – is often called "high-powered money" because of the multiplier effect.

The following example illustrates how the banking *system* can expand the money supply of the economy through its lending operations. Begin with the extension of a loan by Bank A.

The multiple expansion of bank deposits

Bank	Increase in deposits	Increase in loans	Increase in reserves
Bank A		$1,000	
Bank B	$1,000	900	$100
Bank C	900	810	90
Bank D	810	729	81
Bank E	729	656	73
Bank F	656	591	65
	⋮	⋮	⋮
All banks	$10,000	$10,000	$1,000

Thus, it can be seen that total loans have been expanded by a factor of ten times the original loan, and total deposits – assuming that the proceeds of each loan are redeposited in a bank within the system – have also been expanded ten times. Total reserves held by the central bank grow to 100 % of the amount of the original loan. This simplified example is taught to all students of economics to illustrate the power of the banking system to create money. However, it rests on one very important assumption, which may or may not hold true. That is the continued existence of loan demand within the economy. There have been instances, for example, in which the Federal Reserve has lowered the reserve requirement ratio in what was intended to be a stimulative monetary policy move, but found to its disappointment that neither businesses nor consumers wished to borrow from the increased supply of funds, even at a reduced interest rate. This situation is what Keynes referred to as a "liquidity trap" [1]. There will be further discussion of bank reserves in Chap. 12 on monetary policy.

Earning Assets, Investments, Government and Government Agency Securities

Banks have traditionally held investments, not only to earn a return but as backup to meet increases in loan demand. The most conservative banks hold higher proportions of investments relative to loans. Recent trends, however, show that banks are holding investments as trading assets and making loans with the intention of selling them. We shall discuss loans in more depth in the pages ahead, but in both cases, these recent trends have indicated a radical departure from the traditional model of banking, in which earning assets were typically held to maturity, and the bank earned interest income on them during the full term of the obligation.

We have seen these trends demonstrated clearly during the recession that began in 2007, as banks had loaned heavily in the mortgage market in the years leading up to the downturn. In addition, they had invested significantly in mortgage-backed securities – that is, bonds or notes – based on the mortgages that had been sold by the originating banks to investors who converted them into mortgage-backed securities and re-sold them to the investing public, including banks. A serious problem arose because many of these mortgages were subprime loans or other risky mortgages on which adequate analysis – or due diligence – of the borrower's financial situation had not been done. This development was a colossal oversight on the part of the American banking industry, which defies all the logic upon which banking is based. This process, called "securitization," will be discussed in more detail later in this chapter, and its misuse was one of the principal causes of the devastating financial crisis of recent years.

With regard to its investment portfolio, a bank competes with all other investors for the same set of investment opportunities. These competitors include nonbank financial institutions, such as investment banks, mutual funds, hedge funds, insurance companies, as well as private firms and individuals who have funds to invest.

In other words, these are wide-open, private markets subject to all the forces of supply and demand that exist throughout all markets – whether for corn, wheat, oil, or gold, or for bonds, stocks, or other kinds of financial instruments. While many investors rely on bankers to advise them on where to place their funds, the fact remains – as experience has shown – that bankers have no greater insight into what the future holds in these markets than any other analysts or observers.

Treasury Securities

Among the most common investments of the American banks are US Treasury securities (Treasuries). It is also true, incidentally, that US Treasuries are the most popular investments of many foreign banks and investors.[1] They are available to investors in the form of bills, notes, and bonds – typically ranging from 4-week to 1-year bills, 2- to 10-year notes, and 10- to 30-year bonds. US Treasuries are regarded by the markets as virtually risk-free and are treated as such in determining a bank's risk-based capital requirements (more on this subject in Chap. 5).

The market for US Treasuries is highly liquid because secondary markets exist for them all over the world and because they trade in very large quantities so that buyers and sellers are virtually assured of being able to conduct transactions in them almost anywhere and at any time.

Treasury Inflation Protected Securities (TIPS)

In 1997, TIPS were added to Treasury offerings. Investors in fixed-income securities are at a disadvantage in times of significant inflation. Because of the inflationary concerns of investors, the Treasury concluded that to continue to sell its debt in such times would require offering investors protection against inflation. Thus, in 1997, it announced the TIPS program. These securities, which are issued in 5-, 10-, and 30-year maturities, pay interest at a fixed rate twice per year. However, the principal is adjusted – upward for inflation and downward for deflation.

As in the case of other Treasuries, there is a secondary market for TIPS, and the effective rate which they carry in that market is a market-based estimate of the "real" rate of interest. The real rate is defined as the nominal, or market, rate, less the estimated rate of inflation. And, by extension of that concept, a comparison of a TIPS security of a given maturity – for example, 10 years – to a standard Treasury of the same maturity, would give an estimate of the rate of inflation over the period to maturity. Say, for example, that the rate on a 10-year Treasury bond is

---

[1] Of the roughly $16.8 trillion of Treasury securities outstanding at March 31, 2013, $5.6 trillion is owned by foreign investors – governments, central banks, businesses, and individuals. The largest holder at this time is China, with $1.3 trillion, and the rest is spread over virtually every other country in the world.

4.3 % on a given date, and the rate on a 10-year TIPS security on the same date is 2.05 %, the difference (4.30−2.05), or 2.25 %, is a market estimate of the rate of inflation over the time left to maturity. This has proved to be a reasonably reliable estimate over the period since TIPS have existed, which means that the Treasury has been fairly accurate in estimating inflation to set the rate on TIPS.

Real and nominal interest rates on the 3-month treasury bill 1953–2009 (Source: www. federalreserve.gov/releases/H15)

Note in the graph above the difference between nominal and real interest rates on the 3-month Treasury bill over the 55-year period from 1955 to 2010. The period from about 1965 through the 1970s is remembered as the worst inflation that the US economy has experienced in the post-World War II years, attributable to the combination of President Lyndon Johnson's Great Society program and the escalation of the Vietnam War. The spread between the two lines represents the growing pace of inflation. A turning point occurred around 1980, as the Fed pursued rigorous anti-inflation policies for the first time. After that point, inflation was kept under control at an average of around 2 % per year, until after the turn of the 21st century, when it declined even further.

Negative real interest rates occurred during this period – in the late 1970s – because of extremely high inflation and after 2002 because of the sharp decline in nominal interest rates, which, even with low inflation, produced negative real rates. The effect of a negative real interest rate from an investor's perspective means that investors are, in effect, paying others to hold their money for them. Even with this disadvantage, however, an investor might choose to go into 3-month Treasury bills at negative rates, for example, for the "safe haven" argument – that is, they feel their money is safer in the hands of the Treasury than in some other use that they might choose, such as stocks, which might turn out to be even more risky. This, again, helps to explain the attractiveness of inflation-protected securities.

Even nominal rates can become negative, as well, but this usually happens only for brief periods of time, typically within the course of a trading day. This has happened a few times within the past few years of economic decline, when nominal rates were being held low by monetary policy to attempt to stimulate the economy.

Floating-Rate Treasuries

In August 2012, the Treasury announced its intention to offer floating-rate notes, which will be its first new product in 15 years. More recently, they have announced their intention to start issuing them in the fourth quarter of 2013. The timing is expected to coincide with a general rise in interest rates as the economy improves and the Fed backs off the easy-money policy it has pursued since 2007. The rates on these notes will periodically be reset to match prevailing market rates. This move should entice investors to hold on to Treasuries longer since they would not have to be concerned about losing value as interest rates begin to rise again, and it should enhance the stability of the Treasury markets. The notes are expected to be issued in 2-year maturities, and the Treasury will use the yield at auction of its 3-month Treasury bill sales to adjust rates for the floating-rate notes.[2]

Federal Agency Securities

Aside from the direct obligations of the Treasury, there are securities issued by various agencies of the federal government, which implicitly carry federal government backing. These are issued by the so-called "alphabet soup" agencies – Fannie Mae (FNMA), Freddie Mac (Federal Home Loan Mortgage Corp.), Ginnie Mae (Government National Mortgage Corp.), Sallie Mae (Student Loan Marketing Association), FHLBS (Federal Home Loan Bank System), Federal Housing Authority, and the Federal Farm Credit System. All these agencies were created by acts of Congress to provide liquidity to certain sectors of the economy, as their names imply. They operate by buying loans that banks have made for home mortgages, student loans, farm credit, or whatever the case may be, and issuing securities based on those pools of loans which are then sold to the investing public in general. This is the process of "securitization" of debt, mentioned earlier. Investors in these securities range from individuals to large institutional investors, such as insurance companies, mutual funds, and hedge funds.

---

[2] Treasury Decides to Offer Floating-Rate Notes," *The Wall Street Journal*, 2 Aug. 2012, p. C-3. Also, "Treasury is Readying Floating-Rate Debt," *The Wall Street Journal,* 2 May, 2013, p. C-3.

These agencies worked well in carrying out their assigned tasks until excesses occurred, beginning in the early years of the first decade of the 21st century. This was especially true in the housing industry, when the agencies helped to fuel the housing bubble that built up prior to the crash in 2007. Fannie Mae and Freddie Mac, in particular, had reached the point of owning about $5.3 trillion in home mortgages or about half of the $11 trillion of mortgages outstanding in the United States before the bubble burst. We shall discuss further ramifications of the role of these agencies in the recession of 2007–2012 in Chap. 8.

Municipal Securities

Among other securities issued by governments is the broad category of "municipal securities." The reference to municipals in the financial press generally means all debt securities issued by any level of government below the federal level – that is, states, cities, school districts, and other independent authorities such as airports, roads, dams, and bridges. One unique feature of "munies," as they are often called, is that earnings on them are exempt from federal income taxes. Thus, they generally carry somewhat lower rates than other government securities. One anomaly of the recent economic downturn is that, because of the significant cutbacks in federal funding for city and state projects, the credit ratings of municipalities have dropped to a point that they are having to pay higher rates of interest on their debt than ever before.

Earning Assets, Investments, Corporate Securities

Corporate Debt Securities and the Bond-Rating Agencies

Corporate securities may include debt – that is, bonds, notes, and commercial papers – as well as equities, that is, stocks. Corporate debt securities are generally thought of as falling into three categories: investment grade, which is the highest quality, issued by the most creditworthy companies, intermediate grade, and high-risk – "junk"– securities. Debt rating agencies – for example, Moody's, S&P, and Fitch, mentioned earlier – place grades on both new issues of corporate debt and those outstanding issues that are offered for sale in the secondary bond markets. These agencies are private organizations, which virtually all market participants – both issuers and investors – have come to rely upon over the years, and their ratings have significant impacts upon the rates that issuers have to pay.

The bond-rating agencies have come into considerable controversy in recent years, beginning with the Enron scandal of 2002 and continuing with the mortgage-related downturn that began in 2007. In both of these scenarios, the rating agencies were accused of overrating bonds issued by Enron and mortgage-backed bonds issued and sold by a number of large banks. The criticisms alleged that the agencies have an inherent conflict of interest in that they are paid for their ratings by the firms whose bonds they rate, which gives them a disincentive to issue low ratings, even when the financial conditions of the issuers clearly warrant it. Thus, the credibility of the agencies has been seriously damaged during the past decade.

The buyers of corporate bonds, at the time of issue or in the secondary markets, are mainly large institutional investors but also include small investors and individuals. And investment grade corporate bonds are popular investments with banks.

Junk Bonds and Leveraged Buyouts

High-risk or junk bonds have had a spotty history. They became especially popular in the late 1970s and 1980s as vehicles for leveraged buyouts (LBOs). In these instances, the takeover party – either an individual or group of investors – usually attempts to buy all the existing stock of an existing corporation (or at minimum, a controlling interest), and many found they could raise large amounts of money through the sale of junk bonds. The typical procedure is that once the investors have succeeded in purchasing the stock of the target company, they will take it over and place the bonds on its books as debt, with the intention of paying them off from future earnings of the company.

Sometimes this procedure is successful, and sometimes it is not. It is not uncommon to find that the debt burden necessary to obtain the required amount of stock is greater than anticipated and that the acquired company has difficulty servicing the debt. In such situations, the LBO may have to be unwound, and the company must go public again by issuing new stock. One well-publicized example of this was the RJR-Nabisco LBO of 1989 [2]. This episode will be treated further in Chap. 8, as part of the discussion of the role of investment banks.

In the 1980s and 1990s, LBOs acquired a negative reputation in the financial markets and among investors, because on a number of occasions, they were used to take over companies with the intention of breaking up the firms, selling their assets, and putting their employees out of work. Not all were handled in this manner, of course, but enough were to cause them to be suspect in the public's mind. This also affected the market for junk bonds, and as a consequence, they also went into disrepute for several years. One of the best accounts of these experiences is given by James Stewart, in his book, *Den of Thieves* [3]. This extremely well-written book deals with some of the famous and felonious names of Wall Street in the late 1980s

– particularly Michael Milken and Ivan Boesky. Milken, who popularized junk bonds, and Boesky, who made arbitrage into an art form, both crossed the lines of ethics and legality in the process. Despite their unabashed criminal intent, they were interesting and innovative people, and this book lays it all out [3].

It is interesting to note, however, that, despite the experiences of these earlier years, junk bonds have made a comeback over the most recent decade because as market interest rates have declined significantly across the board on investment grade bonds, the spread between investment grade and junk has widened enough to attract investors back into the market.[3]

Corporate Equity Securities

Investments may also consist of corporate equity securities or stocks. While preferred stocks are, in essence, more like bonds in that they pay a fixed dividend and have preferred status – or a higher claim – on the assets of the company in the event of liquidation, it is common stocks, often called "common equity," that represent the real ownership of the company. And they are last on the preference list in the case of liquidation, which explains why many common stockholders are wiped out when a company goes bankrupt.

The Banking Act of 1933 – commonly known as the Glass-Steagall Act – prohibited banks from investing in common stocks, and this prohibition remained in effect until parts of Glass-Steagall were repealed by the Gramm-Leach-Bliley Act of 1999 (GLB). As noted earlier, Glass-Steagall took banks totally out of any aspect of the investment business. Controversy raged over the effect of this act for eight decades, and it is still being debated today. Many observers believed that Congress intended the act to be punitive because of the widely held view in the early 1930s that banks had caused the Great Depression by engaging in stock speculation. While there was some justification for that view, some economists today take a more sober view of the act's impact on the economy and say that it led to a long period of stable banking, that the economy progressed under its restrictions, and that GLB was a mistake, in that its deregulatory effect has led to the chaos we have experienced in recent years.

---

[3] See "Risk Builds as Junk Bonds Boom," *The New York Times*, August 16, 2012, page B-1.

In any event, the result of the passage of GLB has been that banks can now invest in common stocks, which carry an ownership interest in business enterprises. This is a step away from what has been a tradition in the American economy to separate banking and commerce. The philosophy behind this tradition was that the ownership of stocks by banks could pose a conflict of interest – that is, that banks could or would show favoritism to enterprises in which they had ownership interests and would not apply the same standards of credit analysis to such companies, thus lowering credit quality throughout the banking system. A cynic might argue, however, that banks cannot necessarily be counted upon to apply good standards of credit analysis in any event, as a result of the experience we have recently seen in which banks knowingly extended credit – especially subprime mortgage credit – to noncreditworthy borrowers, but not caring because they knew they could sell the loans and eliminate 100 % of the credit risk from their books. And as we now know from the recent experience, this did not eliminate the credit risk from the system, but simply shifted it from the originating banks to unwitting investors who bore the losses that inevitably resulted.

The Japanese have had unfortunate experiences resulting from the lack of separation of banking and commerce. They permit unusually close relationships to exist between banks and their borrowers. The result has been an unwillingness to implement banking reforms that were badly needed, and this reluctance helped to bring about the unusually long recession of the 1990s, which extended into the 21st century. We now call this the "lost decade."

One could therefore say that the historical separation of banking and commerce in the United States is gradually breaking down. This is another illustration of how regulatory policies of various nations are converging – for better or worse.

Real Estate and Other Items

Finally, under investments, banks do not usually show investment in the properties out of which they operate. The other principal exception is the account, "Other Real Estate Owned," – called the OREO account – which represents properties taken in foreclosure proceedings. Banks try to liquidate such accounts as quickly as they feasibly can, because they do not generally wish to be in the business of managing real properties.

Earning Assets: Loans

Loans are the lifeblood of a bank – and usually the bank's most significant asset. The higher the percentage of loans to total assets, the better the bank is serving its market – but one expects the bank to use good judgment in extending loans. For the banking system as a whole, the lending process is its most important role in serving the economy at large.

Historical lending patterns of banks have been that large banks focus on commercial and industrial loans, loans to brokers and dealers to carry securities, foreign loans, credit card loans, etc., while small banks focus more specifically on consumer and small business loans. Thrift institutions – savings and loan associations, credit unions, etc. – have traditionally handled home mortgages, home improvement loans and other housing-related loans, as well as consumer loans.

Economic events can interrupt the lending process of the banking system and cause financial markets to "freeze up," which can impact the entire economy. In earlier years, such situations were called financial panics. Credit crunches still occur, and if the flow of credit is not restored, they can lead to recession. We noted in Chap. 1 that one of the principal reasons for the establishment of the Federal Reserve System as America's central bank in 1913 was to create an "elastic money supply" so that liquidity could be made available to banks to avoid financial panics.

Loans to brokers and dealers, call money, can be highly sensitive to financial crises. For example, the stock market crash of 1987 – the largest percentage drop in prices on the New York Stock Exchange until that time – caused such a crisis, as banks stopped lending to brokerage firms to carry their inventories of securities, which is necessary to keep the industry functioning. Banks stopped lending because the value of the collateral they were carrying – namely, stocks – had declined significantly in value. Then Federal Reserve Chairman Alan Greenspan stepped in to assure banks that the Fed would provide liquidity to them, if they continued lending to keep the brokerage industry afloat. This use of moral suasion was adequate to restore the smooth functioning of the markets.

Again, in the crisis of 2007–2012, similar instances occurred where lending was interrupted – to the housing market and to the commercial paper market, as examples. Here again, intervention by the central bank kept the markets functioning. These examples illustrate both the importance of and the sensitivity to the lending process of the banking system in order to keep financial markets functioning and the economy operating effectively. This is the process we have called intermediation.

Size Distribution, All U.S. Commercial Banks, March 31, 2012
Source: FDIC (http://www2.fdic.gov/sdi/main.asp)

Assets	Number of Banks	Percentage of Banks	Percentage of Assets Held
Less than $100 million	2101	33.5	1.0
$100 million - $1 billion	3637	58.1	8.3
More than $1 billion:			
Below the top 10	515	8.2	34.3
The top 10	10	0.16	56.4
Total	6263	100.0	100.0

Total Assets of the Ten Largest U.S. Banks, March 31, 2012
Source: Federal Reserve System (http://www.federalreserve.gov/releases/lbr/current)

Institution	Location	Assets ($billions)	Share of All U.S. Bank Assets (%)
JPMorgan Chase Bank, NA	Columbus OH	1,842.7	14.4
Bank of America, NA	Charlotte NC	1,448.3	11.3
CitiBank, NA	Sioux Falls SD	1,312.8	10.3
Wells Fargo Bank, NA	Sioux Falls SD	1,181.8	9.2
U.S. Bank, NA	Cincinnati OH	330.2	2.6
PNC Bank, NA	Wilmington DE	287.8	2.2
Bank of NY/Mellon	New York NY	229.7	1.8
HSBC Bank, USA, NA	McLean VA	206.8	1.6
TD Bank, NA	Wilmington DE	193.1	1.5
State Street Bank & Trust Co.	Boston MA	184.0	1.4
Total Assets, Largest Ten		7,217.2	56.4
Total Assets, All U.S. Banks		12,780.9	100.0

Total Assets of the Ten Largest U.S. Financial Holding Companies, March 31, 2012
Source: Federal Reserve System (http://www.ffiec.gov/nicpubweb)

Institution	Location	Assets ($billions)
JPMorgan Chase & Co.	New York NY	2,320.3
Bank of America Corp.	Charlotte NC	2,180.1
Citigroup Inc.	New York NY	1,944.4
Wells Fargo & Co.	San Francisco CA	1,333.8
Goldman Sachs Group Inc.*	New York NY	951.2
Metlife Inc.**	New York NY	819.6
Morgan Stanley*	New York NY	781.0
U.S. Bancorp	Minneapolis, MN	340.8
HSBC North America Hldgs. Inc.	New York NY	340.3
Bank of New York Mellon Corp.	New York NY	300.2
Total Assets, Largest Ten		11,311.7

* formerly an Investment Bank   ** formerly an insurance company

We have noted that the lending patterns of banks have changed markedly in recent years. There are several reasons for these changes. Among them are the increased use of loan participations and syndications, the sales and securitizations of loans, the increased awareness of risks in the lending process and the need for better means of risk management, and, finally, the worldwide trend toward bank consolidation. We shall deal with each of these contributing factors in some depth, but first let us look at the overall financial status of the American banking industry as of March 31, 2012. See the table on page 70.

It is noteworthy that the number of US commercial banks (not including thrift institutions) has declined by almost 60 %, from a peak in 1987 of over 15,000 institutions to 6,263 on March 31, 2012. Many observers believe that this is still far in excess of what is needed to serve the banking needs of the US economy. The large number of banks reflects the American anomaly of the dual banking system, as well as the long-standing prohibition against branch banking in this country, which meant that an institution wishing to do banking business in two or more places had to establish a separately chartered, stand-alone bank, rather than simply opening a branch. That restriction was not finally and totally removed until the passage of the Riegle-Neal Act by Congress in 1994.

From the tables on the preceding page, note that on March 31, 2012, only 8.4 % of American banks held 90.7 % of assets, and 91.6 % of banks (5,738) held only 9.3 % of assets. And concentration at the top is still growing – that is, in 2008, those over one billion Dollars in assets held 86.7 % of assets, which shows an increase in the degree of concentration of 4 % in four years. This simple statistic reveals that a growing share of the nation's financial assets are under the control of fewer people – namely, the officers and directors of the largest banking institutions. This trend correlates very closely with the growing concentration of income and wealth among the wealthiest members of our society.

Numerous economists contend, and studies have shown, that such concentrations of financial resources, which have been building in the United States for the past three decades, tend to reduce investment in industry and result in declines in real output in the economy at large. Nobel-Prize–winning economist, Joseph Stiglitz observes, "The U.S. not only has the highest level of inequality among advanced industrial nations, but the level of inequality is increasing in absolute terms relative to that of other countries" [4].

Evidence of this trend is shown by the "Gini Coefficient."[4] Stiglitz further argues that beyond the costs of instability that inequality causes, it also gives rise to less efficient and less productive economies [4, pp. 92, 117]. Moreover, history shows us that such disparities in income and wealth can result in social upheaval and revolution [5].

The list of financial holding companies in the above tables shows some interesting developments that have occurred since 2007 – the beginning of the most recent economic downturn. Two of the institutions now exceed the two-trillion-dollar level of assets, and four exceed one trillion, raising the issue of the "too-big-to-fail" doctrine, which we shall discuss in more detail in Chap. 5. Also, the

---

[4] The Gini Coefficient measures income equality on a scale of 0 to 1, in which 0 represents perfect equality, and 1 is perfect inequality. Most industrial countries were in the range of 0.2 to 0.3 in 2010. The United States stood at 0.47, the highest level of inequality among all industrialized nations. Source: The U.S. Central Intelligence Agency, *World Factbook, 2010,* ibid. (www.cia.gov/library/publications/the-world-factbook/fields/2172/html).

list contains three institutions that were not banks at the beginning of the recent recession, but which changed their charters to become banks, in order to have access to the Fed's discount window during the crisis. These institutions were the investment banks, Goldman Sachs and Morgan Stanley, and the insurance company, MetLife, Inc.

The lending process of banks has always been subject to certain restrictions, imposed upon them either by law and/or regulation or by rules of thumb that the industry has typically observed in the interest of prudence. In the first category, for example, regulations do not permit a bank to lend over 15 % of its capital to a single borrower. Also, insider lending to a bank's own officers and directors must be reported to regulators. In the area of prudent practice, banks have tended to observe diversification in their loan portfolios in order to avoid putting all their eggs in one basket. And this practice has been underscored and encouraged by the regulators as well. In addition, bank practices have typically stressed thorough underwriting procedures – that is, doing the necessary due diligence with respect to potential borrowers to ascertain whether they can and will repay the loan. Taking this kind of credit risk is a necessary part of banking, and bankers have understood this for centuries.

In light of these sensible and logical rules, it is astounding that ordinarily conservative bankers, on numerous occasions, seem to forget them entirely. We have seen this vividly in the years leading up to the 2007 downturn, as bankers, in their zeal to be competitive and to make as many loans as possible, let greed take over. They made loans and sold them before the ink was dry – without regard to the credit risk being passed along to the unwitting buyers – and led to the failure of many of their own institutions as well as to major losses by thousands of investors.

The path is strewn with the debris of financial institutions that failed by ignoring the diversification principle – for example, the farm belt banks during the agricultural crisis of the 1970s and Texas banks during the energy recession of the late 1980s. If the banking industry were not so central to the well-being of the total economy, perhaps these lapses of judgment would not be of such great concern. But it is central, and the public at large feels the pain of recession and harbors some resentment toward those who caused it. The Dodd-Frank bill of 2010 is a reflection of the reaction by Congress and the public to this debacle.

We noted above that the lending patterns of banks have changed significantly in recent decades. One such development that has enabled banks to handle more effectively large loan demand and still remain diversified is the increased use of loan participations and syndications. In a participation, a bank sells a portion of a loan to another bank. This gets around the capital limit and provides all of the banks involved an opportunity to diversify. A loan syndication is essentially the same but is usually thought of as a more formal structure involving numerous banks, handling huge loans, often global in scope. Both of these techniques are effective ways of diversification and of spreading risk. We shall give more attention to loan syndications in Chap. 8, along with stock and bond syndications.

Risks in Lending

In making a domestic loan – that is, in its own home currency – a bank is mainly concerned with credit risk. If a loan carries a floating rate, as many now do, a bank may also be concerned with market risk, or interest rate risk. In international lending, a bank may have currency risk – or foreign exchange risk. In addition, on occasions, which are fortunately more rare, a bank may have country risk – sometimes called political risk, where a country may, by economic circumstances or by edict, default on its foreign debts, as Russia did in 1998. See the section in Chap. 9, entitled "A Chronology of Financial Crises," on the Russian financial crisis. Also, later we discuss other types of risk – that is, other than those arising from the lending operation – which a bank may face.

Therefore, risk protection is part of the lending process, in both the domestic and the international arenas. This may involve many techniques, but in recent years it has involved the growing use of derivative contracts – which are also discussed in more depth in Chap. 10, section "Managing Financial Risks."

The most basic protections against credit risk are diversification – including the use of participations and syndications – and good underwriting. It has been observed that banks get sloppy when times are good and pay less attention to risk. This happened in the 1990s and up until the crash in the late 2007, as the banking industry fueled the housing bubble, ignoring the economic reality that rising prices in any market can also come down. As a result, as mentioned above, banks have been severely chastened, and many did not survive. Now, risk is on everyone's mind – bankers and regulators alike – and banks have gradually adopted a more conservative approach to lending [6].

Sales and Securitizations of Loans and Asset-Backed Securities

We noted earlier in this chapter that bank balance sheets are changing, reflecting fundamental changes in the industry. We noted also, in our discussion of liabilities, that the trend toward wholesale banking – particularly among larger institutions – is reflected in the growing use of market-based funding, as opposed to reliance on traditional core deposits.

The asset side also reflects this changing trend in several ways – for example, the diminishing percentage of loans to total assets, more use of participations and syndications, increasing sales of loans, and the growing practice of securitizing loans. This practice typically involves the sale of loans by the bank that originated them to third parties, brokers, trusts, investment firms, etc., which pool them into large quantities – that is, hundreds of millions or billions of Dollars worth in face value – and then issue securities in the form of bonds or notes based on those pools of loans. These become "asset-backed" securities, which are collateralized by the pools of loans that are in turn collateralized by the asset on which the loan was based – that is, home mortgages, commercial mortgages, auto loans and leases, and credit card debt. Virtually any loan a bank makes is capable of being converted into securities in this manner. The process has resulted in a large, globalized market for asset-backed securities which has attracted investors far beyond the banking industry itself.

The process is very straightforward and simple in concept, and it enables a bank to restore its liquidity as well as to get rid of its credit risk. The loan is totally eliminated from the bank's balance sheet. Like most other banking practices, however, this procedure is also subject to abuses, misuse, and excessive use.

Securitization has received considerable criticism during the recent financial crisis because of the contribution it made to the housing market crash and the recession that followed. It is important to understand, though, that the procedure itself is a legitimate and useful one, and the fault for its misuse lies not necessarily with any individual institution, but with the failure of the regulators to provide adequate oversight of the lending process and the resulting inability to see the crisis coming. Investors, not only in the United States, but all over the world, wanted to have a piece of the booming American housing market, and they found a convenient way to obtain this by the purchase of mortgage-backed securities.

The result of recent years' experience in this area has brought about a great deal of discussion of "skin in the game." For example, banks were allowed to sell 100 % of their interest in loans, retaining no risk for themselves. This caused many institutions not to care whether the borrower repaid the loan or not because they had nothing at stake. One of the provisions of the Dodd-Frank bill of 2010 is to require banks to keep at least a 5 % skin in the game. Many observers feel that this is an inadequate level of commitment, but it is at least a step in the direction of reinforcing the fiduciary responsibility of banks, and will cause bankers to give more thought to whether their borrowers are creditworthy.

Mortgage-backed securities were the banking industry's first venture into the general class of asset-backed securities, beginning around 1970. They were originally launched by Fannie Mae and Freddie Mac as a means of providing increased liquidity to the housing industry. As mentioned earlier, these two agencies now hold about half of the $11 trillion worth of mortgages outstanding in the United States. Banks themselves are among the multitude of investors in mortgage-backed securities, and many banks have found that by selling their mortgages and investing in these securities – many of which they may have originated themselves – will tend to lower the bank's capital requirements, because, in effect, it moves assets from the loan accounts to the investment accounts, which are generally subject to lower capital requirements than loans.

A further advantage of the securitization process is that it opens access to national – or global – credit markets for a bank. In other words, by selling its loans for securitization into a larger market, the bank brings in funds through which it can make additional loans. The effect of it is to provide capital to the bank's own market area. This practice allows the bank to diversify its assets more effectively if it chooses to do so. Customer relationships can also be maintained in instances where the bank continues to service the customer who originated the loan – which is typical and often totally transparent to the customer – and this usually provides fee income to the bank.

The effectiveness of the securitization process depends upon the ability of the bond-rating agencies – who will rate the securities that are produced by the process – to understand the original, underlying loans. This has become more complex. A value has to be placed on the securities that accurately reflects the value – and risk – of those original loans. Therefore, to reiterate, the most successful banks – whether they securitize assets or not – will be those with the best and more careful underwriting processes for original lending.

The efficiency and globalization of the process of securitization is clear when one considers a simple example. Suppose I go to Big Box Store and buy a TV set, and I put it on my credit card. I now owe someone $1,000 for the TV. Who supplied the money? If I don't pay the credit card bill, my bank that issued the credit card (say BofA) will come after me and collect it. But BofA most likely has sold the credit card debt even before my payment comes due. My TV charge has been pooled with $100 million of other credit card debt and sold to a trust fund, which has converted it to bonds and sold them to a mutual fund. The mutual fund has been converted to a Yen-denominated fund and sold in Japan. Some Japanese family has opened a new mutual fund account, so that Japanese family has actually funded my TV purchase. They will never know it, and neither will I. Everybody is happy as long as I pay my bills and they get their interest on their mutual fund account. The transparency of the financial system to its millions of participants is a miracle of technological achievement.

It should be clear that securitization has provided major advantages to banks, to the banking system, and to the efficiency and effectiveness of the financial markets. It is therefore unfortunate that its misuses and excesses have put it under a cloud of suspicion within the financial community, which is likely to take considerable time to dispel.

Pass-Through Arrangements

Let's consider some examples of the techniques through which mortgage-backed securities (MBS) and other asset-backed securities have come into existence. One such example is the use of a "pass-through," in which pools of mortgages are passed from the bank to a special trust in return for cash. Certificates of ownership in the trust are sold to the public or other financial institutions as securities – bonds or notes. The investors now own the mortgages and assume the credit risk. The bank's balance sheet is modified as it has exchanged loans for new liquidity, and its credit risk is eliminated.

Bank (before)	Bank (after)	Trust	
Step 1:	Step 2:	Step 1:	Step 2:
Mortgages originated by bank	Cash from trust	Mortgages bought from bank	Securities sold to investors (MBS)

Under the pass-through arrangement, repayments of the mortgages go directly to the trust – or via the bank if it is handling this function for the trust – and these repayments pay down the securities. However, securities may be paid down faster than expected if there are substantial prepayments of the mortgages – a potential problem for investors, who often do not want them paid down faster than scheduled if they are receiving an attractive return. This, of course, is likely to happen in periods of low or declining interest rates when borrowers want to lower their interest costs. Such an environment would make it difficult for the investor to find alternative investments at equivalent rates of return.

One factor that helped MBSs catch on initially in the early 1970s was the fact that the mortgages were guaranteed by Fannie Mae, Freddie Mac, and Ginnie Mae. Thus, they have been accepted as relatively low-risk investments, and the market for them has mushroomed. When the subprime mortgage debacle hit in the fall of 2007, this market came to a screeching halt. Investors dumped the securities, and the financial press, in its attempt to portray the situation in graphic terms, called it "the greatest mortgage puke of all time".

Mortgage-Backed Bonds

These are a modification of the original MBSs. Under this procedure, the bank issues mortgage-backed bonds (MBBs) and holds the mortgages as collateral for them. The bonds are the liability of the bank, and the credit risk stays with the bank, as the mortgages stay on its books. No trust or other entity is involved, but the process does restore liquidity for the bank.

Bank (before)	Bank (after)	
Step 1:	Step 3:	Step 2:
Mortgages originated by bank	Cash from sale of bonds (plus original mortgages)	Bonds sold to investors (MBB)

Repayments of the mortgages are made to the bank and, as in the MBS case, are used to pay down the bonds. This technique, however, is also subject to the same disadvantages to the investor if there are substantial prepayments of the mortgages [6, pp. 197–198].

Collateralized Debt Obligations

Still another technique – a hybrid of the first two – has been developed and has become the most popular form of securitization. This is the collateralized mortgage obligation (CMO) – also called collateralized debt obligation (CDO) because it has been expanded to other forms of assets than mortgages. One of the major reasons for the popularity of these instruments is that they avoid the prepayment problem. They are like the MBS and MBB, but with guaranteed maturities. Institutions gather pools of MBSs or MBBs and issue CDOs based on those pools. It is immediately obvious that now the investor is three stages removed from the thing of original value that supports the bank's asset in the first place – the house, other real estate, car, credit card debt, or whatever the asset was upon which the original loan was based.

The convenience of this approach is that CDOs are structured so as to be sold to investors in maturity classes – tranches – of 5-year, 10-year, 20-year maturities, etc. Repayments of the mortgages are organized so as to pay off the CDOs in sequence, and the issuing institution "regularizes" the payments to the CDO holders. This is often done by over-collateralizing their holdings of the underlying securities to provide an additional cushion. Thus, the investor does not have the uncertainty of the early payoffs, as with the other examples [6, pp. 197–198].

Therefore, CDOs became the most popular form of asset-backed securities. However, many of them that were based on mortgage loans went into default during the mortgage crisis of 2007–2012 because the underlying mortgages defaulted. The bond-rating agencies added further confusion by giving top (AAA) ratings to CDOs that they knew were in default, thus misleading investors. This development resulted in CDOs being subjected to considerable bad press. This is unfortunate because the technique itself is legitimate and straightforward, and it had gained widespread acceptance in the financial markets and among the investing public. It had also improved the efficiency of the bank lending process. It was quickly realized, however, that if the quality of the underlying loans is suspect, and if dishonest information is given to investors, serious problems can result.

The holder of a defaulted CDO, in effect, has no place to turn unless the issuing institution can finally make good on it, but this becomes doubtful in the face of a major downturn in mortgage markets, such as that which we have seen in recent years. Being several stages removed from the thing of original value – the collateral – it would be like trying to unscramble an omelet and put it back in the shell to get back to that original asset.

Evaluation of Bank Assets: The Mark-to-Market Issue

International accounting standards require "mark to market" in evaluating bank assets on the balance sheet. This has been a controversy for many years between bankers and accountants. The accounting profession has argued that asset values shown on balance sheets should reflect what assets are worth at the balance sheet date. This means they should periodically be adjusted to current market values. Bankers have argued that they do not hold investments or loans for the purpose of trading or selling them, but hold them for the interest income until maturity, which means that the assets should remain on the books at their original cost.

Banking practices have changed, however, and it is very common now for banks to hold a large portion – or perhaps all – of these assets for trade or sale. Therefore, the current practice has come to reflect a general rule of thumb – which assets held with the specific intent to hold until maturity may be shown at cost, but those that are likely to be traded or sold should be marked to market. The result is that mark to market has virtually become the standard for the industry.

However, because of the huge quantities of defaulted mortgages and mortgage-backed securities on the books of banks during the recent financial crisis, the Financial Accounting Standards Board (FASB) suspended the mark-to-market rules in April 2009 and further extended the suspension in 2011. This currently allows the evaluation to be based on "a price that would be received in an orderly market rather than a forced liquidation." The effect is that banks can delay charging off losses that exist on these assets until they are sold.

This supposedly interim move has avoided many bank failures, but it delays the day of reckoning.

References

1. Keynes JM (1936) The general theory of employment, interest and money. Harcourt, Brace, New York
2. Burrough B, Helyar J (1990) Barbarians at the gate. Harper Perennial, New York
3. Stewart JB (1991) Den of thieves. Simon and Schuster, New York
4. Stiglitz JE (2012) The price of inequality: how today's divided society endangers our future. W.W. Norton, New York, p 22
5. Wolff EN (2004) Recent trends in living standards in the United States. Edward Elgar Publishing, London, pp 3–26
6. Smith RC, Walter I (2003) Global banking, 2nd edn. Oxford University Press, New York, pp 194–203

Chapter 5
Who Owns the Banks? Bank Capital and the Basel Accord

The subject of bank capital has received heightened attention in recent years because of the widespread belief that the level of capital held by banks and other financial institutions prior to the downturn in 2007 was inadequate to protect them from the losses they had to absorb in the recession that followed.

The Nature of Capital

Bank capital, as a percentage of total assets, has historically been lower than that of other types of business corporations. Capital is both a source of funds to the institution and a representation of the depth of ownership – that is, how much of the owners' funds are at risk. This is an important factor in evaluating any business enterprise because it is a measure of strength. Capital is a buffer against losses, and banks are required by their regulators to set aside a fund – normally ranging anywhere from 1.5 % to 3.0 % of the loan portfolio on an annual basis as a "provision for loan losses." This may be thought of either as an offset against the loan portfolio on the asset side of the balance sheet or as an addition to capital on the other side.

The stock of any corporation has a par value, a book value, and a market value. Bankers, as other business managers, want market value to be maximized so as to create conditions in the capital market that will be favorable to the issuance of new stock. But book value has a particular significance to those interested in bank takeovers or mergers.

If market value is low relative to book value, investors may see a potential bargain. The market may be "undervaluing" the stock. This creates conditions favorable to LBOs or other mergers and consolidations. (See the section "Junk Bonds and Leveraged Buyouts" in Chap. 4.) For a number of years, a price of 1.5–2.0 times book value was considered normal for a takeover bid. In 1998, NationsBank paid 2.7 times book for Boatmen's Bank, which was considered outrageous by many in the market. Today, however, offers to 4.0–5.0 times book are not uncommon.

W.H. Wallace, *The American Monetary System: An Insider's View of Financial Institutions, Markets and Monetary Policy*, DOI 10.1007/978-3-319-02907-8_5, © Springer International Publishing Switzerland 2013

Those who engage in takeover activities – for example, T. Boone Pickens and Carl Icahn – argue that shareholders benefit because the activity boosts the market price and shareholders receive more for their stock. Even so, some stockholders resist such change – especially in the case of hostile takeovers – because of uncertainty over what the acquirers will do with the institution.

The practice of paying more than book value creates "goodwill" on the books of the surviving institution. In the banking field, regulators require banks to write off the goodwill against future profits of the bank. The higher the level of credit an investor uses to acquire another institution, the more "leveraged" is the transaction. Thus, a leveraged buyout is one in which the investor or acquirer uses as little of its own capital as possible.

Consider the following example, in which an investor acquires a bank by paying three times book.

Acquired bank (before)				Acquired bank (after)			
Assets	100	Liabilities	90	Assets	100	Liabilities	90
		Capital	10	Goodwill	20	Capital	30
		Total	100	Total	120	Total	120

It is important to note the distinction between capital requirements and reserve requirements, which were discussed in Chap. 3. The terminology is sometimes confusing. Both are, in effect, cushions that are intended to protect the bank against financial difficulties such as runs on the bank or losses in the loan portfolio. Reserve requirements are based on a bank's deposits and are set by the Federal Reserve as a percentage of checkable deposits. Capital requirements are based on the bank's assets – particularly the riskiness of its loan portfolio. Since a bank's losses must be written off against its capital, the riskier its assets, the more capital it should be required to keep. Once the capital of a bank is extinguished – through losses or however it may occur – the bank becomes capital insolvent and must be closed. Federal law requires that when a bank's ratio of capital to its risk-based assets falls below 2 %, the bank must be closed within 90 days unless it can raise more capital [1]. Thus, the question of capital becomes a life-or-death issue for a bank.

The Level of Capital

The appropriate level of capital will always be controversial. In the 1980s, concern began to grow that the low level of capital carried by banks contributed to the high rate of bank failures late in that decade. Some large institutions had capital levels below 2 % of total assets, and banks resisted central banks' efforts to get them to raise more capital. The subject became an international competitive issue because higher capital requirements mean higher costs to the bank. The US banks, for example, felt that they could not compete with foreign banks for global lending opportunities if their foreign competitors were allowed to hold lower amounts of capital.

The Basel Accord: Basel I

The Bank for International Settlements (BIS) – the nearest thing there is to a world central bank but a long way from being a real one – stepped in at the urging of the central banks of many countries to help resolve this international debate.[1] The bank created the Basel Committee on Banking Supervision and assigned this task to it. The Committee still exists and continues to work with central banks on issues related to bank capital, as well as other regulatory matters.

The Basel Committee proposed, and major countries agreed, in 1987, to a risk-based capital plan focused on a target of 8 % (of total risk-based assets) as the standard for total capital of a bank. There is common agreement among nations and central banks that the level of capital required should be related to risks to which the bank is exposed. As noted before, these risks reside primarily in a bank's loan portfolio.

The agreement reached in 1987 became known as the Basel Accord, later designated as Basel I because it was superseded by subsequent agreements. The agreement was initially adopted by the G-7 (or the G-8 as it is known now, since Russia was added in the 1990s), and it was later adopted by over 100 countries around the world. This seemed to be satisfactory to all concerned, and it was readily implemented.

The following is the essential structure of the Basel I agreement, with regard to the calculation of risk-based assets:

- Zero weighted – essentially the bank's own reserves and its holdings of government securities
- 20 % weighted – loans to other banks
- 50 % weighted – municipal bonds and residential mortgages
- 100 % weighted – loans to consumers and corporations

For example, if a bank had $1 million in each of these four categories, for category 1, its risk-weighted assets would be $0; category 2, $200,000; category 3, $500,000; and category 4, $1,000,000. Thus, its total risk-weighted assets would be $1,700,000, and the target rate of 8 % would be applied to that. This means that its capital requirement of this aggregate of $4 million of assets would be $136,000.

Over time, banks began to argue that this simple system was not an adequate representation of its real risks, primarily because the category of loans to consumers and corporations, which is the major portion of most banks' loan portfolios, is most likely a mixed bag of low-risk to high-risk loans. Central banks agreed and asked the BIS to continue the effort, which would result in the creation of Basel II.

Numerous changes occurred in the nature of the banking industry, and the financial system more generally, between the adoption of the original Basel Accord and

---

[1] The BIS was created at the end of World War I to handle reparation payments on behalf of the victorious countries. After the completion of that task, the bank has remained in place and has become, in effect, a consulting organization to central banks around the world. It is located in Basel, Switzerland.

the renewed focus on capital requirements after the turn of the 21st century. Therefore, we shall return to the subsequent Basel agreements in Chap. 6, which deals with supervision and regulation of the financial system.

Too Big to Fail

The occurrence of several mega-bank mergers since the late 1980s has again focused increased attention on the question of capital adequacy. Because of the provisions of Gramm-Leach-Bliley, which repealed the restrictions of Glass-Steagall against the merger of banks and nonbank financial institutions, we have seen the merger of Citicorp with Travelers Insurance, the takeover of the investment banks Bear Stearns and Merrill Lynch by banks, the mergers of JPMorgan Chase with Bank One (each of which had previously taken over numerous institutions), and the mergers of Bank of America and FleetBoston, Wells Fargo and Wachovia, Deutsche Bank and Bankers Trust, etc. As we have seen in the tables on page 70, these mergers have brought into being four institutions exceeding one trillion Dollars in total assets and two exceeding two trillion Dollars. Several of these combinations have been forced by the difficulties of the recent economic downturn, but in any event, they have concentrated the attention of the regulators, the Congress, and the public on the issue of too big to fail.

Could the world afford a failure of a trillion-dollar banking empire? The ripple effect upon other financial institutions and financial markets could be devastating. Among the possible consequences of such an event would or could be (1) cessation of trading in all financial instruments because of a freeze-up of markets and a lack of willingness to trade, (2) immediate bankruptcy of numerous interconnected institutions, (3) inability to settle transactions among institutions, and (4) significant increases in market interest rates. The obvious answer to the question posed above is no!

The too-big-to-fail doctrine has been followed in the past in the sense that the Fed, as well as the Treasury – that is, the federal government, itself – has stepped in to prevent failures through various forms of bailouts [2]. While the final tab is not yet available on the most recent financial crisis – because some of the funds extended are still being collected – the public remembers vividly that such episodes often do carry a significant cost to taxpayers, as in the savings and loan crisis of the late 1980s and early 1990s of $132 billion. Thus, the public is justifiably outraged by the experience it has been through, as well as the prospect that it could occur again.

The questions that too big to fail raises are, first, whether an institution implodes and collapses with all the collateral damage that could cause or, second, whether it can be merged with another institution healthy enough and big enough to save it – even though mergers at this level are often difficult to accomplish and, third, whether the failing firm can be brought down in an orderly way and dismantled piece by piece, thus sparing the markets and other institutions the effects of its collapse.

We experienced a taste of the effect of a collapse of a large institution with the 2008 failure of Lehman Brothers. Though it was not a bank and it has been brought down in a reasonably orderly fashion, the impact was still felt throughout the banking system and the financial sector as a whole, in both the United States and abroad. Among the reasons for the effect it had was the fact that we were still in the midst of a severe financial crisis when the failure happened, and great uncertainty still existed about what it meant for other institutions that were known to be in a weakened condition at the time.

The growing size of banks partially explains the high level of attention currently being given to the subject of bank capital. There is concern that we as a society are allowing institutions to be created that test the limits of manageability and which, because of their size alone, pose significant threats to the stability of the world's financial systems. Some economists have argued that the market values of some of the biggest institutions are less than the sum of their parts. This view is consistent with the conclusions reached in numerous economic studies over many years that economies of scale in banking do not exist. Former Fed Chairman Paul Volcker (among others) has said in testimony to Congress that these institutions are too big to exist.

A number of these issues have been addressed to some degree by the Dodd-Frank bill of July 2010. We shall discuss the specific provisions of the law in more detail in Chap. 9. This law attempts to deal not only with the size question, per se, and the dangers that it presents, but also with the risky practices of banks, which have led to great losses that ultimately fall back upon the depositors and investors in those institutions.

Evaluation of Bank Performance

How do we evaluate bank performance? Analysts look at certain key measures, such as return on equity, return on assets, and net interest margin.

Net interest margin is measured as the difference between the average rate of interest that a bank receives on its assets and the average rate it pays on its liabilities. This statistic is less used than in previous years because a smaller proportion of the total income of banks is derived from interest income and a growing proportion is received from fee income. This reflects to some degree the increasing shift of banks from retail to wholesale modes of operation.

FDIC statistics for the first quarter of 2010, when banks were still struggling and trying to recover from the economic recession of the previous three years, showed return on equity (ROE) – that is, earnings/total capital – was 4.96 % for all the US banks. A rough rule of thumb is that a bank performing well should be in the range of 8–10 %.

Also, FDIC statistics for the same quarter showed return on assets (ROA) – that is, earnings/total assets – to be 0.54 % for all the US banks. Again, a bank performing well should be over 1.0 %.

In the earlier years of the decade, however, the situation was quite different. *The Economist*, on May 20, 2006, stated, "This decade has been the best in living memory for America's commercial banks – so far. Banks have been growing fast around the world, from Tokyo to Moscow. But nowhere does the industry seem more triumphant than in the U.S. In 2005, American banks declared a fifth straight year of record earnings. Their return on equity has been at a 60-year high. No bank has failed for 2 years, an all-time record."[2]

Little did banks know what was about to hit them. The situation changed drastically in late 2007, as the previous five years came crashing down with the mortgage crisis – largely of banks' own making. Profits were slashed by 50 % for the industry, and numerous banks failed.

Gap Analysis

Under normal conditions, the profitability of banks is highly sensitive to changes in interest rates. In a static situation – a snapshot at any one point in time – a profitable bank is one that is earning a higher rate of return on its assets than it is paying out on its liabilities and capital. But time does not stand still, and as time passes over a period of years, months, and even weeks, rates on different financial instruments can change rapidly.

Therefore, among the talents that a banker must have are the ability to analyze quickly the structure of interest rates on both the asset and liability side of the balance sheet and the ability to guess with some degree of credibility the direction of interest rates in the near-term future. To do this in a scientific way is called "gap analysis."

Frederic Mishkin, of Columbia University, uses the following example to illustrate the concept. Total assets and total liabilities are separated into two categories – rate sensitive and fixed rate. Rate-sensitive assets are those that will be paid off within the time period of the analysis – let's say six months. Similarly, rate-sensitive liabilities are those that will have to be paid within that same time period [3]. Consider the following example.

First National Bank			
Assets		*Liabilities*	
Rate-sensitive assets	$20 mil	Rate-sensitive liabilities	$50 mil
Variable-rate loans		Variable-rate CDs	
Short-term securities		MMDAs	
Fixed-rate assets	$80 mil	Fixed-rate liabilities	$50 mil
Reserves		Checkable deposits	
Long-term bonds		Savings deposits	
Long-term securities		Equity capital	

---

[2] *The Economist*, Vol. 397, p. 83

Let's say further that the bank management expects interest rates to rise by 5 % during the six months ahead. The gap is calculated: (rate-sensitive assets - rate-sensitive liabilities), which in this example is ($20–50 mil)=−$30 mil. Apply the expected increase in rates to this gap (0.05×−$30 mil)=−$1.5 mil. This tells us that if the assumption about interest rates is correct, and if nothing is changed on the balance sheet, the bank's profits will decline by $1.5 million.

The logic of this analysis is that while the bank will be receiving a higher rate of return on its rate-sensitive assets, that increase applies to a relatively small amount. On the other side, the bank will be paying a higher rate on an even larger amount of rate-sensitive liabilities, which means that, on balance, the bank incurs a decline in profitability. The outcome would be different if it could be assumed that interest rates would decline by 5 %. The bank would be receiving less on a small amount of assets and paying less on an even larger amount of liabilities, thus giving it an increase in profits.

The convenience of this analysis is that it can be done for any time horizon the bank chooses, and it can be done on the back of an envelope or by high-speed super-computers. The key is making the right assumption about the direction of interest rates. Management can then plan to adjust the bank's balance sheet to stay profitable. In the above example, the bank could liquidate some of its fixed-rate assets and place the funds in the rate-sensitive group, thus making its gap positive. Similar adjustments could possibly be made on the liability side, but in any event, the objective would be to enter the period of rising interest rates with a positive rather than a negative gap.

References

1. Bair S (2013) Bull by the Horns. The Free Press, New York, p 100
2. McKinley V (2011) Financing failure: a century of bailouts. The Independent Institute, Oakland
3. Mishkin FS (2010) The economics of money, banking and financial markets, 9th edn. Addison-Wesley, Boston, pp 245–246

Chapter 6
How Safe Are Our Banks? Supervision and Regulation of the Financial System

Who are the regulators? For the United States, they include the following:

- Federal Reserve System – the central bank
- Treasury Department – Office of the Controller of the Currency (OCC)
- Federal Deposit Insurance Corporation (FDIC)
- Securities and Exchange Commission (SEC)
- National Credit Union Administration (NCUA)
- The state banking supervisors of the 50 states
- And others! (e.g., CFTC, FASB)

A quick glance at the above list leads one to conclude that there must be overlapping responsibilities among the regulatory agencies – and there are. Not only is there overlap among the federal agencies but also between the federal and state agencies. Despite numerous proposals that have been made over the years to combine or consolidate the agencies into a single one, Congress has elected not to do so. The principal reason for not doing it has been the widely held perception that the above system works reasonably well, and the old adage that "if it ain't broke don't fix it" appears to apply here. There is, of course, considerable cooperation and coordination among the agencies, and in recent years, as the financial system has become globalized and more complex, the degree of coordination has greatly increased.

A question my students often ask is, "Why is there so much attention on bank regulation?" What is in the nature of the banking system that makes it "special" or different from other business enterprises? We have seen how the economy depends upon a banking system to support the payment network through which billions of transactions can be functioned efficiently and effectively. We shall develop this concept further in Chaps. 11 and 12, as we see how the central bank depends on a system of commercial banks for the transmission of monetary policy and the achievement of its overall economic objectives.

These factors largely explain the need for bank supervision and regulation – although the degree of it is subject to very much debate. Although supervision and regulation are usually thought of together, there is a subtle difference between the two.

W.H. Wallace, *The American Monetary System: An Insider's View of Financial Institutions, Markets and Monetary Policy*, DOI 10.1007/978-3-319-02907-8_6,
© Springer International Publishing Switzerland 2013

The relative importance of the two varies among different countries. Supervision generally means oversight monitoring, advising and counseling, etc. Regulation means what it says – rules for operations are written; banks are expected to comply; inspections are made to see that they do; and penalties apply when they do not. The Federal Reserve has regulations designated A through Z and AA through GG. Other regulators have similarly long lists.

Often, Congress will pass a law and then delegate to the Federal Reserve – or the FDIC, SEC, or some other agency – the responsibility to write the regulations; seek public comment on them, which is required by law in the imposition of any new regulation; publish them in final form; and finally, enforce them with penalties if necessary. This is the procedure that has been followed, for example, with the passage of the Dodd-Frank bill in July 2010. And the process of completing the steps mentioned above is still underway. Usually, Congress will say what it wants only in very broad terms, which leaves the regulators who are assigned the task of implementing the law considerable leeway regarding the details.

To get a perspective on this, let's look at the important federal legislation that has been passed in recent years impacting the financial industry. Frederic Mishkin lists 15 acts of Congress that most would agree have been important to the banking industry [1]. We can narrow this list to six that have been of primary importance to the American financial system and that have guided it to where it is today:

1. Beginning in 1913, the Federal Reserve Act (the Glass-Owen bill) was passed, which established the central bank of the United States. While it has been amended a number of times, the law on the books today is essentially the same as that passed in 1913. We shall discuss this act further in Chap. 11.
2. The Glass-Steagall Act of 1933 – a.k.a., the Banking Act of 1933 – separated banking from other financial activities, such as brokerage, investment banking, and insurance. It also established the FDIC.
3. The Monetary Control Act of 1980 brought all depository financial institutions under the control of the Federal Reserve System, subjected them to Fed regulations and required that they maintain reserves with the Fed in accordance with Regulation D. Prior to this act, the Fed's rules applied only to banks that were members of the Fed system – that is, all national banks and those state-chartered banks that opted to be members.
4. The Riegle-Neal Act of 1994 approved the ability of banks to branch across state lines.
5. The Gramm-Leach-Bliley Act of 1999 repealed provisions of Glass-Steagall, which prohibited banks from engaging in any financial activities other than the narrowly defined practice of banking – that is, taking deposits and making loans.
6. The Dodd-Frank Act of 2010 – a.k.a., the Wall Street Reform and Consumer Protection Act – provides for an overall reform and update of the federal banking regulatory system. Further discussion of this will follow in Chap. 9.

By comparison to the American regulators' approach to bank supervision and regulation, other nations vary somewhat, reflecting different philosophies of the role of the banking systems of other countries. The British, for example, have historically used what has been called a "light-touch" regulatory system – that is, they have been more supervisory than regulatory. The Germans, on the other hand, have tended to be more regulatory than supervisory. The Japanese system, by contrast, has historically been virtually a hands-off approach.

Our system has been somewhat of a mix of all of the above, but it, along with most of the others, is changing. The recent financial crisis has focused attention on the supervision and regulation process, and other governments as well as central banks are scrambling to close loopholes and repair the laxness of the systems they had in place, which contributed to the difficulties they suffered in the recent downturn.

Chairman Alan Greenspan – who led the Federal Reserve from 1987 to 2006 – was responsible for emphasizing supervision and placed greater reliance on what he called "market discipline." Mr. Greenspan held steadfastly to an anti-regulation ideology, reflecting to a great extent his devotion to the philosophies of Ayn Rand, author of *Atlas Shrugged*, among other books, with whom he had been a personal friend in his earlier years. He believed as she argues, that market forces could do what regulators could not by enforcing restraint, but as he admits, he was proved not entirely correct on this assumption. As a result, he has been criticized for failing to take action in the years immediately preceding the housing market crash of 2007, when the Fed could have – through its regulatory powers – softened the blow of the recession which followed [2].

The increased globalization of the financial world has complicated the process of bank supervision and regulation. As banks have become global in scope, which is necessary to handle the financing needs of their multinational customers, the question arises as to whose responsibility it is to supervise the activities of banks that have a physical presence all over the world. One of the first incidents to bring this to the attention of regulators around the world was the Bank for Credit and Commerce International (BCCI) scandal of 1995. BCCI was a Luxembourg-based bank that had operations in numerous European countries as well as the United States. It became involved in a number of illegal activities in support of drug trafficking and arms trafficking. Luxembourg had a lax regulatory system and the systems in place in other countries, as in the United States, virtually ignored it because they didn't know what was going on, and it wasn't their responsibility in the first place.

By the time this activity was discovered and people were arrested, the embarrassment was palpable among central bankers all over Europe and in the United States. This episode brought to an end the very distinguished career of Clark Clifford, who had been a counselor to every democratic president since Truman. He had become chairman of the BCCI-owned bank in the United States and claimed to be unaware of the activities that brought down BCCI. He was convicted in his 1990s of conspiracy but did not serve jail time. There is further discussion of this episode in Chap. 9, "A Chronology of Financial Crises."

The BCCI scandal was only one of a number of developments that helped to bring about a realization by regulators that a greater and more tightly coordinated level of cooperation was needed among central banks to see that regulators of any country have access to information about the activities of banks that operate in their territories. This development has resulted in a great deal more consistency in the regulatory approaches of central banks. Again, the BIS, through its Committee on Bank Supervision, has assisted in the development of new procedures. While the responsibility and authority for oversight and regulation of banks is still vested in national governments or individual central banks, financial crises tend to be global in scope. Thus, under these new agreements, bank supervisors in the United States, for example, have access to foreign branches of American banks in any other country and also to American affiliates of foreign banks located in this country. And the same is true for supervisors from the central banks of other countries. We did learn from the BCCI scandal.

The traditional approach to bank supervision and regulation in the United States has been to try to answer the question, "Is the banking system safe and sound?" In the past, the answer was largely based on on-site examinations. The principal questions examiners tried to answer were as follows:

- Do the financial statements, in general, reflect the financial condition of the bank?
- Are the assets in place and properly valued – that is, marked to market or stated at fair value?
- Are the underwriting procedures sound – adequate due diligence, arm's-length review, etc.?
- Is there insider dealing?
- Is credit administered fairly in accordance with consumer protection laws – that is, no allocation of credit on any basis other than creditworthiness, such as race and sex – no redlining?
- Are the bank's funding sources stable enough to sustain its asset structure?
- Is there sufficient liquidity?
- Are there serious mismatches between assets and liabilities – that is, as in the S&L example?
- Have there been adequate loan reserves established or write-offs made?
- Are the bank's earnings adequate and properly planned for the future – that is, gap analysis?
- How difficult would it be for the bank to raise new capital?
- Is capital insolvency a possibility?
- What recommendations should be made to the bank – that is, examination as consultation?
- Is a memorandum of understanding (MOU) or, in the extreme case, a cease and desist order necessary? (A MOU is a written agreement between the chief examiner and the bank CEO that the bank will take certain actions recommended by the examiner within a certain time period. A cease and desist order has the force of a legal agreement and can impose certain penalties on the bank for not following its orders).

The CAMELS Ratings

At the conclusion of the examination, the bank is given a CAMELS rating, based on the six attributes: capital, assets, management, earnings, liquidity, and sensitivity to market risks. A bank is rated from 1, which is the highest, to 5, which is the lowest, on each attribute. Examiners have certain guidelines to follow, as well as a range of latitude of judgment on the first five attributes. For years, a bank with an overall rating in the 4 or 5 categories was considered a "troubled institution," in need of counseling to improve its condition, or perhaps a merger. Banks in category 5 were almost invariably headed for failure. Those in categories 1 through 3 were considered to be in satisfactory condition.

Courses of action might be recommended by examiners – for example, disposition of selected troubled assets and raising more capital. Management has always been a more subjective and controversial category. Regulators can recommend management changes and, in extreme circumstances – that is, imminent failure due to management ineptness, and fraud – can remove management.

The last attribute, S, for sensitivity to market risks, was added by agreement among regulators in 1996. It was clear in the late 1990s, for example, that banks that score very well on all the other five attributes might still be subject to risks of which bank management was not aware. Adding the S measure reflected regulators' concerns about the growing size of banks and their increasing use of market-sensitive products, as well as other highly risky activities, such as (1) acting as counterparties in derivative transactions in which the banks take on the risks of other parties for fee income; (2) trading of derivative contracts over the counter without adequate information (see the Barings Bank crisis in Chap. 9); (3) increased usage of bank financing (loans) by highly leveraged individuals and entities, such as LTCM and other hedge funds, or direct investments in these entities by banks (see the LTCM crisis in Chap. 9); (4) the growing globalization of banking and vulnerability to multinational economic shifts, as in the 1997 Asian Crisis (see Chap. 9); and (5) the increased speed of financial transactions and the need to adjust positions and spreads frequently within a business day.

In addition, the concerns of regulators about banks' exposure to risks have been heightened by practices of banks during the recent financial crisis, such as short-circuiting good underwriting procedures, abdication of responsibility for the credit-worthiness of borrowers by the excessive use of securitization, and the selling of loans which were destined to go into default to unsuspecting investors without caring whether those investors would eventually bear the brunt of the bank's defective analysis.

All these developments have contributed to the increased emphasis that regulators now place on the sensitivity to risk measure. The Federal Reserve System explains this change of direction of the supervision and regulation of banks as follows:

> With the largest banking organizations growing in both size and complexity, the Federal Reserve has moved towards a risk-focused approach to supervision that is more a continuous process than a point-in-time examination. The goal of the risk-focused supervision process is to identify the greatest risks to a banking organization and assess the ability of the organization's management to identify, measure, monitor, and control these risks. Under the risk-focused approach, the Federal Reserve examiners focus on those business activities that may pose the greatest risk to the organization. [3]

The way a bank would be evaluated on the sensitivity question would vary sharply between the small, locally based bank and the large, globally based one. The trend in the past five years has been to place more emphasis on the S issue, for large banks in particular. And there is by no means general agreement among regulators on how to measure sensitivity to risk, or the riskiness of the institution. Thus, emphasis has shifted from the traditional bean-counting examination to one focused on risk and on the capability of the bank to assess and manage its own risk.

Therefore, the choices the regulators face, particularly with regard to the large, so-called too-big-to-fail institutions, are as follows: (1) let institutions fail if they become excessively risky and overexposed – that is, get rid of them – or (2) constrain their activities and limit their growth and/or limit their ability to take excessive risks, that is, learn to live with them. The first choice would evoke the too-big-to-fail question, in which some banks are large enough that their failure could entail the systemic risk of causing the entire financial system to break down. The second choice would keep banks from being innovative, or being able to take advantage of technology, and keep them from serving the needs of their markets. Therefore, neither choice is desirable.

Basel II

Before the recent financial crisis, a new approach to bank regulation was already being developed in response to the growing concern about risk. This effort, also led by the BIS, became, in 2004, Basel II. As we noted earlier, this work was started because the original Basel Accord (Basel I), which had lasted 20 years, had become inadequate in measuring bank risk. Unfortunately, Basel II came about five years too late, because, if it had been in place early in the last decade, the recent crisis might have been avoided, or its impact might have been softened. Basel II was implemented in some countries, but the United States lagged far behind because of disagreements over how to measure and manage risk.

Basel II, like Basel I, would have been an agreement among regulators of the leading financial countries, but would have relied on national laws for its implementation. The uniqueness of its approach was to have been that it would rely upon banks themselves to determine what they believe their risk exposures are, to quantify them, and to allocate their capital accordingly. Their decisions would have been subject to the review of regulators, and the effect was expected to reduce the capital requirements of a number of large banks.

But the onset of the financial crisis intervened in the implementation of Basel II, especially in the United States. And, in view of the nature of the crisis and the way in which it developed, some – including Congress – questioned the advisability of allowing banks to assess their own risks. The thinking here was that banks' own inaction in the face of serious impending loan losses, and their greed in expanding lending even to non-creditworthy borrowers cast, doubt on both their honesty and their competence to assess and report accurately their levels of credit risk. Therefore, it would be fair to say that the movement toward implementation of Basel II was politically sidetracked in the United States.

Basel III and Subsequent Proposals

The Basel Committee on Banking Supervision, as well as the regulators of most major countries, realized that Basel II was in trouble, especially in the United States, where it was unlikely ever to be fully implemented. The global financial crisis had changed the ground rules and had recast the whole issue of bank supervision as a much more urgent matter. Therefore, work immediately started on Basel III. Preliminary recommendations were made in October 2010, in time for consideration by G-20 countries at their meeting in November 2010.

The Committee stated its objectives for Basel III: to improve the banking sector's ability to absorb shocks arising from financial and economic stress, whatever the source, to improve risk management and governance, and to strengthen banks' transparency and disclosures.

The Committee's targets for reform were, first, to develop bank-level – or "microprudential"– regulation, which will help raise the resilience of individual banking institutions to periods of stress. Second, it stated it planned to develop regulations to deal with system-wide – or "macro-prudential" – risks that can build up across the banking sector, as well as the pro-cyclical amplification of these risks over time, which leads to increasing volatility and instability in the banking system.[1] Thus, the Basel Committee took a different approach with Basel III in that it focused on both individual bank risks and system-wide risks. They further stated that Basel III represents a fundamental strengthening and a radical overhaul of global capital standards.

To accomplish these objectives, the Basel III specifications are that banks must hold a "common equity" of 7 % of risk-based assets. Common equity simply means the value of common stock outstanding. Basel III breaks down the 7 % into two parts – a 4.5 % base common equity and a 2.5 % conservation buffer. The conservation buffer is an amount set aside to provide for any unrecoverable costs of future financial crises – that is, so that the financial industry itself would pay the costs of any future crises, rather than taxpayers.[2]

In addition to common equity, Basel III will require a total "Tier 1 Capital" of 8.5 % of risk-based assets. Tier 1 capital is common equity plus retained earnings of the bank.

Finally, "total capital" is required to be 10.5 % of risk-based assets. This is Tier 1 capital plus preferred stock outstanding and long-term debt with maturity of greater than five years. Total capital might also include contingent convertible bonds, referred to as CoCo bonds that are automatically convertible to equity if common equity falls below the required levels. Thus, it is clear from these

---

[1] The term prudential in this usage means special care and/or attention.

[2] The US banking system is required to provide for this coverage under the Dodd-Frank bill. The BIS Committee is, in effect, suggesting that other countries do the same. The development of Basel III was concurrent with the debate on the Dodd-Frank bill in Congress in the summer of 2010. Thus, there was interaction between the two.

specifications that if a bank has no retained earnings, preferred stock, or any form of debt that qualifies as capital, it would have to come up with common equity equal to 10.5 % of risk-based assets. This is a large increase in capital requirements from earlier years, such as the 8 % target under Basel I.

The system of weights to determine risk-weighted assets is much more detailed and complex than the simple system imposed by Basel I. Under the Basel III approach, banks will be required to use ratings from external credit-rating agencies to classify assets, ranging from the highest level of creditworthiness to the lowest, such as the following, from least to most risky: loans to sovereign entities, loans to bank and securities companies, loans to corporations, loans on residential property, and loans on commercial real estate – ranging down to overdue loans. It immediately stands out that residential mortgages have been considerably downgraded from the older system as a result of recent experience.

Weights in the Basel III system will vary, from least to most risky, from zero to as much as 150 % of face value of loans on extremely risky or defaulted loans. This represents a powerful disincentive for banks to grant loans that might go into default [4].

While it is expected that major countries – that is, the G-20 and others – will adopt the Basel III provisions, this has not been completed as of this writing. US banks began implementing some provisions on January 1, 2013, but all countries that participate in Basel III will have until January 1, 2019, to complete the task.

There remain many facets to this debate. The banking industry continues to fight capital increases because they claim this will raise their costs and make it more difficult for them to extend loans and to make a profit. However, regulators – and apparently Congress – are adamant that capital be increased because it is obvious that one of the factors in the severity of the recent downturn was the lack of an adequate capital buffer. Sheila Bair, the recently retired chair of the FDIC, advocated that another 1 % on top of the Basel III requirements be added for any bank that has not developed a "living will," as required by the Dodd-Frank bill. The living will is a plan to be developed by all large banks outlining how they could be dismantled in event of a crisis that would minimize damage to outsiders.

Others have suggested adding even more to the Basel III requirements, with some proposals ranging as high as 17.5 % of risk-based assets. While it is unlikely that these higher proposals will be adopted, there are many who argue that, in light of the agony caused for the country by the banking industry in the recent crisis, whatever proposal is adopted should be punitive – as Glass-Steagall was in 1933.

In the United States, for example, much discussion has taken place within the banking industry and among regulators regarding whether to implement Basel III, as such, or some modification of it with other provisions that seem more appropriate for American banks. In July 2013, the Federal Reserve, the Comptroller of the Currency, and the FDIC announced an alternative plan that would, in effect, go even further than Basel III for certain banks. That plan is to require the largest eight bank holding companies to hold capital consisting of common stock and retained earnings to a level of at least 5 % of *total assets* – not just risk-based assets as Basel III would require. This is defined as a "leverage ratio." In addition, the proposed US rules would require the bank subsidiaries of these holding companies to hold similar leverage ratios of 6 % of total assets. Clearly, the US proposals are intended to discourage banks from becoming large enough to be subject to these requirements. The concern is obviously with the largest institutions, while smaller banks, say those below $50 billion in total assets, are likely to be allowed to remain under Basel I rules.

When a Bank Fails

When a bank becomes capital insolvent – that is, liabilities exceed assets – it must be closed. A bank can be illiquid – that is, being unable to meet current obligations – without being capital insolvent. Today, in the United States, primarily because of deposit insurance and the central bank's ability to provide liquidity through the discount window, banks rarely have to close because of liquidity problems. This was not the case in the years of the Great Depression, when liquidity problems could cause runs on banks and ultimately lead to capital insolvency.

Usually, a bank is declared insolvent by the central bank or other supervising authority. The act of closure is taken by the chartering authority, which cancels its charter and appoints the FDIC as receiver. The receiver collects assets and pays liabilities to the extent that it can.

The FDIC tries to avoid an outright liquidation, where they pay off all depositors at $250,000 or less, take all assets, and attempt to collect or sell them to another institution. This is usually the most costly form of bank resolution for the FDIC, and it may require the FDIC to take over and run the bank temporarily. This temporary arrangement is called a "bridge bank" [5]. This step was recently taken in the case of IndyMac of California, where FDIC took over and changed the name to IndyMac Federal Bank, to distinguish it from the original.

The alternative to liquidation is a purchase and assumption (P&A), where the FDIC, working with the Fed, attempts to find a merger partner – a bank that is willing to purchase all assets and assume all liabilities. Thus, the FDIC, to make the deal work for the acquiring bank, may inject funds in the form of a loan, which the acquirer would pay off over a period of years. This way, the FDIC doesn't lose anything, nor do any of the depositors, regardless of the deposit size.

The P&A approach has worked over and over again in recent years, but the management of the failed institution is always ousted, and common stockholders generally lose everything.

References

1. Mishkin FS (2010) The economics of money, banking and financial markets, 9th edn. Addison-Wesley, Boston, pp 270–271
2. Greenspan A (2007) The age of turbulence: adventures in a new world. The Penguin Press, New York. Chaps. 10 and 11

3. Board of Governors of the Federal Reserve System (2005) Purposes and functions of the Federal Reserve System, 9th edn. Board of Governors of the Federal Reserve System, Washington, DC, p 63
4. Bank for International Settlements, Basel Committee on Banking Supervision, Basel III (2010) International framework for liquidity risk measurement, Basel, Dec 2010
5. Bair S (2013) Bull by the Horns. The Free Press, New York, p 110

Part III
Financial Markets and the Management of Financial Risk

Chapter 7
What Makes the System Work? The Discipline of the Markets

As we broaden our focus from just banks to all types of financial institutions and to the financial markets, we shall consider the roles that financial institutions play in the markets and look at their interdependence. We shall also consider the impact of changes in market conditions on the institutions. Finally, we shall examine financial risk and how it is managed – or in some instances, mismanaged.

The Evolution of the Capital Markets

The banking system depends upon an efficient system of markets to handle its business, and markets depend on the banking system for funding sources, liquidity, and to connect savers and investors – that is, intermediation. The terms "market" and "exchange" are used in the financial press almost interchangeably, but in reality, they mean different things. A market may or may not be a physical place. They are entities through which buyers and sellers come together and through which trade occurs. There are markets for services as well as goods – for commodities as well as financial instruments. An exchange is a place where trading occurs. If I buy a bond, my trade will go through the bond market somewhere, but my broker will decide which exchange to use to access the bond market, or whether to go over the counter for my trade. The broker would have a membership in the relevant exchanges.

We usually refer to the market for equities as "the stock market" and the market for debt instruments as "the bond market." The term "capital market" is used to refer to both the debt and equity markets. The "money market" has a more specific meaning, as the market for debt instruments that are issued with a year or less to maturity – such as Treasury bills, short-term certificates of deposit (CDs), repurchase agreements (repos), Federal Funds, commercial paper, and any other such short-term financial instrument that may be invented. The "foreign exchange" market – often called the "forex" – is the market for currencies.

W.H. Wallace, *The American Monetary System: An Insider's View of Financial Institutions, Markets and Monetary Policy*, DOI 10.1007/978-3-319-02907-8_7, © Springer International Publishing Switzerland 2013

In economic policy discussions and in the financial press, you often hear or see references to "the money and capital markets" or "the money and credit markets." These are references to all the financial markets in general. We also see mention of "market sentiment," or statements that "the market reacted favorably or unfavorably" to an event, or that "the market was pleased or displeased." Such comments suggest that the market has humanlike qualities. Market analysts seem to think of the markets in that manner, that is, whatever the market suggests about prices of commodities or financial instruments is something that should be respected because it represents the collective wisdom of traders everywhere.

As we shall see, the bond market is especially important in the economy because it is the market in which interest rates are determined. To the central bank, the bond market is the most important of the markets. All the hype that we typically see about the stock market during economic crises and turning points is often unwarranted, especially in the long run.

The Importance of Capital Markets to the Economy

Businesses and governments depend upon the capital markets to raise funds – either debt, by issuing bonds, or equity, by issuing shares of stock – for long-term financing purposes. Governments, which of course do not issue shares, depend upon the debt markets, while business firms can and do utilize both debt and equity markets. Businesses and governments similarly depend on money markets for their short-term financing needs, such as working capital – governments through the issuance of short-term bills and businesses through commercial paper. Thus, it is clear that the capital markets are critical to the economy at large.

It is important to keep in mind the distinction between the capital markets and the use of bank loans for financing purposes. The principal distinction is that security is provided for instruments issued in the capital markets in the form of the collateral of the assets of the issuing companies or the sovereign guarantees of the governments, and this in turn is supported by the secondary markets that exist for all such securities. Bank loans may or may not be secured, depending upon the lending policies of the bank.

The adequacy of the underwriting process that investment banks use in the pricing of original issues of stocks and bonds is critical to the success of these securities in the secondary markets. As they are bought and sold by investors in the secondary markets, the prices and yields of these instruments will continue to reflect the credit standing of the issuing entity. The same argument could be made about the importance of the underwriting process for bank loans in determining the quality of the loans. Recent experience in the mortgage market certainly bears out the consequences of lax underwriting procedures for mortgage lending by banks. This has become even more important in recent years as secondary markets have developed for bank loans. A current controversy still lingers about the amount of skin in the game that a bank should keep in the loans it originates when it sells those loans to third-party investors.

Without the requirement that the skin in the game be significantly above zero, banks have no incentive to care about the creditworthiness of their borrowers, and this leads to unwise lending decisions.

On the other side of the market, in addition to their use for fund-raising purposes, the capital markets and the money markets are depended upon by investors as vehicles through which to place funds for income-producing purposes. Investors range from individuals to large institutions, both banks and nonbanks, and investment instruments range from bonds and stocks on the long-term side to money market accounts, savings accounts and commercial paper for short-term uses. In addition to making outright purchases and sales in the secondary market, entities with money to invest for a brief period can acquire a security temporarily, and holders of debt instruments can borrow short term by selling securities temporarily through such vehicles as repurchase agreements and reverse repurchase agreements [1]. These instruments, known as repos and reverse repos, were discussed in Chap. 3.

The Federal Reserve also depends on an efficient system of capital markets in the execution of monetary policy. As it attempts to ease or tighten overall money and credit conditions in the economy at large, the Fed's activities in buying or selling securities in the capital markets raise or lower the money supply and hence ease or tighten credit conditions throughout the economy. This is the process of open market operations which we shall discuss in detail in Chap. 12. Ann-Marie Meulendyke, formerly of the Fed's open market desk in New York, notes, "If active markets in financial instruments did not exist, the Federal Reserve would not be able to make open market operations its primary policy instrument, and a very different, less efficient set of monetary policy procedures would have developed" [1].

The Markets for Derivatives

Unlike the capital and money markets, which provide funding for businesses and governments, the derivative markets serve a different, but related purpose. Derivative markets can be used to hedge against risk as well as to take risk for a fee. In the case of financial derivatives, the risks involved are the future movements of prices of financial instruments and rates of return on those instruments.

Derivative markets involve the trading – both over the counter and through exchanges – of derivative contracts, such as forwards, futures, options, swaps, and credit-default swaps. These instruments are in the form of contracts in which value is *derived* from an underlying financial instrument – for example, bonds, notes, stocks, and currencies. In this chapter, we are focusing on "financial derivatives," which have been in existence only since the 1970s. Derivative contracts in commodities, particularly agricultural products, have been available much longer, as farmers have used them to hedge against losses on crops due to unexpected price declines. It is appropriate to think of trading in derivative contracts as making bets on the future value of financial instruments. In fact, the press often refers to derivative markets as casinos.

The markets for derivatives have received some bad press because their use – and misuse – have resulted in serious financial losses for some individuals and institutions during the recent financial crisis. Some of this criticism is warranted, and some is not. Until very recently, derivative markets have been essentially unregulated, as opposed to the capital markets mentioned earlier. Many individuals and institutions have engaged in derivative trades without understanding the nature of the contracts they were trading. The Barings Bank crisis represents a good example and was a wake-up call to the financial world as to the risks involved in derivative trading.[1] A provision of the recently enacted Dodd-Frank bill will apply more extensive regulation to the derivative industry in the future. The use of derivative contracts as risk-control measures has not been in question. They have been shown to be highly useful in that regard. But, speculation on their value in the markets is the issue that has generated controversy and has led to substantial losses. This market illustrates, perhaps more clearly than any of the other markets, how important it is to keep in mind that *anything* that trades is subject to speculation.

Markets and Exchanges

For years, the markets were basically domestic in nature. Today they are global. Borrowers and lenders of funds and buyers and sellers of financial assets now have many choices: Customers are not locked in to local banks; Internet-based and other electronic banking systems allow access to financial services anywhere; and, as a general rule, brokers and dealers operate across all markets and have access to numerous exchanges. This means one might go to the same broker to buy or sell stocks, options, futures, forex, bonds, etc.

Securities and all manner of financial instruments are bought and sold in these markets, either over the counter or through exchanges. If I meet you on the street, and I see that you have in your pocket a certificate for 100 shares of XYZ Corp., and I say to you that I'll give you $1,000 for that stock certificate, and you say, okay, we have just conducted an "over-the-counter" trade – an OTC trade. OTC trades can be that informal, or they can go through brokers who trade them in the same manner with other brokers.

On the other hand, trading through exchanges is a more formal process in which a record is made of the details of all transactions – prices, volumes, dates, etc. One current controversy focuses on this distinction. Regulators contend that they need the information, which trading through exchanges generates, in order to monitor, and perhaps impose restrictions on certain trades if they perceive a potential danger to the functioning of the market. For example, one of the regulatory provisions under Dodd-Frank is to force trading in derivatives through exchanges in order to provide better information, and hence better control. It is widely held by regulators,

---

[1] More details on the Barings Bank case are presented in Chap. 9.

such as the SEC, that having such information could have prevented some of the recent crises that occurred in that market.

Exchanges are simply institutions that conduct trades in the various markets, or they may be thought of as places where trading occurs, either physical places or networks. The New York Stock Exchange,[2] for example, is an exchange that operates across numerous markets, stocks, bonds, and others, and conducts business in a given physical location, Wall Street and Broad Street in New York City, where its trading floor is located. An exchange such as NASDAQ[3] operates only on an electronic network and has no physical location or trading floor other than an administrative office at Times Square in New York. Trading takes place only in electronic form on the network. The Chicago Board of Trade (CBT) and the Chicago Mercantile Exchange (CME) are other examples of American exchanges that specialize in certain instruments. These two exchanges have become dominant in financial derivative trading, which grew out of their earlier lead in commodities trading, associated with their location in Chicago as the heart of the farm belt.

What are the major exchanges?

- New York: NYSE, NASDAQ, American Exchange (Amex)
- Chicago: CBT, CME (Commodities and Futures)
- London: London Stock Exchange (LSE)
- Frankfurt: The Deutsche Borse
- Euronext: (A merger of the Paris, Amsterdam, Brussels, and Lisbon stock exchanges) now merged with NYSE

    - Also, Euronext, as of 2008, owns Amex

- Eurex: a German-Swiss future exchange – seeks operations in the United States to compete with CBT
- Tokyo, Hong Kong, Shanghai, etc.

The total market capitalization of the major exchanges on December 30, 2011 – that is, the total market value of all shares listed – were as follows (in Dollars or Dollar equivalent)[4]:

- NYSE-Euronext: $14.2 trillion, also largest in US trading volume at 24.8 %
- NASDAQ-OMX: $4.7 trillion, second in trading volume, 21.1 %

---

[2] Now a unit of NYSE-Euronext, Inc.

[3] NASDAQ's name stands for the National Association of Securities Dealers Automated Quotation system, which began simply as a data base for the NASD to monitor prices of OTC trades in stocks, specializing in technology issues. It was quickly realized that the existence of that information on an electronic network provided all the ingredients for a market and that it could conduct trades. Hence, it has become the second largest stock exchange in the world, in terms of volume of shares traded, and has developed from a trading system to a comprehensive exchange operating in a wide variety of markets.

[4] It is worth noting that in the year preceding the date of this table, the 12 largest stock exchanges in the world lost $5.6 trillion in market capitalization, or 13.3 % of their total value, due to the worldwide recession.

- Tokyo: $3.3 trillion
- London (LSE): $3.3 trillion
- Hong Kong, Shanghai: $2.3 trillion each
- Toronto: $1.9 trillion
- Sydney: (Australian Securities Exchange) $1.2 trillion
- Brazil (Bovespa): $1.2 trillion
- Frankfurt: $1.2 trillion
- Bombay and NSE of India: $1.0 trillion each

In addition to those listed, there have been several new exchanges created, such as BATS Global Markets in Kansas City, now number 3 in the United States with 12.1 % of trading volume, and Direct Edge Holdings in New Jersey with 9.3 % of trading volume.[5]

Market Competition Between the United States and Europe

The above lists clearly show that there has been quite a bit of merger activity among securities exchanges around the world, and the feeding frenzy still continues. A major catalyst for these combinations was the introduction of the Euro in 1999 in 12 countries of Europe, which has now expanded to 19 countries (see table on the next page). The existence of a common currency vastly simplifies not only securities trading but trading of all kinds in Europe and between the Euro-zone and the rest of the world. A consolidated European exchange system would accommodate large financing needs in Euro-denominated stocks and bonds. These needs have been heavily dependent upon the Eurodollar market since World War II because it has been the only market large enough to handle multinational financing in a single currency, the Dollar, which is beyond the capacities of some individual countries.

Membership in the European Union and the European Monetary Union (Euro-zone)[a] July 1, 2013

European Union	European Monetary Union (Euro-zone)
The initial 15:	The initial 12:
Austria	Austria
Belgium	Belgium
Denmark	
Finland	Finland
France	France
Germany	Germany
Greece	Greece
Ireland	Ireland
Italy	Italy

(continued)

---

[5] "Taking Stock," *The Wall Street Journal,* 12 July 2012, p C-1.

European Union	European Monetary Union (Euro-zone)
Luxembourg	Luxembourg
Netherlands	Netherlands
Portugal	Portugal
Spain	Spain
Sweden	
United Kingdom	
Joining after the initial 15:	Joining after the initial 12:
Bulgaria	
Croatia	Croatia
Cyprus	Cyprus
Czech Republic	
Hungary	
Malta	Malta
Poland	
Romania	
Slovakia	Slovakia
Slovenia	Slovenia
Estonia	Estonia
Lithuania	
Latvia	Latvia
Total: 28	Total: 19

[a]Two major European countries that chose not to join either the EU or the Euro-zone are Norway and Switzerland. Several candidate countries are still under consideration. The EU has said that no country may join the EU in the future without also joining the Euro-zone

Competition is intense among exchanges. For example, London (LSE) and Frankfurt (Deutsche Borse) vie to be the leading exchange for the European Union. The LSE, now thought to have that distinction, rejected mergers with the Deutsche Borse as well as others, though NASDAQ has acquired a 31 % interest in LSE. Meanwhile, Frankfurt considers itself to be the financial center of continental Europe and is headquarters for the European Central Bank (ECB).[6]

One major combination proposed in 2011 was the merger of the Deutsche Borse with NYSE-Euronext. This prospect generated controversy on both sides of the Atlantic, and the plan was finally abandoned as regulators in both the United States and Germany signaled their opposition to creating an entity that could dominate the industry. It seems likely, however, that the pressure to merge in this field will continue because the synergies and efficiencies involved are too obvious to ignore.

---

[6] The United Kingdom is one of the three countries (along with Denmark and Sweden) that are original members of the European Union, the free trade zone, but chose not to join the Euro-zone. They retain their own currencies. Many observers believe that the reason that London has maintained its dominance as Europe's financial center is because the English language remains the principal business language of the world. See the table on the following page showing member countries of the EU and the Euro-zone.

Operating Methodologies and High-Frequency Trading

A difference in operating methodologies has been one complication that has stood in the way of some proposed mergers of exchanges. The NYSE, for example, is an auction-based exchange, whereas NASDAQ is a dealer-based exchange. The auction method depends upon a "specialist" who functions as an auctioneer. The concept goes back to the days when trades were entered into a book with pencil, and even though it has been automated and is much more efficient today, it is still slower. Proponents of the auction-based system argue that they get the best price for the customer – that is, lowest available price for the buyer and the highest available price for the seller.

I remember being allowed to go onto the floor of the NYSE as an undergraduate student in the late 1950s when I had a summer fellowship to attend a Forum on Finance at New York University. I talked with a specialist who was standing there with a book and a stubby pencil entering orders to buy and sell, which were handed to him by brokers on slips of paper. It is almost inconceivable today to think that things were once that primitive, but I was so impressed as a 20-year-old being there in the center of activity, that I thought it was really high tech. Now, we can see the action on the floor of the exchange on cable TV channels that cover the markets, and we see that the specialist, now called the "designated market maker," has several computer screens in front of him. He or she is receiving information on those screens and entering trades on a handheld electronic device.

Under the dealer-based system, which operates exclusively on an electronic network, the broker-dealers who are members of the exchange are directly connected to the network, and trades are executed much faster. Proponents of this system argue speed is more important to the customer, and surveys show that customers agree. NASDAQ now claims that its average speed per transaction is 98 microseconds, or 98 millionths of a second.

Preference for speed is evident in numerous new developments, such as high-frequency trading, flash orders, naked access, and dark pools, which pose the issue of unfair advantage being allowed to "selected" traders. High-frequency trading has developed by allowing individuals or firms with supercomputers to gain access to the exchange itself to conduct their own trades, rather than going through a broker. This is called naked access. Since ordinary traders would not have such capability, it raises questions of fairness. This type of access permits a trader to enter thousands of orders to buy or sell a stock in rapid-fire succession, thus manipulating the value of a stock. This happened in April of 2011, when a broker in the midwest entered and cancelled thousands of sell orders within a few seconds, causing the value of a given stock to drop to the extent that trading had to be stopped in that stock, and it took several days of research to figure out what happened.

A dark pool is a technique of trading in which individuals or firms get together, do their trading off line, and then run only the net of their settlements through the exchange. This has the effect of hiding transactions and defeats the purpose of the exchange to monitor and to regulate, if necessary, the flow of trading in the markets. The exchanges can intervene in the trading process by stopping the trading of a given stock if its volatility becomes too great and threatens to spread to the rest of the market. The practice of dark pools has become so popular that brokerage firms are now offering to set them up for their customers who either believe that they can negotiate better deals for themselves within the pool or have some other reasons to hide their trading activity.

The SEC has these unfair trading practices under review and has recently adopted a system to track orders, cancellations, and executions of all US-listed stocks and options across all markets that will produce uniform data for the SEC by the next trading day. This will enable the SEC to intervene and reign in activities that might cause market disruption, although it does not deal with the fairness question raised by naked access [2]. This is another example of how technology has led to greater efficiencies in the way we do business, while at the same time creating opportunities for unethical or even fraudulent practices to develop.

The differences in operating methodologies will ultimately be resolved in favor of what most customers want, and that trend seems to favor the NASDAQ approach. Some people believe this will ultimately mean the abandonment of the trading floor of the NYSE, which would represent a major culture change, since the floor is looked upon as the epicenter of stock trading throughout the world. Traders every-where closely watch what happens there and typically wait until the NYSE opens to get a sense of direction on the day's trades and a feel for market sentiment. It has been noted, for example, that three-fourths of the trading on the LSE on a typical day waits until after the NYSE has opened.

The NYSE began as the "Buttonwood Exchange" in 1792 at a spot near #68 Wall Street, where traders gathered to buy and sell shares under a buttonwood (sycamore) tree. Similarly, the American Exchange began as the "Curb Exchange" at a place on the curb on Broad Street. It didn't take the traders long to see the benefits of moving indoors, and since their earliest days the exchanges have usually been sensitive to investor needs and preferences and quick to change when necessary. Both of these exchanges were initially organized as mutual, or member-owned associations, and had certain regulatory functions to perform for the public interest to assure orderly trading activity. In the past decade, both have converted to stock-based, publicly owned, for-profit corporations and have given up all regulatory functions. Also, NASDAQ has become a full-fledged exchange, as opposed to an "interdealer trading system," as it had been known, and it has spun off its regulatory role which it had previously conducted for the NASD. Now, it is possible for investors to own stock in the stock exchanges.

The process of change is continuous within these exchanges because of the intensity of competition that prevails in the industry. All major exchanges have incorporated automation and state-of-the-art telecommunications technology to enhance speed, accuracy, and security. Automated trading technology has replaced the "open-outcry" systems of trading that characterized the floor of the exchanges and the "pits" in the commodities markets. Thus, yelling and throwing of paper have been replaced by electronic signals.

Measures of Market Activity

There are numerous indices of market performance. The three most popular of the stock indices are the Dow Jones Industrial Average (DJIA), the NASDAQ composite index, and the Standard and Poors 500 index. These three are published every business day by the financial press and many other news outlets, and updated in real time, so that analysts, brokers, and traders have virtually continuous access to prices and volume of activity in the markets. The DJIA, published by Dow Jones since 1896, is based upon a sample of the stock prices of 30 industrial corporations in the United States. Even though the sample is small relative to the total of 3,129 publicly traded American companies listed on the exchange, it is generally regarded as remarkably accurate in reflecting US industry in general.[7]

The NASDAQ composite is calculated on the basis of all 2,711 common stocks, both foreign and domestic, listed on that exchange. Standard and Poors, a division of McGraw-Hill, publishes the S&P 500, based on a sample of 500 publicly traded American stocks. The correlation among the movements of these indices is extremely high.

---

[7] The DJIA is arguably the most widely used and most frequently quoted of all stock indices. The sample of 30 stocks, upon which it is based, is revised periodically to keep it reflective of American industry in general. To calculate the DJIA, add the market prices of the 30 stocks at any given point in time, and divide that total by a "divisor," which is calculated and published daily by Dow Jones in the *Wall Street Journal*. The result is the DJIA. The divisor takes into account any adjustments in the sample, such as added or deleted stocks, stock dividends, etc. For example, on a randomly selected date, say July 12, 2012, the total prices of all 30 stocks was $1,665.27, and the divisor was .132129493. The calculation gives you $12,603.31, which was the DJIA just before closing on that date. One can simulate, by this technique the impact on the DJIA of movements in price of any given stock or group of stocks.

The graph on page 110 provides a 112-year perspective on stocks measured by the Dow Jones Industrial Average (DJIA). A perusal of this chart gives the reader an interesting snapshot of American financial history over the last century.[8] One can see clearly, for example, the impact of the Depression era crash from 1929 to 1933, as well as the second recession of the 1930s, due to misguided Federal Reserve policy, beginning in 1937 and lasting until the beginning of the buildup for World War II in 1942. This is followed by the postwar growth spurt, then the difficult years of the late 1960s and the 1970s as we struggled with "stagflation" – stagnating growth accompanied by high inflation – something which, according to economic theory, isn't supposed to happen. Then, the boom of the 1980s and 1990s came, which included two small recessions – of 1990–1991, which was labeled the "white-collar" recession, and the dip of 2001–2002, labeled the "dot-com" recession. Finally, the dip of 2007, the effect of which lasts to the present, is highly visible.

We also see on the chart, the DJIA's all-time peak, prior to the beginning of the recent downturn, of 14,164.53, which occurred on October 9, 2007. It shows a drop during that downturn to a low of 6,547.05 – a loss of 54 % of its value. The human cost associated with that decline was devastating to millions of people, because, behind these numbers are job losses, home foreclosures, business failures, and interrupted lives. While the DJIA has recovered from that low and has set a new all-time high of over 15,000 in 2013, all the devastation of that downturn has not been repaired. This is especially reflected in the unemployment statistics, which remain inordinately high.

On the NASDAQ, a similar picture emerges, but for somewhat different reasons. The NASDAQ composite reached its peak at 5,048 on March 10, 2000. This was at the outset of the dot-com recession, during which many high-tech firms did not survive. The NASDAQ, being heavily weighted with high-tech companies, bore the brunt of this downturn very heavily. It had not recovered from that crisis before it was hit again by the downturn in 2007. By July 2009, it reached its low of 1,790 and had lost 65 % of its value. By mid-2013, it had recovered only to about 3,600, or 71 % of its peak.

---

[8] Note that the chart is logarithmically scaled, which has the effect of muting the overall impact of the changes – that is, an upward-sloping straight line on the chart represents a constant percentage rate of change.

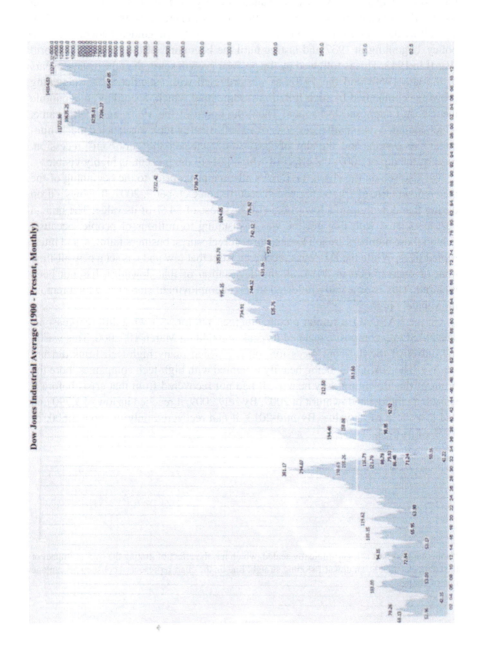

Investor Behavior in the Markets

Investors often make their choices between stocks and bonds on the basis of the outlook they perceive for the economy, and increasingly that has come to mean the global economy. Bonds, especially Treasuries, are considered safer investments than stocks. Yet stocks are viewed, at least over long periods, as yielding greater returns to investors. Therefore, in periods of volatility in the stock market, or in periods of uncertain outlook for the economy, we typically see investors move out of stocks into bonds. This depresses prices of stocks while it boosts prices of bonds, and consequently lowers the yield of bonds. Conversely, as the economic outlook becomes brighter and/or markets become stable, investors become willing to take on higher risk, and we typically see movement out of bonds into stocks. Of course, this oversimplifies the process of investor choice because there are many other factors that can affect the markets, such as wars and conflict, here or elsewhere, political events, and natural disasters.

Some of the increased volatility in the stock market during the recent downturn has been attributed to the increased use of short sales. A case in point has been some recent behavior by Goldman Sachs, which brought renewed attention and scorn from the public as well as Congress about short-selling in competition with their own customers. Goldman was highly touting a new issue of CDOs and selling them to investors at the same time it was short-selling the same securities, expecting them to drop in value. Other instances of similarly deceptive activity have been noted, which has raised the question of whether short-selling is ever in the public interest.

Naked short-selling of any securities – bonds, stock, or any financial instruments – is not permitted under SEC rules. Normally, an investor who sells short borrows the shares or instruments from a broker and sells them in the hope they will drop in value. The investor can then buy them at a lower price, replace the borrowed shares, and pocket the difference as a profit. This is legal. But, in naked short-selling the investor never borrows the underlying shares, in effect manipulating the market, because the investor gets by with taking the risk without posting collateral to protect the buyer of the shares. While the SEC has established stiff penalties for naked short-selling, it is difficult to enforce because of the lack of information. The SEC has also imposed an "uptick rule," which means that no one can short-sell a security that is already declining in price until there has been an uptick in the market price. But many observers continue to feel that short-selling is not in the public interest at all, and this debate is likely to continue as regulators define market rules and regulations for the future.

Financial markets, like commodity markets, are extremely efficient due to high-speed telecommunications and due to the fungibility of items traded – shares, bonds, etc. Financial instruments, such as a bundle of 10-year government notes or a bundle of MBSs or CDOs, are just as tradable as commodities, such as barrels of oil, tons of coal, or bars of gold. Therefore, banks and brokers and dealers lend and borrow bonds and other securities as easily as I might borrow a cup of sugar from my neighbor.

Because of this efficiency, conditions in one market transfer quickly to all other markets. The Southeast Asian crisis of 1997–1998 was an example that came to be called "the Asian contagion." More on this crisis will be discussed in Chap. 9, but it illustrated that the free movement of capital around the world, while highly beneficial to growing markets, also has a downside. Capital can leave a country as quickly as it comes in, and this is what the Asian countries discovered – leading to devaluations of currencies, bank failures, recession, and market collapse. We shall see later that this was also a situation that required defensive monetary policy to protect against the contagion effect. The subprime mortgage crisis, starting in 2007, also quickly became global in scope. American-produced CDOs and MBSs were just as popular with investors in Germany, France, and Japan as in the United States. While it was unintentional, this resulted in our exporting the economic problems of US markets to theirs. In 2012, we began to import the financial problems of Europe, as well as the effects of the economic slowdowns in China, India, and Brazil – all of which are further examples of the globalization of markets.

The Changing Role of Financial Institutions in US Markets

We have previously noted that the nature of the banking industry, as well as that of the shadow banking industry, have changed markedly in recent decades, and we have remarked on several components of that change:

- The movement of some banks from retail to wholesale banking
- The increased competition between the regulated banking industry and the virtually unregulated shadow banking industry
- The decline in the importance of deposits as funding sources for banks and the increased use of market sources of funding
- The availability of other avenues for traditional customers of banks to place their money aside from deposits and to obtain funding other than through bank loans
- The increased opportunities for banks to sell and securitize loans to restore liquidity and remove credit risk
- The increased awareness of risk in the industry and the availability of new techniques to control it
- The increased pressure to hold higher levels of capital to buffer against unexpected losses

Consumers and business borrowers are also finding the capital markets easier to use because of new technologies, online access, discount brokerages, etc. Therefore, customary banking functions have diminished in importance, such as seeking stable deposits from the community, using those funds to make loans, and holding the loans at risk until maturity. As evidence of change, checkable deposits, which in 1960 funded 60 % of bank assets, funded only 11 % in 2011. These shifts are often referred to as "dis-intermediation," that is, obtaining banking services while bypassing the banking system itself. Note the extent of these changes in the table below, over the period of 1980–2008.

Total assets held by all financial institutions in the United States[a]

	1980	%	2008	%	Factor of change
All depository financial institutions	$2,340 bil	57.9	$14,591 bil	36.0	6.2
Mutual funds	$70 bil	1.7	$6,588 bil	16.3	94.1
All others[b]	*$1,628 bil*	*40.3*	$19,344 bil	*47.7*	11.9
Total	$4,038 bil	100	$40,523 bil	100	10.0

[a]www.federalreserve.gov/releases/Z-1
[b]Includes insurance companies, pension funds, state and local government retirement funds, finance companies, and money market mutual funds

The table shows that total assets of all financial institutions grew from $4.0 trillion to $40.5 trillion over the 28-year period. The table was constructed to highlight the disparities in rates of growth among certain types of institutions. While the growth of depository institutions was positive, their share of total financial assets declined from almost 58 % to 36 % of the national total, significantly outpaced by the growth of non-depository institutions, especially mutual funds.

What do these figures portend for the future of the banking industry? It is clear that the traditional banking model no longer exists and that banks, which have dominated the financial markets for generations, will have to share those markets with other kinds of institutions to a much greater extent and, in order to compete, will be required to perform many different functions than they have in years past.

Commercial Paper

By 1995, only 20 % of US businesses were borrowing from banks, accounting for about 18 % of American corporate finance. So, where is the financing of business coming from? Much of the gap has been filled by commercial paper (CP) – a market that has expanded from $33 billion in 1970 to $1,544 billion in 2000 and has reached the equivalent of about one half of the total of bank credit outstanding.

The commercial paper market is a large, easily accessed, highly liquid market, and is one of the oldest in the American financial system, dating from the early 19th century. It is a means of direct financing. A corporation issues an IOU and sells it directly to an investor or through a dealer. Why has there been such phenomenal growth in this market? Once again, we can say that technology has made it possible by making this market easier to access by corporate borrowers. Relative interest rates are also a major factor. CP rates have historically been somewhat lower than bank lending rates. See the table of money rates on pages 42–43.

Commercial paper has developed not only as an alternative to bank loans for corporate borrowers but as an attractive investment for individuals as well as institutional investors and banks. The paper is short-term – 9 months maximum – and is sold without documentation, at a discount, by the most creditworthy borrowers. Improvements in information technology have made it easier to issue and for investors to analyze the risks involved. Secondary markets for commercial paper exist, and the role of CP brokers and dealers has grown, particularly as the use of the market has begun to appeal to smaller borrowers in more recent years. Smaller borrowers who may not be as well-known as the corporate giants of the world have often found it more convenient and effective to go through dealers rather than trying to sell their paper directly to investors. The added risk of this segment of the market is reflected in the slightly higher rates for dealer-placed commercial paper. Note also in the table on Pages 42–43 that there is Euro-commercial paper, which is Dollar-denominated CP issued outside the United States. Like other Dollar-based financial instruments, this market also has a foreign constituency.

Therefore, the use of CP has mushroomed in the market as a credit instrument, and this growth has enhanced the liquidity of the market, which means that buyers and sellers are readily available.

The CP market has encountered some difficulties in the past decade. The Enron scandal in 2002 was one event that sent shock waves through this market. Buyers of the paper were alerted to the declining credit quality of formerly creditworthy corporations – Enron, WorldCom, Tyco, etc. This was further exacerbated by the onset of the mortgage crisis in late 2007. Since this is an unsecured market, and therefore highly sensitive to overall market conditions, nervous investors stopped buying CP and caused the market to "freeze up" in 2008, putting a major crimp in corporate finance and hurting business generally. This caused the Fed to start buying CP for the first time in history in order to get the market moving again. The Fed has since disposed of all its holdings of the paper, but their actions did save the CP market from total collapse.

References

1. Meulendyke A-M (1998) Purposes and functions of the Federal Reserve System. Board of Governors of the Federal Reserve System, Washington, DC, pp 79–82
2. Ackerman A (2012) SEC arms itself to better track trades. The Wall Street Journal, 12 July 2012, p C-3

Chapter 8
Who Finances American Industry? The Relative Roles of Commercial and Investment Banking

The Role of Banks in Corporate Finance: An International Comparison

In their book, *Global Banking*, Smith and Walter argue that there are three models of bank-industry linkages [1, p. 431]. The first is what they call the "outsider system," which is essentially the English/American system. The typical industrial firm is semidetached from banks. Financing is done mainly through the capital markets, with short-term needs satisfied by commercial paper and longer-term needs through bonds or medium-term notes. Bank relationships are important for backstop lines, etc., but relationships remain at arm's length.

Their second model is the "insider system," which is the German approach, and is typical of other continental European countries. It involves close bank-industry relationships, with business financial needs met by bank lending and retained earnings. Bank roles often extend beyond credit to stock ownership, share voting, and board memberships. Unwanted takeovers are rare, and the use of capital markets is limited.

The third model is the "ultra-insider system." This is a cross-holding system, typified by the Japanese *keiretsu*.[1] Interfirm boundaries are blurred through equity cross-holdings and long-term supplier-customer relationships. This system has diminished in recent years – but only slightly – with the growth of the Japanese capital markets. The following table shows the extent of reliance on various forms of corporate finance by firms in the United States, Germany, and Japan.

---

[1] *The Economist*, Oct. 16, 2009, Vol. 401, defines *keiretsu* as a Japanese word meaning headless combine – a form of corporate structure in which a number of organizations link together, usually by taking small stakes in each other and, therefore, having close business relationships. It is often criticized because it implies restricting business only to members of the "family."

W.H. Wallace, *The American Monetary System: An Insider's View of Financial Institutions, Markets and Monetary Policy*, DOI 10.1007/978-3-319-02907-8_8, © Springer International Publishing Switzerland 2013

Sources of external corporate finance: United States, Germany, and Japan[a]
(Non-financial Businesses – 1970–2000)

	United States	Germany	Japan
Bank loans	18 %	76 %	78 %
Non-bank loans (Including CP and other direct financing)	39	10	8
Bonds	32	7	9
Stock	11	7	5
Total	100 %	100 %	100 %

[a]Andreas Hackenthal and Reinhard H. Schmidt, "Financing Patterns: Measurement Concepts and Empirical Results," J.W. Goethe-Universitat Working Paper No. 125, January, 2004

The US trends are in sharp contrast to Europe, where bank financing of business is dominant. Many people expect this to change over time as Europe-wide capital markets develop in response to the growth of the Euro. And they contrast sharply, as well, with Japan where 78 % of business financing is from banks. Change in the Japanese financial system, however, has been much slower to occur. These differences in the role of banks in corporate finance are mirrored in the fact that total bank assets in the EU are about three times total EU GDP, while in the United States, they are about 80 % of GDP.

Businesses in need of longer-term funds essentially have two broad choices: loans through banks or sales of stocks or bonds through investment banks. To compare the role of commercial banks in extending loans with that of investment banks in underwriting new issues of stocks or bonds, let us look first at loans. Loans can be domestic in nature, that is, in the domestic currency. They can be cross-border, in the home currency of the lender, or in that of the borrower. Finally, they can be multinational in nature, perhaps in a variety of currencies, through foreign branches or affiliates.

Commitments to lend, whether domestic or international, are often referred to as "lending facilities." The terminology simply means lending arrangement. These may be *revolving credit facilities*, which are agreements to supply credit as needed. See the "tombstone" on page 120 announcing the revolving credit facility for Dow Chemical. This is a syndicated loan arrangement.

Another approach might be a *committed facility* or an agreement to provide a specific amount of credit at a designated time. This is often a legally binding commitment on the part of the bank, in which case it is a contingent liability of the bank – or an off-balance sheet item – until the loan is made. Often, this arrangement is necessary to enable the borrower to make further commitments to suppliers, etc.

Finally, the arrangement might be simply a *backstop line*, which is a commitment to supply credit if needed. The borrower may be seeking other credit sources, such as bonds or stocks, but needs a backstop if these other sources become unavailable or if other credit markets are not conducive to the borrowing firm's needs. Interest rates may have risen, which makes the issue of bonds more expensive, or the stock market may have dropped, which means that issuing stock in a down market is costly and unwise. During the recent financial crisis, many firms have had to rely on backstop lines, which were set up years earlier because other market sources dried up.

Investment Banking

As noted, the alternative to bank loans for business finance is the capital markets. This is the bailiwick of investment banks. These institutions underwrite new issues of securities – stocks, notes, and bonds – by offering them to investors on behalf of the issuing corporation. The purposes may be to raise additional capital for an existing enterprise, to raise capital in an initial public offering (IPO) for a new startup company or for an existing company going public for the first time, or to finance mergers and acquisitions.

These activities have been among the most lucrative on Wall Street in recent years, but they have generated much controversy lately due to some highly publicized conflicts of interest and unethical deals involving a number of well-known firms – Enron, Goldman Sachs, Citigroup, etc.

Most investment banks are also brokers and dealers in securities, meaning that they also buy and sell securities – stocks and bonds as well as government securities – in the secondary market. Some dealers in government securities, called "primary dealers," are authorized to buy and sell directly with the Federal Reserve. We shall discuss their role further in Chap. 12 under monetary policy.

Therefore, an investment bank, which is also a broker and dealer and a commercial bank, can handle all financing needs of business. Many large institutions are all of these under the terms of the Gramm-Leach-Bliley Act of 1999 (GLB). This act has become the subject of controversy recently because it is alleged to have led to conflicts of interest and caused other moral hazards, such as making a loan agreement with a firm contingent upon getting its investment banking business or bidding against their own customers in their trading operations, as Goldman was accused of in 2010.

Who are the major investment banks, and what has happened to them during the recent financial crisis? As noted in Chap. 1, recent years have not been kind to various kinds of financial institutions, and investment banks head that list. The top five in this industry, all of which encountered severe financial difficulties at the start of the recent recession – around 2008 – were Bear Stearns, Merrill Lynch, Goldman Sachs, Morgan Stanley, and Lehman Brothers.

One of them, Lehman Brothers, failed and has since been dismembered and sold off in pieces. The other four would have failed had it not been for action by the Treasury and/or the Federal Reserve to save them. Bear Stearns has been taken over by a bank, JPMorgan Chase, which allowed it to have access through the bank to the Fed's discount window. Merrill Lynch has been taken over by the Bank of America, which also gave it access to the Fed. The remaining two, Morgan Stanley and Goldman Sachs, converted their charters to financial holding companies, which also gave them access to the Federal Reserve. There are others – Deutsche Bank, UBS Warburg, Smith Barney – which have survived, but one can look back on this experience and say in all honesty that we almost lost the industry.

It is likely to be argued for years to come whether the recombination of commercial banking and investment banking under GLB was a good idea. In view of the pain associated with the recent recession, many people, including Massachusetts Senator Elizabeth Warren, have argued for a return to Glass-Steagall, which GLB partially repealed.

Investment banks are expected to provide advice to clients about markets. The choice between bonds and stocks is important to the issuing company because secondary issues of stock can dilute existing shares, while bonds can often be costly to service. The timing can be crucial, in terms of both market receptivity and cost. And the investment bank, depending upon the type of commitment made to the issuer, may be stuck with buying and holding part of a new offering. The industry continues to be a dog-eat-dog world.

The question arises as to why, with all these lucrative lines of business, the top investment banks went bankrupt during the recent recession and required bailouts? The simplest answer is they invested in securities and often got stuck with those they issued. They sometimes made bad choices, and in the recent episode, they invested heavily in mortgage-backed securities, which turned out to be poison. *The Economist* recently dubbed the investment banking world as one "where angels fear to trade."

Bond Ratings

For bond financing, cost and market receptivity are influenced by ratings assigned by bond-rating agencies. There are nine such agencies presently registered with the SEC, which are "Nationally recognized statistical rating organizations (NRSROs)." Two of these – Moody's Investors Service, Inc., and Standard & Poor's Ratings Services – are most prominently recognized in this field. They evaluate issues of bonds and other fixed-rate debt instruments in categories of investment grade, intermediate grade, and speculative instruments, respectively, from highest quality to lowest. The lowest category is alternatively referred to as high-yield or junk instruments.

The highest quality, investment grade, is designated by Moody's as Aaa, Aa1, Aa2, Aa3, A1, A2, and A3 and by Standard & Poors (S&P) as AAA, AA, A, and BBB. This group is defined as ranging from the best quality with smallest risk to medium quality with "some vulnerability" to changing economic conditions.

Intermediate grade is designated by Moody's as Baa1, Baa2, and Baa3 and by S&P as BB and B. This group is defined as having some speculativity or some risk of default in the future.

High-yield or junk instruments are designated by Moody's as Ba1, Ba2, Ba3, B1, B2, B3, Caa1, Caa2, Caa3, Ca, C, and D and by S&P as CCC, CC, C, and D. The group is defined as ranging from poor quality with high risk of default to actually in default. It is worthy of note, however, that in this market, even securities that are in default will sell with deep discounts. For example, some mortgage-backed securities, almost immediately after the onset of the downturn in December 2007, went into default and sold at $0.27 per Dollar of face value.

Prior to about 1970, investors paid for ratings provided by these agencies, and the ratings given were presumed to be independent. That changed in the 1970s to the present system in which the issuers of the securities being rated pay for the ratings. This has tended to create a conflict of interest in which the rating agencies apparently have developed a reluctance to give their paying customers unfavorable ratings. This first became obvious to the entire financial community with the Enron scandal of 2002, when the agencies continued to give AAA ratings to Enron's bonds even after its stock prices dropped from above $90 to $4. While the rating agencies do not rate stocks, this highly visible drop in share prices was a signal that all was not right with the company financially and should have raised a red flag. Again in 2008, the agencies gave AAA ratings to CDOs which they knew were based on defaulted mortgages.

The rating agencies have been severely criticized for these misdeeds and for their overall reluctance to alert the financial world sooner about credit risks. The agencies are private in nature and are therefore totally unregulated. They are targeted by Congress for reform, and in July 2011, the SEC announced plans to bring charges against them for deliberately misleading investors during the recent crisis. Nothing has been done thus far.

It was recently noted in *The Wall Street Journal* that the rating agencies are getting the rug pulled out from under them because they are not being used as much today – at least not to the extent that existed before their failures became widely known.[2] Company policies, as well as laws that once required that bond issuers obtain ratings from these agencies, are gradually being changed to eliminate the requirement, and companies are increasingly finding that they can issue bonds without the ratings – that is, the markets will accept them.

Syndications of Loans and Securities

We have noted earlier that syndication is a process by which financial institutions share large loans with each other or divide responsibility for new issues of securities. The process of syndication is relatively new in the financial system and has been used to a significant degree only since the early 1960s. We shall consider first the role of commercial banks in syndicated lending.

The process involves a formalized arrangement among banks, with an announcement of the loan in the financial press – often involving a "tombstone," similar to the one pictured in the left panel on the following page [1, pp. 24–38 and 318]. A lead institution usually arranges the syndicate and is designated as the manager of the effort, or it is possible for several banks to share the lead role. The leader then recruits the syndicate partners. The leader will usually take a significant stake in the loan in order to instill the confidence of the partners. The underwriting process,

---

[2] *The Wall Street Journal*, 27 July 2010. Section C.

including the due diligence, is also typically handled by the lead institution, although syndicate partners, unless otherwise specified, would have the right to do due diligence as well.

There are advantages to lenders in the process of syndication, such as better diversification of a bank's loan portfolio, avoidance of capital limitations on loans to a single borrower, and access to large customers which smaller banks might not otherwise have. The three billion Dollar Dow Chemical revolving credit facility is a good example. There is cooperation among multiple banks, which opens the door for many of them to future business, and there is reduced credit risk because there is often better underwriting expertise in the lead institution, allowing for more thorough analysis and legal protection.

From the perspective of the borrower, there are also advantages, such as the ability to obtain larger loans, usually greater efficiency, and perhaps lower cost. Consider what alternatives might have been available to Dow Chemical, for example, if bond and stock markets were not conducive to their needs at the time. The lead institution in the Dow example is Citibank, and it is assisted by others in Britain, France, and Canada.

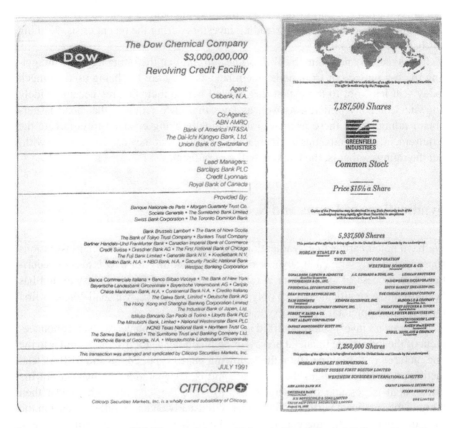

Tombstones announcing a $3 billion revolving credit loan to Dow Chemical (left panel) and the sale of 7.2 million shares of common stock for Greenfield Industries (right panel)

The lead institution will prepare an information memorandum detailing financial and economic information on the borrower, including historical and political information. Smith and Walter note, "Lead managers in syndications carry heavy responsibilities to both borrowers and lenders. They must be absolutely forthright and reliable in their dealings with participants" [1]. Sometimes, this trust in the lead manager goes awry in unexpected ways.

After retiring from the Federal Reserve, I was asked in 1999 to serve as a consultant to a law firm representing the Bank of Montreal, which had joined a lending syndicate, led by Signet Bank of Richmond, Virginia. This case involved bank fraud, in which a person, representing himself as an official of Phillip Morris & Co., approached Signet Bank for a $120 million loan to purchase computers and set up operations to conduct research on smokeless cigarettes outside the United States.[3] The borrower's name was familiar because he had been an official of Phillip Morris, so the bank did not inquire further into his background.

Many red flags were raised: suspicions about a letter that had been forged from the CEO of the company confirming the project, in which the signature differed from all other legitimate letters in the bank's files from the CEO; the requirement that all banks in the syndicate sign confidentiality agreements not to disclose the existence of the project; the refusal by the borrower to allow the banks to confirm the existence of the equipment and/or the location of the facilities; the assertion that the reason they were conducting the research in foreign locations was to avoid FDA restrictions on research on human subjects; and the list went on and on. All members of the syndicate surprisingly agreed to these terms and conditions.

The law firm with whom I consulted represented the Bank of Montreal, which had agreed to take a $24 million piece of the loan. The funding of the loan began in December 1993. The Bank of Montreal signed on as a participant in the syndicate in November 1995 and funded its share. Other banks joined the syndicate, most of whom raised questions about some of the irregularities but were told by Signet to keep quiet about it because of the confidentiality agreement with the borrower. One participant, the Bank of Tokyo, ignored Signet's instructions and placed a call to Phillip Morris to inquire about the individual who was the borrower. The bank was told that he had retired several years earlier.

The fraud was then revealed in March 1996. The Bank of Montreal sued Signet for the return of its money on the grounds that Signet had not revealed to syndicate members the irregularities involved in the case. The case was tried before a six-person jury in the US District Court for the Eastern District of Virginia in January 1998.

Signet's rather weak defense was that the Bank of Montreal, as well as others, had the right to do due diligence if they wished. I was asked as an "expert witness" what the obligations were of the lead institution in a syndicate to the other members. Relying on the Smith and Walter book, *Global Banking*, I stated that the lead bank in a syndicate had the obligation to report to all members of the syndicate any

---

[3] Information about this case in all its detail is now entirely in the public domain. See *The Richmond Times Dispatch*, Jan. 22, 1998, B-9, Jan 23, 1998, B-6, and Jan. 24, 1998, C-1.

information that came to its attention regarding the creditworthiness of the borrower and that Signet had plenty of information that should have been revealed. The Bank of Montreal won its case, and other syndicate members followed with lawsuits. The perpetrator of the fraud and several accomplices went to prison. Lenders ultimately lost a net of about $100 million. Signet Bank was facing failure as a result of this incident, and it subsequently was taken over by First Union Bank, one of the ancestors of the current Wells Fargo Bank.

What was shocking about this case was the cavalier manner in which banks that had been successful lenders for generations approached this very large loan. Obviously, they thought they were dealing with the real Phillip Morris and did not want to vex a valued customer.

Consideration of this case causes one to wonder whether we learn from past experience. I am not entirely convinced that we do. In light of numerous incidents similar to this one, although not necessarily involving fraud, which have occurred since the turn of the 21st century, it is clear that defective underwriting procedures and lack of due diligence continue to abound. If bank loan officers can treat the sanctity of customer deposits with such carelessness, it lends credibility to the argument that the successive increases in deposit insurance that have been approved over the years have added considerably to the moral hazard of the banking industry.

The syndication process for bonds and stocks is similar to that for loans. Bonds and stocks all have well-developed secondary markets, but the initial process of underwriting remains a critical ingredient because it determines the underlying quality of the financial assets that result. We learned this again, to our dismay, during the recent mortgage crisis in which banks willingly lent to non-creditworthy borrowers. The forces of competition and greed kept them doing so until it all collapsed in the fall of 2007.

See the tombstone on page 120 for Greenfield Industries. Shares are to be issued partially in the United States and partially outside. The latter are Euro equities, that is, Dollar-denominated shares issued outside the United States. The offering is priced to raise $112 million. Investment banks will try to time their entry when the market for stocks in the given industry is high or, in this case, when the market for the stock of Greenfield Industries is high. Share prices will vary once they go into the secondary market. Occasionally, when the stock experiences a significant increase immediately with the issue of new shares, the issuing company can opt to increase the offer. This is referred to in the industry as the "Green Shoe" option, named for the company that first did this.

Not all new issues, or new loans, warrant a tombstone such as those illustrated. These are not solicitations to investors; they are simply announcements of the issues, and they are done for public relations purposes primarily. It is usually thought of as good publicity for the financial institutions to show that they are handling such large issues, as well as for the borrowers, so that their investors and customers will know that they are expanding and presumably doing well to be obtaining the credit. The financial press regularly publishes lists of new securities issued and bank loan syndications for those borrowers who do not warrant tombstones.

Another feature of this process is "shelf-registration," in which a company issuing new stocks or bonds, and after obtaining SEC approval, will decide to wait, usually because conditions in the market have shifted, making the existing market un-conducive to the issue. So, the stocks or bonds are put "on the shelf." Therefore, the financial press will also regularly publish lists of stocks or bonds that are taken "off the shelf" for issue.

There are several types of syndication mandates – for stocks or bonds: a fully committed syndication in which the lead investment bank guarantees the full amount and then attempts to sell it; a partially committed syndication in which the leader agrees only to part of the total but attempts to sell the full amount; and a "best-efforts" syndication in which the leader makes no guarantee but does the best it can. Obviously, credit standing and previous experience with the borrower dictate what the lead bank will be willing to guarantee. However, the high degree of competition in the investment banking industry means some institutions go out on a limb to guarantee an issue in order to get the business ahead of some other investment bank. The press often refers to competition in this industry as a "feeding frenzy."

Some investment banks have been stuck for years with holding issues of stocks or bonds on which they have made the mistake of overcommitting to the issuer. A good example is the syndication of RJR-Nabisco junk bonds by the investment banking firm of Kohlberg Kravis Roberts (KKR). They sold these junk bonds in 1989 into a market in which demand for them began to decline precipitously [2].

The Bond Market and the Behavior of Interest Rates

Investment banks can also adapt the nature of the securities they issue to the preferences of potential buyers. For example, the traditional bond – both Treasury and corporate issues – is issued on a coupon basis. This terminology is based on the fact that bonds were issued historically with coupons attached that represented the interest payments the bondholder would be paid at the fixed "coupon rate." The holder would simply clip the coupon, mail it to the bank that was the agent of the issuer, and would receive a check for the interest by mail. Now, bonds and almost all other marketable securities are no longer issued in paper form, but rather in "book-entry" form only. The bondholder receives a computer printout from the issuer or its agent as evidence of ownership of the bond. Payments of interest are handled by wire transfer directly to the bank account of the bondholder, and no paper changes hands. But the bonds that pay interest in this manner are still referred to as "coupon bonds." This is true whether the bond is bought new at original issue or in the secondary market at a later date through a broker.

Certain types of bonds and other fixed-income instruments are not issued with a coupon rate but are sold at a discount by the issuer. This is true of Treasury bills (T-bills) – short-term instruments ranging in maturity from four weeks to one year – as well as commercial paper, zero-coupon bonds, and the like. Investors typically bid for these instruments by stating what they are willing to pay. Thus, the rate of return on the instrument is the difference between its face value and the amount actually paid for it, calculated over the length of time it is held. For example, if you pay $9,500 for a $10,000 face value T-bill that matures in exactly one year, your rate of return is $500/$9,500 × 100, or 5.26 %.

Other types of securities that have been invented to meet particular interests or needs of investors or issuers, by either the Treasury, corporate issuers, or investment banks, have been Treasury TIPS and Contingent Convertible (CoCo) bonds, mentioned in Chap. 6; synthetic convertible bonds; Treasury cash management bills (CMBs) with maturities of only a few days; and savings bonds that were issued during wartime to encourage citizens to save and support the war effort. Also, as we have noted earlier, asset-backed securities, beginning with mortgages, have developed continuously since about 1970 and have appealed to a wide variety of investors, both foreign and domestic. Others that we shall discuss are zero-coupon bonds and strips and "when-issued" securities.

Markets seem to develop readily for every type of issue that comes along, and each apparently fills a particular niche that investors desire. Driven by historically low rates on long-term bonds, the New York Port Authority, in mid-2012, began to issue $1 billion of 40-year taxable municipal bonds, rated Aa2 by Moody's, to fund the World Trade Center redevelopment. This came after a successful issue of 100-year tax exempt municipals – the so-called Century Bonds – by the Port Authority in 1994. Also, in recent years, an advisory panel to the US Treasury has been urging the government to lock in current low interest rates for several decades by issuing Century Bonds. The Treasury, however, has said that it has no plans to do so at this time.[4]

Let's consider some examples of bond yields in the tables from *Barron's* on pages 126–128. Prices are quoted as of July 16, 2012. See the Treasury bill maturing June 27, 2013, the last item in the list of T-bills. If you buy this bill at the ask price on the date of the table, you pay $9,981.06 and receive $10,000 on June 27, 2013. Thus, you receive the annual equivalent of the 0.18 % yield. Even though the return is low, notice that it has the highest yield in the table because it has longer to go to maturity than any of the others. The yields on those bills maturing in October 2012, for example, are about half this one. The price is calculated as the present value of $10,000, discounted for 11.5 months at the annual rate of 0.18 %.

Next, see the Treasury 3.0 % coupon bond maturing in May 2042, the last item under US Notes and Bonds. This is a 30-year bond, issued in May 2012. If you pay the ask price of $10,862.50 for the bond, you get a 2.58 % annual yield if you hold it until May 2042. You would have bought this bond at a premium, meaning that bond prices have risen in the market since it was issued 1½ months earlier. You will receive $8,962.50 in total interest at 3 % of the face value of $10,000 for 29.875 years.[5]

---

[4] *The Wall Street Journal*, February 3, 2011, Section C.

[5] One quirk of reading bond tables is that the financial industry continues the maddening practice of quoting bond prices in 32nds of a point. Therefore, the ask price in this example is 108:20 or 108 20/32 = 108.625. This is 108.625 % of the face value or $10,862.50.

Look also in the Barron's tables (p. 127) for a Treasury TIP security, due February 2042. It has 29 years and 7 months to maturity. If bought at the ask price, its yield is 0.371 %, which is, as we have noted, a proxy for the real interest rate. Also, in Chap. 4, we noted that the difference between the yield on TIPS and that of regular Treasury bonds of the same maturity is a market estimate of the expected rate of inflation. In this example, the yield on a 30-year coupon bond due in February 2042, if bought at the ask price, is 2.57 %. Thus, 2.57–0.371 = 2.20. This could be viewed as an estimate of the average annual rate of inflation over approximately the next 30 years. This is a bit above the Fed's target inflation rate, but this is what the market thinks it will be.

Some Treasury issues are watched by analysts more closely than others for a variety of specific reasons. Long-term Treasury rates, for example, are key indicators of capital market conditions for years ahead based upon expectations of participants in the market.

Historically, the most closely watched of the Treasury long-term issues has been the 30-year bond, called the "long bond." We know on a priori grounds that rates on long-term issues tend to be higher than short-term rates. We shall see further evidence shortly of this structure of rates in our study of bond yield curves. The principal reason for this is the "time value of money" argument, simply that investors will require a higher return the longer they tie up their money. The prospect for inflation, for example, is more likely over longer periods of time than it is for the short horizon. And, as we know, inflation erodes the value of any investment over time. Thus, investors lose real value when this occurs, whereas borrowers benefit from it. In other words, borrowers will pay off their debt with cheaper money, but investors will receive money of less value than that they originally lent.

The long bond is regarded as the most risk-free of long-term issues. The rate on it sets the pace for other long-term rates, such as mortgages. This places the long bond into a particularly sensitive role for a large number of people, ranging from average homeowners to sophisticated investors.

During the period of 1998 through 2000, the United States ran budgetary surpluses, and the Treasury actually began to pay down the debt, beginning with the long-term issues. They began to buy back long-term government bonds and retire them. Analysts in the Treasury and the Federal Reserve were actually beginning to think in terms of "what if" we paid off the entire federal debt. The Treasury then declared a moratorium on the issue of any additional 30-year bonds. After 2000, the situation changed, and the United States went back into deficits, but the moratorium lasted 4½ years. The Treasury resumed the issue of long bonds in the middle of the last decade.

While the moratorium was in place, the 10-year bond, which became the longest-term Treasury issue, increased in popularity and took upon itself some of the burden that had been carried by the long bond. The result has been that the 10-year bond continues to get more attention than it did in years past, along with the 30-year bond, and they are both now considered bellwether issues. It has been considered highly newsworthy that the rate on the 10-year bond has dropped below 2 % during 2012, and at midyear it stood at 1.4 %, indicating that long-term Treasuries are still

U. S. Treasury Bonds, Notes and Bills
From *Barron's* July 16, 2012

much in demand all over the world and that the cost of long-term credit is lower than it has ever been. All the hype in the financial press about this development prompted me to ask my students at the university in the Fall of 2012 whether the fact that the 10-year bond had dropped below 2 % was among the things that excited them. I could tell that most of them were not particularly turned on by it.

The 10-year bond did not creep back above 2 % until mid-2013, when concerns began to surface that the Fed might soon end its easy-money policies and allow interest rates to rise again.

U.S. Treasury Zero-coupon Bonds and Inflation Indexed Treasury Securities (TIPS)
From *Barron's* July 16, 2012

Instruments of other maturities also seem to attract a certain following in the market. I remember that when the two-year note was introduced in the late 1970s, I was invited to a party at the Treasury to celebrate its coming out. As the Secretary of the Treasury stood on a desk, holding high a glass of champagne, he loudly exclaimed, "Let's hear it for the two-year note!" I could not help thinking that this party was a little different from any I had attended before. Now, this note is very popular. It is the shortest term of the coupon notes and is regarded as sensitive to expectations about Federal Reserve policy.

Investment Grade Corporate Bonds
and High-yield (Junk) Corporate Bonds
From *Barron's*, July 16, 2012

CORPORATE BONDS

For the week ending Friday, July 13, 2012
Forty most active fixed-coupon corporate bonds

COMPANY (TICKER)	COUPON	MATURITY	LAST PRICE	LAST YIELD	**EST SPREAD UST†		EST $ VOL (000's)
Goldman Sachs Group (GS)	5.750	Jan 24, 2022	108.309	4.659	316	10	740,513
Anheuser-Busch Inbev Worldwide (ABIBB)	2.500	Jul 15,2022	100.786	2.411	92	10	708,807
Community Health Systems (CYH)	7.125	Jul 15,2020	102.250	6.663	516	10	582,245
Sumitomo Mitsui Banking (SUMIBK)	1.800	Jul 18,2017	100.103	1.778	115	5	489,200
Sumitomo Mitsui Banking (SUMIBK)	3.200	Jul 18,2022	100.057	3.193	169	10	419,690
Anheuser-Busch Inbev Worldwide (ABIBB)	1.375	Jul 15,2017	100.207	1.332	71	5	366,005
Anheuser-Busch Inbev Worldwide (ABIBB)	3.750	Jul 15,2042	102.496	3.613	105	30	346,297
Citigroup (C)	4.500	Jan 14,2022	104.857	3.883	238	10	306,567
Sumitomo Mitsui Banking (SUMIBK)	1.350	Jul 18,2015	100.404	1.212	86	3	282,850
General Electric Capital (GE)	2.300	Apr 27,2017	101.459	1.978	135	5	265,752
Citigroup (C)	4.450	Jan 10,2017	105.586	3.104	247	5	253,191
Primerica (PRI)	4.750	Jul 15,2022	102.813	4.399	290	10	246,922
JPMorgan Chase (JPM)	3.150	Jul 05,2016	104.019	2.087	146	5	242,347
Telefonica Emisiones Sau (TELEFO)	5.462	Feb 16,2021	91.563	6.774	527	10	237,631
JPMorgan Chase (JPM)	4.500	Jan 24,2022	110.084	3.259	178	10	236,524
Occidental Petroleum (OXY)	2.700	Feb 15,2023	103.243	2.344	84	10	233,126
Goldman Sachs Group (GS)	6.750	Oct 01,2037	101.496	6.626	405	30	232,248
United Technologies (UTX)	4.500	Jun 01,2042	114.464	3.896	112	30	216,712
Telefonica Emisiones Sau (TELEFO)	4.949	Jan 15,2015	98.000	5.823	548	3	204,742
Time Warner (TWX)	4.900	Jun 15,2042	107.085	4.468	190	30	203,665
Goldman Sachs Group (GS)	3.625	Feb 07,2016	101.420	3.199	257	5	197,296
General Electric Capital (GE)	1.625	Jul 02,2015	100.756	1.363	102	3	195,506
Morgan Stanley (MS)	4.750	Mar 22,2017	100.627	4.598	397	5	194,758
Anheuser-Busch Inbev Worldwide (ABIBB)	.800	Jul 15,2015	100.094	0.768	42	3	188,705
Morgan Stanley (MS)	5.750	Jan 25,2021	101.389	5.543	405	10	186,445
Hewlett-Packard Co (HPQ)	2.600	Sep 15,2017	100.110	2.577	195	5	184,351
Bank Of America (BAC)	3.875	Mar 22,2017	103.493	3.067	244	5	181,831
Nippon Telegraph And Telephone (NTT)	1.400	Jul 18,2017	100.419	1.313	69	5	180,490
Bank Of America (BAC)	5.700	Jan 24,2022	112.965	4.045	255	10	179,640
Cabot (CBT)	3.700	Jul 15,2022	101.743	3.492	200	10	178,000
Rabobank Nederland (RABOBK)	3.875	Feb 08,2022	103.318	3.464	197	10	174,254
Morgan Stanley (MS)	5.500	Jul 28,2021	101.411	5.301	380	10	172,639
Westlake Chemical (WLK)	3.600	Jul 15,2022	99.767	3.628	212	10	166,770
Telefonica Emisiones Sau* (TELEFO)	5.877	Jul 15,2019	94.063	6.964	549	10	165,315
Target (TGT)	4.000	Jul 01,2042	103.120	3.824	125	30	161,886
Monsanto Co (MON)	3.600	Jul 15,2042	101.755	3.504	93	30	158,450
AT&T (T)	3.000	Feb 15,2022	104.633	2.454	96	10	152,474
Wells Fargo (WFC)	2.100	May 08,2017	101.369	1.801	117	5	150,949
Telefonica Emisiones Sau (TELEFO)	3.729	Apr 27,2015	94.000	6.110	576	3	142,255
Lloyds TSB Bank (LLOYDS)	4.200	Mar 28,2017	104.000	3.273	265	5	141,067

Volume represents total volume for each issue; price/yield data are for trades of $1 million and greater. * Denotes a security whose last round lot trade did not take place on the last business day prior to publication. ** Estimated spreads, in basis points (100 basis points is one percentage point), over the 2, 5, 10 or 30-year hot run Treasury note/bond. 2-year: 0.250 06/14; 5-year: 0.750 06/17; 10-year: 1.750 05/22; 30-year: 3.125 02/42. †Comparable U.S. Treasury issue.

Source: MarketAxess Corporate BondTicker - www.bondticker.com

HIGH-YIELD BONDS

Friday, July 13, 2012
Ten most active fixed-coupon high-yield, or "junk", corporate bonds

COMPANY (TICKER)	COUPON	MATURITY	LAST PRICE	LAST YIELD	**EST SPREAD UST†		EST VOL (000's)
Supervalu (SVU)	8.000	May 01,2016	82.500	14.112	1349	5	401,252
Patriot Coal (PCX)	8.250	Apr 30,2018	41.765	30.050	2942	5	241,239
Supervalu (SVU)	7.500	Nov 15,2014	91.750	11.640	1140	2	237,852
Community Health Systems (CYH)	8.000	Nov 15,2019	107.125	6.397	491	10	227,230
Community Health Systems (CYH)	7.125	Jul 15,2020	102.250	6.663	516	10	218,015
Navistar International (NAV)	8.250	Nov 01,2021	92.000	9.565	808	10	211,277
Chrysler Group LLC (CHRYGR)	8.250	Jun 15,2021	103.250	7.634	613	10	160,686
ATP Oil & Gas (ATPG)	11.875	May 01,2015	44.500	51.320	5097	3	157,679
New Albertsons (SVU)	7.250	May 01,2013	97.550	10.548	n.a.	2	155,166
Goldman Sachs Capital II (GS)	5.793	Jun 01,2043	70.250	8.529	596	30	142,084

Volume represents total volume for the market; price/yield data are for trades of $100,000 and greater. * Denotes a security whose last round lot trade did not take place on the last business day prior to publication. ** Estimated spreads, in basis points (100 basis points is one percentage point), over the 2, 5, 10 or 30-year hot run Treasury note/bond. 2-year: 0.250 06/14; 5-year: 0.750 06/17; 10-year: 1.750 05/22;

Zero-Coupon Bonds and Strips

Among recent developments in Treasury securities are zero-coupon bonds and strips. These instruments began by investors stripping the interest coupons from the bond and selling them separately. Zero-coupon bonds, which are now issued in that form originally, have no stated interest. They are sold at a discount and redeemed at maturity at face value – the same method that Treasury bills have always followed. Yields on these instruments track other market rates for similar maturities.

Again, look at the *Barron's* table (p. 189) for the zero-coupon note maturing in May 2042 or 29 years and 10.5 months to maturity from July 16, 2012. If you buy at the ask price, you pay $4,400.00 for the bond, and your yield, if held to maturity, is 2.77 %. You will earn no interest, but will collect the principal of $10,000 at maturity.

Strips have no principal and are sold at the discounted present value of the stream of interest payments. See the strip in *Barron's* maturing in May 2042. If you buy at the ask price, you pay $4,275.00 for the stream of interest payments for the next 29 years and 10.5 months. No principal is involved, and your yield will be 2.79 %, which is the market rate.

Market activity in zero-coupon bonds and strips has been virtually limited to Treasury issues, although there is no reason why corporate issuers could not also offer them.

Cash Management Bills

Still another type of security that has developed in recent years among Treasury issues is the Cash Management Bill (CMB). When the Treasury's balances are low for some reason and the normal turnover of bills, notes, and bonds will not supply adequate cash, CMBs are used. They are also sold at a discount, like Treasury bills, but can be issued for whatever number of days the Treasury specifies, often fewer than 21 days.

When-Issued Securities

A hybrid that has developed, particularly in the Treasury field, is that of "when-issued" securities. This is the practice of a securities dealer selling a Treasury security before it is actually issued. Trading begins in this market as soon as a formal announcement of the forthcoming issue is made. Settlement of transactions in the market is made on the issue date of the actual security.

One cannot discuss this market without mention of the case of Salomon Brothers, a once prestigious investment bank that no longer exists [3]. To put their experience in perspective, the Treasury places limits on the proportion of a new issue of securities that may be obtained by individual dealers, in order to spread the issues equitably among all dealers. The Federal Reserve, which auctions Treasury securities at their original issue, monitors this process for the Treasury. At a sale of new two-year notes in May 1993, Salomon faked bids in the name of other dealers to get a larger share than it was entitled to receive because it had oversold the issue in the when-issued market. This was a serious breach of Treasury rules. What Salomon should have done was to go into the secondary market and acquire the notes after they had been issued to settle its oversold position. But this would have cost it more money. Salomon attempted at first to cover it up but ultimately was forced out of business. The firm was taken over by new investors headed by Warren Buffet and resold. It was first merged with Smith Barney and became part of JPMorgan Chase, who spun it off to Morgan Stanley. The Salomon name has since been dropped.

The name associated with the Salomon debacle was John Meriwether, who managed it for the firm. His name appears again in connection with the failure of one of the largest US hedge funds in 1998. The financial press has described him as one of the few who has presided over two major financial disasters within the space of five years.

Corporate Debt

Finally, we shall compare Treasury and corporate debt securities. Consider, for example, in the *Barron's* table for corporate bonds, on page 128, the United Technologies 4.50 % coupon bond, maturing June 1, 2042. If you buy it at the last price of $11,446.40, you will earn a yield of 3.696 %, and if you hold it to maturity, you will receive $13,443.75 in interest over its remaining life. The yield is lower than the stated coupon rate because bond prices rose during the interval between its issue date and the table date of July 16, 2012. Thus, you have paid a premium for the bond, which lowers your yield. The table shows that there are $216.7 million of this issue of the United Technologies bonds outstanding in secondary markets.

For comparison, look at the high-yield (junk) bond table. See, for example, ATP Oil and Gas. The deep discount reflects its financial trouble. You are paying $4,450 for a $10,000 face value bond, which matures in less than 3 years. If you hold it until maturity, you will get an annual yield (if it pays off) of 51.32 %, based on the amount invested. Also, you will receive the gain in principal of $5,550. It is still a gamble.

Note that corporate bond tables show an estimated rate spread from the most comparable US Treasury security. This is called the "risk premium," a measure of how much more risky the corporate bond is than the comparable Treasury. The United Technologies bond, which matures in 29 years and 10.5 months, is invest-ment grade; its yield is 112 basis points above the 30-year Treasury bond – a small margin. The ATP Oil and Gas bond, which matures in 2 years and 9.5 months, has a yield of 5097 basis points, almost 51 %, above the 3-year Treasury note. The bond is clearly junk. Remember, however, that bondholders are in a preferred status in bankruptcy proceedings. These tables reveal a great deal about the financial conditions of the listed companies.

Callable, Convertible, and Synthetic Convertible Bonds

Corporate bonds may also be issued in the form of callable, convertible, or synthetic convertible bonds. A callable bond is issued with the stipulation that the issuer may at its discretion pay off the bond at a specific date prior to maturity. Convertible bonds are issued with the stipulation that they may be paid off in stock of the company, again at the discretion of the issuer. Synthetic convertibles, which are of more recent origin, are issued with the understanding that they may be paid off in stock, but not necessarily the stock of the company. For example, I may own a Home Depot bond and find that it is being paid off in Starbucks stock of equivalent value. This last technique was used extensively by high-tech companies in the late 1990s. Buyers, of course, are fully aware of these stipulations when they purchase the bonds.

The existence of large, efficient, and highly liquid secondary markets for both Treasury and corporate securities means that holding securities until maturity is often not an issue in an investor's mind. Investors know they can liquidate holdings in a flash if they need liquidity or see opportunity for profit. Many securities are held in a variety of trust funds, retirement funds, mutual funds, and other institutionally managed funds. Managers of such funds trade frequently in secondary markets to obtain the best returns possible for their respective constituencies. This task has become increasingly difficult in recent years due to the pervasively low level of interest rates throughout all markets.

Investment Banks' Role in Mergers and Acquisitions

Another role of investment banks is that of handling mergers and acquisitions, including LBOs, briefly discussed earlier in connection with junk bonds. The investment bank contracts with an acquiring entity to obtain controlling interest, or all of the stock, of another company. This typically involves either new issues of stock to swap for outstanding stock of the acquired company or bonds to finance purchases of those stocks. These instruments would presumably become the obligations of the acquired or merged company. As we noted earlier, junk bonds are often used for this purpose, but the quality of whatever debt is issued for this purpose would depend on the credit standing of the acquiring entity.

If the buyers have to pay high premiums to obtain the stock, the debt burden on the acquired company may be so high that it cannot be serviced out of future earnings. An example of an acquisition in which this happened was RJR-Nabisco, in 1988–1989. The company's CEO, Ross Johnson, tried to buy out the company – that is, to take it private – because he was "bored." The purchase of all stock was expected to cost about $20 billion, the largest LBO on record at that time [2].

Competition developed between investment banks – Shearson Lehman representing Johnson's management group and Kohlberg Kravis Roberts (KKR), who wished to buy the firm and replace the management, including Johnson. This turned into a feeding frenzy among the investment banks. Ultimately, the bid of KKR was accepted at the equivalent of $108 per share, and Johnson's bid of $109 per share was rejected because of his stated plans to dismantle the company, among other things. The market price at the time was about $80. KKR's debt level had to go to $25 billion to acquire the stock.

The flow of cash to handle this transaction was so large that the US money supply statistics showed a temporary surge as the funds roared through the system. Funds from the sale of securities by KKR were temporarily parked in banks and then flushed out into the economy to buy the existing stock of RJR-Nabisco. This sharp reduction in bank reserves caused a temporary spike in the Federal Funds rate of over 150 basis points. RJR-Nabisco ultimately could not pay off the debt, and after some structural changes, it issued new equity and came back together as a publicly held company.

Investment banks may also work the other side of the fence by contracting with companies to defend them against takeovers. The investment bank will help plan and finance "poison pills," sometimes called shareholder protection plans, as defensive measures against hostile takeovers. A poison pill approach would be to issue rights to existing shareholders to obtain additional stock at a substantially reduced price once a bidder acquires more than a stated level, say 15–20 %, of existing stock outstanding. This makes it more difficult for the bidder to acquire enough stock to take over the company. They can also help implement legal changes, say in the voting rights of stock, to prevent new shareholders from having any voice in merger considerations. Investment banks are typically the most aggressive of all financial institutions and will "sniff" on both sides of the fence for business.

The Pricing of Credit: The Libor Rate

How does a bank know what interest rate to charge on a loan – or an investment bank – on a new issue of bonds? In a free-market system, the forces of competition apply here as well. The supply of funds available within a given market and the demand for those funds ultimately determine the price – the interest rate.

Syndicated loans all over the world are typically priced at the London Interbank Offer Rate (Libor), plus or minus some spread. The Libor is simply the reference rate, and the lending institution will adjust the spread around that rate to whatever competitive conditions exist at the time the loan is made. This would be a floating-rate loan, in which the actual amount being paid would be adjusted at specifically agreed-to intervals as Libor changes. For example, if 1-year Libor is 1.069 % on a given date (see table on p. 62) and the lender offers the loan at Libor plus 300 basis points, the borrower will pay 4.069 % for the loan. It may also be agreed that the rate will be adjusted every six months. Let's say that in six months, Libor is 1.345 %. The borrower will then pay 4.345 %. The same system would apply to new issues of bonds or notes.

There are other commonly used reference rates. It has been traditional in the United States to price loans or bonds at the US Prime Rate or the Treasury bill rate, plus or minus a spread. However, in recent years, as Libor has become more popular globally, its use has grown in the United States. *The Wall Street Journal* noted, "Libor is an important benchmark for everything from adjustable-rate mortgages in the U.S. to giant floating-rate bank loans taken out by global corporations."[6] It is now estimated to be used in $350 trillion of contracts worldwide.

Libor began in the early years of the Eurodollar market in London as the rate at which Dollar-denominated interbank loans were made. It is an individual bank rate, set by each London bank as the rate at which it is willing to extend credit to other banks. But, at the same time, it is a published rate, calculated by the British Bankers Association, as an unweighted average of the rates quoted by the 18 largest banks, with the highest four and lowest four removed, as the rate at which they were paying or would have to pay to obtain credit from other banks. Individual bank rates then cluster closely around the published rate. As noted in The *Wall Street Journal* comment, however, its applicability is now far broader than interbank lending.

In the previously discussed case of Signet Bank versus the Bank of Montreal, the leader (Signet) priced the syndicate participation to the Bank of Montreal at Libor + 50 bp. The Bank of Montreal held out for more and finally agreed to Libor + 58 bp – a difference of only $19,200 per year on a $24 million loan. Later, of course, they regretted participating at any price.

For comparison, the prime rate in the United States is the base rate on corporate loans posted by at least 70 % of the nation's ten largest banks. It is also set by each bank, but all cluster around the published rate. Often when a change in monetary policy is announced in the United States, banks will compete to see who can be the first to announce a change in its prime rate, either up or down, depending on the direction of monetary policy. Then, others would be expected to fall in line, and this usually happens. There have been occasions, however, in which an individual bank has jumped the gun and announced a change that was not followed by others. In those cases the bank that announced the change usually backs down and returns to the original rate because the others were not ready.

Another reference rate gaining increased attention in the European community is the Euro Libor, also called the Euribor (see table on p. 62). This rate is calculated by the European Banking Federation from a sample of 57 banks, with the highest nine and lowest nine removed, on loans denominated in Euros. Many large European banks now use the Euribor as their reference rate.

In midyear 2012, a scandal hit the world financial community regarding the authenticity of Libor. The Libor rate has traditionally been somewhat predictable in that, under normal conditions, it tends to track the US Federal Funds rate. It had been rumored for several years that Libor was offtrack, and suspicion was raised that it was being manipulated. In July 2012, Barclays Bank admitted that it had submitted fallacious information to the British Bankers Association (BBA) and suggested that other banks had done the same. Because of the financial crisis that began in 2007, banks found they were having to pay higher rates for credit, and they did not want this fact to be discovered because it would reflect unfavorably on their financial conditions. Thus, they submitted lower rates in their BBA reports, and the collective effect of this substantially understated the Libor rate. Civil as well as criminal charges are being considered by regulators, and Congress is holding hearings; the top management of Barclays has been forced out, and the bank has paid a

---

[6] *The Wall Street Journal*, September 5, 2007, Section C.

$451.6 million settlement with British and American authorities;[7] central banks are embarrassed; and the overall impact that this situation has had on the world financial community is yet to be determined. Investors are irate about lost income, and the finger-pointing continues. If anyone had doubts about the global significance of the Libor rate, those doubts have been put to rest by this incident.

Bond Yield Curves

Treasury bond yield curves show a relationship between yields, or current market rates, on Treasury securities, from those of short maturity – 30-day bills – out to long-term 30-year bonds. See the graph below.

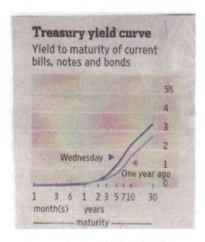

Treasury bond yield curve (From *The Wall Street Journal,* June 13, 2013)

The typical yield curve is upward-sloping, reflecting the "time value of money" phenomenon noted earlier. The yield curve shows the effects of numerous factors in the economy – monetary policy, market conditions, inflationary expectations, economic growth outlook, and significant changes in federal budget deficits. This is a principal reason that analysts study yield curves over a period of time to get a perspective on what is happening in the financial sector of the economy.

The yield curve depicted above, for example, shows that for Wednesday, June 12, 2013, rates on the short-term issues from the one-month bill out to about the one-year bill are virtually at zero. Rates rise from that point to 3.37 % for the 30-year bond. The graph also shows a similar pattern for the short-term rates for a year earlier, with rates beyond the two-year note somewhat lower. Both curves on this graph reflect the downward pressure on rates in recent years due to the Fed's efforts to stimulate the economy. But the spread between the curves shows the rise in rates

---

[7] *The Wall Street Journal*, July 17, 2012, p. C-2.

over the past year for issues longer than about two years because of the anticipation that the Fed will soon allow rates to rise due to the expected recovery of the economy and the likely tightening of monetary policy. The yield on the long bond – the most sensitive – has risen over 50 basis points in the past year. It is noteworthy also that the yield on the 10-year note, another bellwether issue, has climbed to 2.21 %. These increases in rates also denote declines in bond prices in the secondary markets.

See the graph on the following page for a comparison with other points in time when economic circumstances were different.[8] For example, the curve for January 15, 1981, is what would be called an "inverted yield curve," in which short-term rates are higher than long-term rates. That curve reflects the Fed's pursuit of an extremely tight monetary policy in order to kill inflation, thus elevating rates in short maturities and inverting the yield curve. The curve of March 28, 1985, shows a return to a more normal shape after the period of tight money was over and the economy had resumed moderate growth.

Another date to note is February 6, 2006, about a year and a half before the onset of the recent financial crisis. The Fed was tightening because of concerns about inflation. It had raised the Federal Funds rate to 5.25 %, and other market rates were following suit, producing a "flat yield curve." Again, the curve of January 15, 2009, is a little over a year into the period of significant easing that the Fed has pursued to deal with the recession that began in the late 2007. This curve shows a more normal

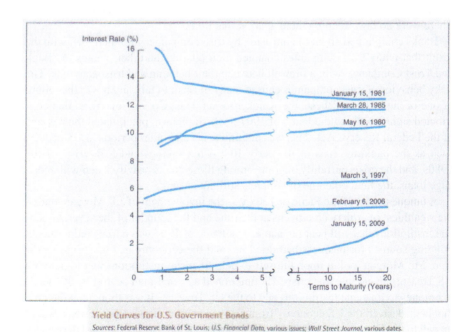

Yield Curves for U.S. Government Bonds
Sources: Federal Reserve Bank of St. Louis; U.S. Financial Data, various issues; Wall Street Journal, various dates.

Treasury bond yield curves for selected dates

---

[8] This graph is drawn from Frederic Mishkin [4], p. 142.

shape and reflects the fact that short-term rates are approaching zero, but it is not as flat along the horizontal axis as the current yield curve.

The one inescapable conclusion to be reached from an analysis of the yield curves shown in both the above graphs is that US Treasuries hold their own in global markets. This has been true despite persistent rumors that foreign investors and foreign central banks would like to dump Dollar-denominated assets. The truth is that they cannot afford to do so, because losses from dumping securities would be too great. In addition, there is no incentive – other than a purely political one – to do so because the safe-haven argument still prevails. Despite its many problems, the US financial system engenders confidence, and foreign investors still obviously believe their funds are safer in US Dollar-denominated securities.

A Note on Trust Companies: The Panic of 1907

Trust companies, historically important institutions, operate under a traditional concept of managing assets for clients. Around the turn of the 20th century, banks and trust companies were separate institutions. Trust companies handled both corporate and personal trusts and managed financial assets for clients, functions that have since become the business of hedge funds, equity funds, etc., in addition to trust companies. In the early 20th century, trust companies became jealous of the profits earned by banks and gradually began to move into traditional banking activities. There were no laws keeping them apart at that time.

Banks complained about the intrusion by trust companies into their turf, with the result that many trust companies changed their charters and their names to "Bank and Trust Company," with a firewall between their banking and trust activities. The risky behavior of trust companies caused many of them to fail, and it was the failure of one of the largest of these, the Knickerbocker Trust Co. of New York, that contributed significantly to the Panic of 1907 – which, in turn, precipitated the passage of the Federal Reserve Act. This was not unlike several other periods in US history, such as the banking crisis of the early 1930s, the savings and loan crisis of the 1980s, and the crisis currently ongoing among those banks heavily laden with mortgage loans, the final outcome of which is still not clear.

A unique aspect of the Panic of 1907 was the involvement of J.P. Morgan, one of the wealthiest of American citizens at the time and the founder of the several financial institutions that still bear his name. The Panic of 1907 was a true credit crunch. Funding sources for business had dried up, and the economy had gone into recession. Mr. Morgan took it upon himself to help financial institutions and to help the US Treasury overcome this crisis. He functioned as a one-man central bank – lending money to financial institutions and to the US Treasury. It was thought at the time that he had saved the US economy from an even greater disaster, but it was a wake-up call to the Congress and to the public at large that the nation could not depend on an individual to bail it out to the extent that the US financial community had relied on J.P. Morgan. This gave impetus to the discussion that was already ongoing about attempting one more time to establish a central bank.

The Fannie Mae and Freddie Mac Problem

Many people first became aware of the significant roles played by the Federal National Mortgage Association (Fannie Mae) and the Federal Home Loan Mortgage Corporation (Freddie Mac) in 2008 when it became obvious that they had fueled the housing bubble that led to the collapse of the mortgage market. These institutions began as agencies of the federal government to assist in housing finance. In later years, they were privatized and their stock sold to the public. They are not banks, so what are they?

These agencies assured the liquidity of the housing market by buying mortgages from banks, mortgage companies, and other lending institutions. Typically, they securitized the mortgages in the form of mortgage-backed bonds, which they sold to the public – institutional investors, banks, and individuals. They served the purpose for which they were created very efficiently. As housing prices rose in the years preceding the 2007 downturn, and the clamor for home ownership grew, these agencies fueled the expansion on the implicit assumption that this growth would continue forever and that housing prices would never decline. Even Alan Greenspan, Chairman of the Fed, when asked about where this exuberant expansion might lead, remarked that we had not seen a decline in housing prices since the Great Depression. While that was technically true, most economists know that prices can both go up and come down. He regretted that statement later, because it made him appear to be naive and out of touch.

At the onset of the recent downturn, Fannie Mae and Freddie Mac together held about $5.3 trillion in mortgages, approximately half of the home mortgages outstanding in the United States. Thus, their importance to the housing industry was obvious. It was never quite clear in the minds of the public whether the quasi-governmental nature of these agencies meant that the mortgage-backed securities they had issued were guaranteed by the federal government. In view of the significance of the agencies to the financial markets in general, however, both the Treasury and the Federal Reserve treated their securities as though they were fully federally guaranteed. This was, in fact, the impetus behind the TARP (Troubled Asset Relief Program), passed by Congress on October 3, 2008. Under this program, the Federal Reserve began buying mortgage-backed securities from banks that held them as investments and at the same time began pumping capital into banks by buying stock in banks that held substantial amounts of mortgage-backed securities. And the Federal Reserve also bought stock of Fannie Mae and Freddie Mac, themselves, in order to keep them operating and to keep the housing market from totally collapsing. This, in effect, partially re-nationalized them.

In light of the financial disaster that followed the bursting of the housing bubble, questions have been raised in Congress on what to do with these agencies – totally nationalize them, re-privatize them, or close them down completely and replace them with some other entity that would take over their assigned task. *The Economist* noted at the height of these troubles that we had succeeded in privatizing the profits but nationalizing the risks.

The more conservative elements in Congress advocate a complete abolition of federal guarantees regarding housing, which would mean the elimination of Fannie Mae and Freddie Mac. A more centrist view argues that some federal role is needed to preserve liquid markets for mortgages. This latter idea, however, still leaves open the question of whether the entity that succeeds Fannie and Freddie would be public or private – or perhaps, private with some degree of government backing or support. The dissatisfaction with previous experience runs so high that finding a solution becomes problematic. It remains a long way from being settled.

References

1. Smith RC, Walter I (2003) Global banking, 2nd edn. Oxford University Press, New York, p 431
2. Burrough B, Helyar J (1989) Barbarians at the gate: the fall of RJR-Nabisco. Harper & Row, New York
3. Mayer M (1993) Nightmare on Wall Street. Simon and Shuster, New York
4. Mishkin FS (2010) The economics of money, banking and financial markets, 9th edn. Addison-Wesley, Boston

Chapter 9
What Went Wrong, and What Are We Doing to Fix It? A Chronology of Financial Crises

As we noted at the beginning, the US financial industry has been subject to mismanagement, unethical behavior, greed, corruption, excesses and abuses, fraud, and other outright criminal acts. While the industry has suffered some serious blows from these incidents, it has not been destroyed. In fact, one would hope that legislators, policymakers, and the public at large have learned from such incidents and that the industry in the final analysis has been strengthened by them.

It is useful, therefore, to review some of these scenarios of the past two to three decades and to consider the impact that they have had on the financial industry of today.

The Bankhaus Herstatt Failure, 1974

The failure of this German bank came about as a result of risk in the payment system. It was a time zone-induced risk. The bank failed in the midst of a mark-dollar transaction. German authorities closed it down at the end of the German business day, which was the beginning of the business day in New York. The date was a Friday. A number of banks had made payments to or had sent securities to Herstatt and were anticipating payments or securities from it. Herstatt was a major clearing bank.

For example, Chase had $50 million of Herstatt's money that was to be sent to them, but held it once they knew of Herstatt's closure. Banks that had agreed to put payments on the wire to Herstatt became concerned that they would not receive the value expected in return, such as other currencies and securities. They therefore stopped their transactions, and everything froze over the weekend. The Federal Reserve had to contact all New York clearing house members to assure them that, by agreement with the German authorities, funds would move in order to settle.

This incident provided a serious wake-up call to the industry of the risks associated with failure to settle. The Herstatt experience forced the entire banking community to improve its systems. Electronic funds transfers, including book-entry transfers of

W.H. Wallace, *The American Monetary System: An Insider's View of Financial Institutions, Markets and Monetary Policy*, DOI 10.1007/978-3-319-02907-8_9, © Springer International Publishing Switzerland 2013

securities, are now settled by Fedwire on an instantaneous "gross-settlement" basis. The Federal Reserve guarantees settlement by any depository financial institution that it allows to connect to Fedwire. This is part of the Federal Safety Net, discussed earlier. The type of risk in the payment system that this incident represented is still referred to as "Herstatt Risk."

The Continental Illinois Bank Crisis, 1984

One of the first major domestic bank failures in recent years, which introduced regulators to the concept of too big to fail, was Continental Illinois of Chicago. Through a series of mismanagement steps, such as sloppy underwriting, failure to do adequate due diligence, and failure to diversify its loan portfolio, the bank, then one of the US top ten, allowed itself to be sucked into vast amounts of loan participations, particularly in oil and gas lending. It was learned that Continental had over 400 accounts with other smaller banks, and regulators feared that all these banks would go down with Continental, causing a systemic failure of the financial sector. Under pressure, the FDIC paid off all depositors, including those above the $100,000 limit. Outrage in Congress over this action ultimately led to passage of legislation prohibiting payoffs beyond the legal limit. As we have noted, the limit was raised to $250,000 in 2008.

The Dodd-Frank bill of 2010 prohibited the use of the too big to fail doctrine in future banking crises in which the taxpayers have to pay the costs. Instead, the bill puts the burden of the cost of any collateral damage on the financial industry itself. The implementation of this provision is still under debate. It is safe to say, however, that in 1984, no one anticipated multitrillion-dollar institutions. Future policy will emphasize procedures to prevent institutions from becoming too big to fail.

The Japanese Financial Crisis, 1990–2005

Japan's economic bubble burst in 1990, and the economy did not fully recover until about 2005. In many ways, it is still struggling as a result of outdated banking regulations and policies. The 1990s are often referred to as "the lost decade" for Japan. Until 1990, other Asian countries were buying 40 % of Japanese exports, but by the turn of the 21st century, this had dropped to 11.5 %.

The very paternalistic Japanese government propped up failing institutions and refused to recognize reality by writing off losses, which regulators in most other countries would have insisted upon. Therefore, unrecognized bank failures were rampant in which banks were kept open by government support when they were financially dead.

Japan sought to recover by cheapening the Yen and trying to grow exports. This did not work. Meanwhile, Japanese debt continued to grow, and today it stands at 200 %

of the nation's GDP. The Japanese economic plight contributed substantially to the Southeast Asian financial problems later in the decade. Today, Japan is continuing to have economic troubles resulting from the spillover effect of the mortgage-related worldwide crisis, but under its new Prime Minister, Shinzō Abe, it has begun to take corrective measures in 2013 that it should have taken two decades earlier. These actions are viewed as cautiously hopeful in leading to economic recovery.

The BCCI Financial Scandal, 1995

One of the most egregious scandals to occur involved the Bank for Credit and Commerce International, a Luxembourg-based bank that owned banks in several European countries and in the United States. Its problems began as a result of a lapse in international regulatory standards. Luxembourg had a lax system of regulation, and other countries in which BCCI's banks were located ignored them. The bank was heavily involved in money laundering, supporting drug trade and weapons trade throughout the world. When its problems were revealed, the bank became a major embarrassment to the central banks in the United States, United Kingdom, and the rest of Europe.

This scandal awakened regulators around the world regarding the gaps in their regulatory systems and alerted central banks to the need for international cooperation in the supervision and regulation of banks that have branches, affiliates, or subsidiaries in numerous countries. Now, virtually all central banks have been given authority by their peers to enter each other's countries to examine the affairs of banks that operate beyond their own borders. This resulted in more standardization of regulatory rules.

Since this affair, multinational banking operations have grown substantially. As a result, the Federal Reserve is no longer permitted under US law to approve any foreign acquisition of an American bank unless it can be shown that the foreign bank is adequately supervised by its home country. This rule was applied, for example, in the recent acquisition by the Industrial and Commercial Bank of China of the American unit of the Bank of East Asia, which had been organized as an American bank.

The Barings Bank Demise, 1995

The failure of Barings Bank was the first major crisis attributed to derivative problems. Barings was one of the oldest and most respected British banks with offices all over the globe. It became enamored of the derivative markets and began trading in derivative contracts as well as acting as counterparty to derivatives in which it sold protection against risk to others. Barings delegated this operation to a young trader, Nick Leeson, who seemed to be making lots of money for the bank in this field.

The senior management of the bank did not understand what he was doing and gave him unlimited authority to trade using bank funds. Leeson went beyond prudent trading in the futures market, however, and got the bank in so deep that it failed. He also exceeded legal limits in his use of customer funds and served time in prison. A popular movie, *Rogue Trader*, is based on this episode.

The Barings crisis was another warning to the banking industry that risks are large in the derivative market and alerted the regulators to the fact that numerous banks were engaging in such trades without adequate knowledge of the markets. In the years since Barings, a number of other instances like this have occurred – especially during the mortgage crisis – suggesting that the industry is learning very slowly, if at all, from this experience.

The Southeast Asian Financial Crisis, 1997–1998

This problem began in Thailand; moved to Indonesia, Singapore, Hong Kong, and the Philippines; and ultimately hit South Korea and China. And, it was made more serious by the preexisting economic problems of Japan. The heavy dependence of this group of countries on foreign trade meant that a global – or at least a multinational – impact might be expected. But, because of early attention to the problem and defensive measures that were taken, the impact upon North America and Europe was somewhat muted.

Prior to the summer of 1997, the Asian economies were basically sound and were growing rapidly. They were attracting considerable foreign investment, and interest rates were high enough to keep capital flows coming in. But this group of countries had a high proportion of government-directed investment. Banks were pressured to lend heavily to government-sponsored projects – that is, graft. The banks were not strong enough to withstand heavy political pressure, and corruption became evident. For example, the self-serving interests of former President Suharto's family projects in Indonesia ultimately drove him from office. Many projects were unsound and would have been judged so if subjected to proper underwriting procedures. This meant that competitive markets were not making proper credit allocation decisions because of bureaucratic intervention.

Money was readily available because of the large capital inflows, and these countries were awash in liquidity. This rush to put money where high returns existed, without adequate analysis, was reminiscent of the "third world debt crisis" of the late 1970s and early 1980s, in which a tremendous increase in liquidity developed in association with "petrodollars," that is, the buildup of Dollars in the hands of oil-exporting countries. Remembrance of this should have raised a red flag when the Southeast Asian crisis began.

The inevitable happened in Southeast Asia as projects did not pay off and loans began to default. The result was the failure of banks, and when banks failed, currencies came under pressure. Speculators took over, and the crisis spread. A few analysts had noted this potential crisis as early as 1994 as they saw the rapid capital inflow to these countries. The initial problems started in Thailand in late 1996, as foreign investors, sensing problems, began to pull funds from the country. The "take-the-money-and-run" philosophy took over. What was witnessed here was the downside effect of allowing free movement of capital.

Thailand raised interest rates, normally a correct move to attract more foreign capital, but this was not adequate to stem the outflow. Hence, the Thai currency had to be devalued, and this was done by the central bank raising the price it was willing to pay for other currencies. This is typically viewed as a move of desperation by a central bank, and it was recognized as such in this case. The contagion effect took over, and devaluations spread across the Southeast Asian countries. Several of the countries had their currencies tied to the US Dollar, and those ties had to be severed to permit the devaluations.

These developments were preceded by a wave of "dollarization" moves across the region, in which countries who were nervous about the weakness of their own currencies pegged them to the Dollar, or to some other stable currency, at a fixed – although sometimes arbitrary – rate. This move is often made to combat inflation, and it sometimes is very effective, as in numerous Latin and South American countries. It is a unilateral action; the United States has nothing to say about it. Its ultimate success, however, depends on whether the country can acquire enough Dollars to hold in reserve to support the currency at the rate of exchange they have established. Historian Niall Ferguson notes, "The difficulty of pegging currencies to a single commodity-based standard, or indeed to one another, is that policymakers are then forced to choose between free capital movements and an independent national monetary policy. They cannot have both" [1].

Worries mounted that Hong Kong would be affected, even though its economy was stronger and its markets more stable. Thus, when Hong Kong's Hang Seng (stock) index plunged in October 1997, the crisis was recognized as a full-blown Asian problem. The nervousness about Hong Kong was heightened by persistent rumors that China would devalue its currency, and this would have created additional problems for all of China's neighbors. But China, in a surprise move, pledged not to do so, and it actually helped Hong Kong out of the crisis by intervening to buy $HK to support the currency.

Hong Kong had used a "currency board" since 1983, in which it tied the $HK to a fund of US Dollar-denominated reserves – currency, bonds, and other financial assets. Hong Kong weathered the crisis because of its strength going in, and with China's help, it was able to avoid devaluation, or having to let its currency freely float, as the other countries did. The problems finally spread to South Korea, the largest of the economies in the region affected by the crisis, aside from China.

China's role in the Southeast Asian crisis was also interesting apart from its assistance to Hong Kong. In 2003, China took the unusual step of pegging its currency, the Yuan – often also called the renminbi – to the Dollar. This has hurt other nations' ability to sell goods to China, but China apparently made this move to keep its own exports competitively priced. The United States advised against this development and has continuously urged China to release the peg. Holding the peg to the Dollar means the Yuan is undervalued; to let it float would mean it would rise, and China's exports would be more costly, which China does not wish to see happen. Nevertheless, in mid-2010, after more than five years of negotiations, China relented under world pressure. But, it simply raised the peg rather than letting it float, and even today it refuses to allow the Yuan to float. The result is that most countries continue to have large trade deficits with China.

The Russian Financial Crisis, 1998

As the Asian crisis was at its peak in 1998, the drumbeat of rumors about problems in Russia grew louder. But in June of that year, Goldman Sachs managed to sell $1.25 billion in Eurobonds for the Russian government at a modest (for Russia) 12 % annual interest rate. This news falsely convinced investors that Russia's economy was improving, and Goldman quickly sold the issue. The group of "traders that never sleep," however, began to pick up signals that all was not as well as it seemed. Finally, on August 17, Russia defaulted on its foreign debt. It simply announced that it would rather use what Rubles it had left to pay Russian workers than Western bondholders.

This shock came at the height of the Asian crisis and worsened the Asian problems. The United States again became the only safe haven, and the US Treasury market soared. In the meantime, central banks in the United States and Europe began defensive actions. The Fed lowered the Federal Funds rate and the discount rate three times between September and November 1998. This move was contrary to the monetary policy that would have been called for at the time because the US economy was booming. Concern existed about inflation, and monetary policy had been on a tightening agenda. Whether the 1998 move was effective with either the Asian or Russian situations is arguable, but at least these policy actions sent signals that we were going to protect our economies against the contagion effect.

The old adage that "nuclear powers don't default" was quoted daily on Wall Street. The price of oil dropped, hurting Russia's exports; the Russian stock market dropped 75 %; and short-term interest rates went to 200 %. The world waited for a ruble devaluation.

Ironically, this situation did not get the coverage in the United States than it did in the rest of the financial world because it coincided with President Clinton's admission of his relationship with a White House intern, which flooded the front pages.

Hedge Funds and the LTCM Debacle, 1998

We have previously referred to Long-Term Capital Management (LTCM), which presented the financial markets with yet another crisis in the late 1990s. LTCM was a hedge fund – a private financial institution that accepts typically very large investments and invests the funds in virtually anything the managers of the fund choose. Hedge funds are conceptually like mutual funds, but they differ in that they, until very recently, have been totally unregulated. Hedge funds are characterized by a high level of secrecy, and their investments – particularly their investment strategy – are known only to themselves.

These features alone do not necessarily make hedge funds a menace to the financial system, which they are thought to be in the minds of many investors. However, when their activities become so large that the decisions they make can cause systemic risk, within a market, or within several markets, they then become a potential danger. This is what happened with LTCM.

This type of institution is called a hedge fund because, in theory, it hedges against loss on any given transaction by making a companion transaction that will offset any loss on the first. The initial idea, developed by investor, Alfred Winslow Jones in 1949, was that for every instrument the fund purchased, it would short-sell another, but this strategy is not necessarily followed today as it was originally.

Let's look at an example that was an actual transaction by LTCM [2]. The firm buys $1 billion in 30-year Treasury bonds; it borrows the $1 billion from a bank. At the same time, it sells short $1 billion in 30-year Treasury bonds of about the same time to maturity; it borrows these bonds from a dealer. It lends the bonds it purchased to a dealer and receives cash from that dealer as collateral. Thus, it now has $2 billion in cash on its balance sheet without using any of its own money. It has selected these particular issues of bonds because there is a 12-basis-point difference in their yields; the ones it bought have the higher yield, and the ones it short-sold have the lower.

Therefore, it will receive income from the bonds it bought, and it will have to pay the income on the bonds it short-sold to the dealer from whom it borrowed them, thus making the 12-basis-point profit. It would seem that 12 basis points is a minuscule difference, but remember that on the basis of $1 billion in face value, the spread is worth $1,200,000 on an annual basis. Further, remember that LTCM was buying and selling tens of billions of these instruments. Since the maturity values of the two issues of bonds are the same, they can be swapped out at maturity or liquidated at any time. If the market were not highly liquid, this would not be possible, because unless the transactions can be done in huge amounts and quickly, they would not be profitable.

LTCM was unusual because of its size. It got into financial difficulty in September 1998 because of a decline in the value of its assets. The Russian debt repudiation the month before was the trigger that set off the decline. LTCM's investments were so large, and the degree of leverage was so great that when the problem began, failure was nearly inevitable. The fund was faced with having to cover its debts with assets whose total value was insufficient as collateral. It would have had to dump all of its holdings to cover obligations, and the markets knew even that would not be sufficient. There was therefore immediate concern that because of LTCM's size, a forced liquidation would undermine the financial markets and pose a systemic risk. This would have meant trouble for banks that were financing brokers and dealers, not to mention banks that had invested in and loaned to LTCM. To illustrate, LTCM had total positions in financial assets of $90 billion just before it failed. Its capital had dropped to 0.6 % of total assets.

While it had no responsibility or regulatory authority over hedge funds, the Federal Reserve Bank of New York decided to act within the category of its "unspecified" duties in order to stabilize and protect the financial markets. They believed, and the Dodd-Frank bill has since confirmed, that any potential systemic risk is the business of the central bank. It sidestepped the use of Section 13(3) of the Federal Reserve Act and put together, instead, a consortium of 14 private banks and prevailed upon them to lend to LTCM enough to cover its position. As a result, and by agreement with the lending banks, LTCM's owners were removed, and they wound up losing 90 % of their value. Many observers and market participants felt that they should have lost 100 %, because the firm was highly unpopular in the financial community due to its arrogance toward its competitors and its high level of secrecy about its operations.

One irony of the LTCM situation and the origin of the title of the cited book, *When Genius Failed*, is that the fund had on its board two Nobel-Prize–winning economists, Myron Scholes and Robert C. Merton, who had developed "a new method for determining the value of derivatives." They were advising LTCM, and they were the geniuses to whom the book refers. Another irony is that this was the second financial disaster in five years presided over by Wall Street mogul, John Meriwether, as mentioned earlier.

The Enron Situation, 2002

Because of the obscure and complex nature of many derivative contracts, there have been examples of their use which push ethical limits. Several of these were present in the Enron case.

Enron obtained loans from Citigroup totaling $1.2 billion from August 2000 to May 2001. Citigroup wanted to hedge this exposure, indicating that it knew there might be financial difficulties associated with the company. Citigroup set up a trust which, in turn, issued securities to investors totaling $1.4 billion. Investors would receive a steady return on these securities that was competitive in the market. However, a stipulation agreed to by the investors was that if Enron could not pay its loans to Citigroup, the bank would stop paying a return to its investors, keep the investors' principal, and issue them securities of Enron instead. Thus, Citigroup had effectively transferred all its risk to its investors. The securities that Citigroup sold were called "credit-linked notes" and are a type of credit derivative.

It was presumed that investors knew what they were buying, though many denied that later. The credit-linked notes paid 7.37 % because Enron still carried a Baa1 investment grade rating from Moody's. The solicitation by the trust to sell the notes stated, "The notes are subject to the same credit risks as Enron's regular bonds."

In addition to the credit-linked notes, Citigroup arranged a further $4.8 billion loan, and JPMorgan Chase arranged a $3.7 billion loan to Enron. These were accounted for by Enron as sales, not loans. These transactions doubled Enron's cash flow and profits and understated its total debt by 40 %. Enron's financial statements were complete fiction.

A derivative technique used by Enron that helped get debt off its books was to account for still another $3.9 billion in bank loans from the same banks as prepaid swaps. By labeling them as swaps rather than loans, the credit rating agencies were not alerted to the increased debt. For clarification, a swap is an aboveboard agreement whereby two parties trade income from investments over a given period of time. In this case, however, rather than swapping any payments, the banks funded all their commitments up front as in a loan, and the company was to pay it back over time. This has all the features of a loan, and indeed, it was a loan, not a swap. This has been cited as one of the most serious infractions that Enron made. The fact that substantial debt did not show on its balance sheet caused its credit rating to be much higher than it would otherwise have been.

This sequence of transactions raises many questions, not only about Enron but also about the banks involved. For example, how much did these banks know about the way that Enron was accounting for the transactions? Congressional hearings after the fact suggested that the banks not only knew but helped Enron plan the strategy and even tried to sell that strategy to other companies. Another question is, should Citigroup have used its role as a widely trusted investment bank to sell notes to the public if it knew the real credit status of Enron? Why didn't it know this, since it had the right to do due diligence? Why wasn't it severely penalized for it?

Another important fact about the Enron scandal was that Arthur Andersen & Co., its auditor, did not blow the whistle on any of these egregious and deceitful practices. This was clearly accounting subterfuge, and Arthur Andersen was driven out of business because of it. These examples represent some of the most blatant conflicts of interest imaginable – of exactly the kind Glass-Steagall was passed to prevent in 1933. It is ironic that they should have occurred so soon after the passage of GLB, which repealed most of Glass-Steagall.

The Dot.Com Crisis, 2000–2002

During the 1990s many new companies were started which operated exclusively on the Internet and offered services and products of all kinds. Hence, the term "dot.com companies" was born. These firms required very little in terms of initial capital, often operating out of garages, attics, etc. Many of them were inspired by people like Bill Gates, and a number of them were successful. When they began to go public, through initial public offerings (IPOs) or other fund-raising techniques, many people bought into them, having the effect of driving their stock prices out of sight.

When the economy began to turn down in early 2000, some of these companies found themselves on the skids. While some were successful, such as Google and Yahoo, a majority of them actually faced bankruptcy. This hit the NASDAQ exchange particularly hard since it had specialized in listing high-tech companies.

The loss in market capitalization in the recession that followed was around $7 trillion for the exchange.

The recovery from that downturn was especially sluggish, but the economy did recover, just in time to prepare itself for the onset of the subprime mortgage crisis in which the economy was still mired as recently as 2013.

The Subprime Mortgage Crisis and Related Recession, 2007–2012

This episode has turned out to be the most serious economic crisis in American history, aside from the Great Depression of the 1930s. It stemmed from an unsustainable easing of credit standards and financing, which fueled the prior expansion but also created the imbalances that led to the recession.

The first hard evidence of the crisis came in August 2007, when mortgages and mortgage-backed securities began to go into default in massive quantities. There were earlier warnings, going back to at least 2005, that a bubble in the housing market was developing. Interest rates began to rise, and under floating rate lending, homeowners were unable to make payments. Many mortgages became delinquent. Yet, housing prices were rising at an unprecedented pace, and home buyers bought into the market, sometimes obtaining multiple properties with as much debt as they could possibly take on, all on the assumption that the rise in prices would never stop, and they could liquidate at any time with a handsome profit. This assumption defied all logic of economic theory and practice, and as we have seen, it all came tumbling down with a crash.

Among the first questions people ask about this crisis are as follows: How did we get into this? And, whose fault was it? These are important questions, despite their simplicity, because the answers to them shed some light on what we must do to prevent the recurrence of such a disaster.[1]

As we try to answer the first of these questions, look first at the roles played by Fannie Mae and Freddie Mac. They fueled the bubble, assuming that housing prices would never decline. Second, banks picked up the momentum and started scrambling to make more and more mortgage loans, and to do this, they began to lower their lending standards. Competition thus turned into greed, and banks started making loans to borrowers who were not creditworthy and who the banks knew would not be able to pay off the loans.

The banks did not care, however, because they knew they could sell the loans, restore their liquidity, and be rid of the credit risk. Thus, they had no "skin in the game." Fannie and Freddie, as well as many other institutional investors, were there to buy the loans. This was moral hazard in the purest sense.

---

[1] For a detailed account of how officials dealt with these issues at the beginning of the crisis, see Henry M. Paulson [3].

In addition, the regulators, particularly the Fed and the SEC, were complicit in this because of their lack of adequate oversight of the banking industry. Some critics say the Fed is guilty on two counts. First, it held interest rates too low for too long in the 2002–2004 period, in the aftermath of the dot.com recession. This, it is argued, provided liquidity to lending institutions and helped to fuel the housing bubble. Second, it did not take action through its supervisory powers to rein in banks by placing tougher lending restrictions on them and by not insisting on higher capital requirements to cushion the impact of losses. Both the Fed and the SEC have appropriately taken a lot of heat for their lack of oversight in this regard.

The first attempt to control the problem was taken by the Fed in lowering the discount rate in September 2007 and the target Federal Funds rate the next month. Later, further moves to ease credit conditions, by lowering rates and by other means of pumping liquidity into banks and financial markets, continued into 2009. The Term Auction Facility, which we discussed in Chap. 3, was a radical move to increase liquidity throughout the financial markets at a rate of about $500 billion per month into early 2010. How much any of these stimulative efforts helped is arguable, but it is generally conceded by most economists that they kept the downturn, from being considerably worse.

The costs of the crisis have been enormous. Banks and other financial institutions have failed, including AIG, previously the world's largest insurance company. In addition, many nonfinancial firms have gone into bankruptcy, including two of the big-three automakers, which, with the help of the Treasury, have since emerged from bankruptcy status. From the start of the downturn to July 2010, losses on residential mortgages had reached $370 billion, and higher losses were in prospect as financial institutions continued to hold defaulted mortgages on their books. The human cost was one of the worst consequences of the downturn, as unemployment reached 10.5 % of the work force. While it has been reduced since the trough of the recession, it still stands in mid-2013 at 7.6 %, an unacceptably high level.

The Wall Street Reform and Consumer Protection Act (The Dodd-Frank Bill)

The severity of the economic recession has resulted in pressure to improve regulatory control of the financial industry, in an effort to prevent this disaster from happening again. Congress responded in July 2010 with the passage of the Dodd-Frank bill. The purpose of the law is to "provide for financial regulatory reform, to protect consumers and investors, to enhance Federal understanding of insurance issues, to regulate the over-the-counter derivative markets, and for other purposes" [4, p. 280]. The bill is very extensive and detailed; thus, only its major provisions are highlighted here.

First and arguably the most celebrated of its provisions is the elimination of the too big to fail doctrine. This provision does not change the reality that there are institutions large enough that their failure would cause systemic disruption and chaos, including failure of additional institutions, inability to settle transactions, and interruptions or breakdowns of market functions. It simply states that institutions headed for failure will be allowed to fail, regardless of size and interconnectedness. The difference under this law is that the cost will not be borne by taxpayers, as it has been in the past, but will be the responsibility of the financial industry itself.

The bill provides (Section 214) that funds will be provided to cover future financial crises by asset sales, recoupment of payments made to creditors, or special assessments on the industry. Debate in Congress on this bill during the months leading to its passage coincided with the work underway in the BIS on Basel III, which as we have noted will significantly raise capital requirements on banks. The banking committees in Congress that were drafting Dodd-Frank were aware of the Basel III proposals and took into account that banks would have more capital in the future that could be tapped for financial crises. This was the purpose behind the inclusion of the conservation buffer as a part of the common equity that Basel III requires banks to keep, as we discussed in Chap. 6. In addition to these specific provisions, the bill gives the Federal Reserve added authority to increase capital requirements further if needed (Sections 112 and 171).

Another major provision is the creation of the Financial Stability Oversight Council (FSOC), headed by the Secretary of the Treasury and made up of members of all federal financial regulatory agencies, which will be responsible for identifying and responding to risks throughout the financial system (Sections 111–176).

The law gives the Federal Reserve the power to regulate and set standards for nonbank financial institutions at the request of the FSOC (Sections 113–115 and 161–176). This was a weakness in the system during the recent crisis in that numerous nonbank institutions were totally unregulated, and no agency had any authority over them, even at the time their actions were adding to the destructive impact of the crisis. Related to this is an additional power given the Fed to require divestiture of certain assets or holdings if the Fed determines that they pose a grave threat to stability (Sections 121 and 165).

In addition, the FDIC is given the power to unwind systemically significant financial institutions and provides that shareholders and unsecured creditors will bear losses and that management and directors will be removed (Sections 201–217). Heretofore, the FDIC has had to wait until the institution had been declared insolvent by its chartering authority.

The law prohibits emergency lending to an individual institution or to an insolvent entity (Sections 1101–1103). This is a restriction on the use of Section 13(3) in that an individual entity could not be singled out for an emergency loan (such as AIG was) unless that entity is part of a "broad-based eligibility" program that makes emergency credit available to all other entities in that group. In all cases, collateral must be adequate to cover any losses, as is the case at present [4, p. 282].

Another provision of the bill provides for the adoption of the "Volcker Rule," a proposal made by former Fed Chairman, Paul Volcker, to limit banks' ability to engage in proprietary trading. Volcker's concern was that during the crisis, banks were gambling with depositor's money by excessive trading, and some lost considerable amounts as a result. We witnessed the effect of this type of trading in June 2012, with JPMorgan Chase's loss of $6 billion. The problem that regulators are wrestling with in the implementation of this provision is that it is extremely difficult to define the dividing line between the legitimate trading that banks must do to meet customers' needs, and to provide for earnings on their own assets as opposed to that which is gambling. Though still not resolved, the last date for compliance with the rule is July 2014.

Other provisions are that derivatives will be required to trade through exchanges, which will add a degree of regulation to that industry; hedge funds, previously unregulated, will be required to register with the SEC, to submit reports on investment practices, and to submit to SEC examinations; and a new consumer protection bureau was set up, housed at the Fed but not under Fed control, to protect consumers from hidden fees, abusive terms, and deceptive practices. Finally, an Office of Credit Ratings was established under the SEC to regulate and monitor the rating agencies and attempt to resolve conflicts of interest. So far, nothing has been to deal with such conflicts.

Economist Joseph Stiglitz states, "The Dodd-Frank bill represented a carefully balanced compromise between the ten biggest banks and the 200 million Americans who wanted tighter regulations" [5, p. 117].

References

1. Ferguson N (2008) The ascent of money: a financial history of the world. Penguin Press, New York, p 58
2. Lowenstein R (2000) When genius failed. Random House, New York, pp 44–45
3. Paulson HM (2010) On the brink: inside the race to stop the collapse of the global financial system. The Hachette Book Group, New York
4. McKinley V (2011) Financing failure: a century of bailouts. The Independent Institute, Oakland, CA
5. Stiglitz JE (2012) The price of inequality: how today's divided society endangers our future. WW Norton, New York

Chapter 10
Why Have Financial Risks Skyrocketed, and How Is the Industry Dealing with It?

Managing Financial Risks

We discussed briefly in Chap. 4 the variety of risks present in the financial industry that arise from the lending process. The most basic and pervasive of these is credit risk. It was the fundamental cause of the financial disaster of 2007–2012. Other risks of importance to financial institutions are market risk, associated with movements in interest rates, and foreign exchange risk, linked to movements in currency values. Finally, country risk, or political risk, may exist on rare occasions when governments or other sovereign entities repudiate outstanding debt and refuse to pay it. This type of risk may be controlled to a degree through careful country analyses and political assessments.[1] Thus, the identification and measurement of risk, as well as the ability to control it, are basic requirements for the successful operation of financial institutions, bank, or nonbank.

Banks have the tools to control credit risk effectively through good underwriting – still the most important – and through sales and securitization of loans and sharing of risk through loan participations and syndications. Credit risk can also be controlled by the use of credit derivatives, as we shall see. Market risk and foreign exchange risk are often controlled by hedging with derivatives – forwards, futures, options, and swaps.

In this chapter, we shall consider how institutions or investors in general control risks by the use of derivatives, and we shall also look at other ways in which financial institutions become involved in derivative contracts.

---

[1] See Smith and Walter [1], Chap. 5, for excellent examples.

W.H. Wallace, *The American Monetary System: An Insider's View of Financial Institutions, Markets and Monetary Policy*, DOI 10.1007/978-3-319-02907-8_10, © Springer International Publishing Switzerland 2013

The Nature of Derivatives: Where Is the Value?

Financial derivatives are contracts in which value is "derived" from an underlying financial instrument – bond, stock, currency, etc. Banks or other investors often buy derivative contracts to control their own risk. They may also be sellers or dealers in derivatives if they sell a contract to control someone else's risk, such as a bank customer. In this instance, the bank is a "counterparty" to the risk hedger. It is assuming someone else's risk for a price. Determining the appropriate price or fee for a derivative contract by the seller is one of the trickiest aspects of the derivative business because that party has to know within reasonable bounds what the probability of a loss is and must be able to estimate the amount of the loss if it should occur.

Consider an example of a bank as a buyer of a derivative. A US bank may extend a loan payable one year hence in one million British Pounds. This resembles the example we used in Chap. 4. The bank may enter into a forward contract to exchange one million Pounds one year hence at today's exchange rate. It has thus protected itself against any decline in the value of the Pound over the year ahead. This is a one-time, unique, binding contract between two parties.

In this example, the "notional"[2] value of the contract is one million Pounds. But this is not an estimate of the risk assumed by the seller, since the real exposure to loss is a small fraction of that amount or whatever might be the decline in the value of the Pound. In other words, it would be unrealistic to assume the Pound would go to zero, in which case the risk would be the entire one million. Therefore, some estimate of what is likely to be the decline in value is key to the ability of the seller of the contract to price it appropriately. Let us say, for example, that the current exchange rate is £1 = $1.56, and the seller of the contract decides to take the risk of a decline to $1.50. The seller then puts a "floor" on the contract of that amount. The seller's actual exposure is $60,000 on the £1million contract, and the seller must decide what to charge for taking that risk for one year. Obviously, a fully open-ended contract would be much more expensive to the buyer, and whether it is even feasible would depend on some assessment of the stability of the currency market.

Estimates vary widely on what is the total global notional value of derivative contracts. *The Wall Street Journal* recently estimated it to be $583 trillion, worldwide.[3] But the notional value is not relevant, except to the extent that it shows how much the derivative market has grown in recent years.

The financial press unfortunately quotes these wild estimates of notional value to scare people because they make good headlines. But they are misleading because of the very small percentage of these amounts that is actually at risk. Recent BIS data have shown that the at-risk amount is less than 1 % of the notional total.

In the above example, the seller of the contract is betting against the buyer's fears that the Pound will decline. The seller is betting that it will remain the same or rise

---

[2] In the context of derivative markets, "notional" simply means the total value of the financial instruments involved in a derivative contract, whether that value is exposed to risk or not.

[3] *The Wall Street Journal,* April 13, 2011, Section C.

in value. If the Pound does rise in value, the buyer, who is bound by the contract, foregoes the profit that would have been made by accepting Pounds of a higher value. But, at least, the buyer has been protected from a loss.

Futures

The situation illustrated above of a forward contract assumes that two parties who have offsetting needs can find each other and come together to form a contract that satisfies the interests of both. A much more practical extension of this concept has developed in the form of the futures market. Futures contracts are bought and sold through exchanges such as the Chicago Board of Trade (CBT) and the Chicago Mercantile Exchange (CME). Therefore, buyers and sellers do not know each other. These are, in effect, secondary markets in the sense that the contracts traded in them are based on financial instruments that already exist in other markets.

Interest Rate Futures

See the table of futures contracts below for July 19, 2012.[4] Consider the first item under Interest Rate Futures, that of Treasury bond futures, which are traded on the CBT in units of $100,000 in face value. You will see that the table lists futures contracts for either September or December 2012 settlement. Look at the September line, and see the open, high, low, and settlement (closing) prices and the number of such contracts outstanding – called "open interest" – in the futures market on the date of the table. The number of units given in the table translates to $62,236,400,000. This number alone tells you that the futures market for Treasury bonds is a very large and highly liquid market.

A person, a bank, or any investor buying a September contract might pay the closing, for example, of 150–300 or $150,937.50.[5] This means the buyer is entitled to receive on the settlement date, September 21, 2012, $100,000 face value of Treasury bonds. The buyer now owns the contract and can either hold it until settlement or sell it at some interim date through the exchange. The buyer is said to be in a "long" position. Both buyers and sellers of such contracts will be asked by the exchange to post a margin requirement, usually about 2 % of the contract value or, in this case, $3,018.75. In other words, the buyer does not have to come up with the full purchase price, but if prices in the market are volatile and rise significantly before settlement, the exchange can issue a "margin call" and ask the buyer to post some additional amount. It can easily be seen why this market is popular with

---

[4] *The Wall Street Journal,* July 19, 2012, p. C-5.

[5] Again, the table is stated in 32nds of a point, so that 30/32 = .93750. The quoted price of 1.509375 is multiplied by the unit size to obtain $150,937.50.

Futures Contracts
From *The Wall Street Journal*, July 19, 2012

traders of all kinds because one can manipulate large sums of money while actually operating on a very small margin. The margin amounts are refunded to buyer and seller upon settlement.

Settlement dates in the derivative markets are set by the exchanges, as the third Friday, in the months of March, June, September, and December. These are sometimes referred to in the financial press as "triple-witching dates," because they are the dates on which futures, options, and swaps are all settled.

Now, consider the position of the seller of a contract of this same amount on the same date. The seller is obligated to deliver $100,000 in face value of Treasury bonds on the September settlement date. The seller may or may not actually own the bonds, but that doesn't matter. In any case, the seller is said to have taken a "short" position. The seller may remain in this position until the settlement date, or if he or she chooses not to, he or she can buy a contract to offset the one sold, and the exchange will settle out of both contracts.

Let's look at the relative positions of the buyer and seller in this transaction. If the *seller* chooses to wait until the settlement date, he or she is obligated to deliver to the exchange the actual bonds or an amount of money equal to their purchase price on the settlement date. If the *buyer* waits until the settlement date, he or she is entitled to receive either the bonds or an amount equal to their sale price on the settlement date. However, whatever the buyer or seller is technically obligated to do, in the vast majority of trades, never takes place. Instead, the exchange simply settles with them by either paying or receiving the net amounts that each has lost or gained in the transaction.

Assume, for example, that you are the buyer, which means that you have bet that the price of Treasury bonds will rise. You have guessed correctly, and the price of a unit has risen by $5,000. You will be paid this amount by the exchange. On the other side, a seller who sold a contract on the same date that you bought has bet that the price will decline. The seller has guessed wrong and has lost $5,000. Therefore, he or she will have to pay the exchange the $5,000. Both contracts are settled, margin requirements are refunded, and one party is richer, while the other is poorer by $5,000. Generally speaking, if you are the buyer of a futures contract, you are betting that the value of the underlying instrument will rise. If you are the seller, you are betting its value will decline.

Neither the buyer nor the seller has actually taken possession of the bonds at any point in this transaction. The actual bonds on which these bets were placed have a life of their own, and they go on their merry way in the bond market itself, untouched by whatever may be happening in the futures market. The only connection between the two markets is that the price of the actual bonds in the bond market and the price of the futures contracts in the futures market will converge so as to be the same on settlement day. This virtually never fails to occur and is attributable to the phenomenon of arbitrage. The traders in both markets make this happen. Smith and Walter explain this as follows:

> "Arbitrage is the simultaneous purchase and sale of substantially identical financial assets in order to profit from a price difference between the two. For example, if ABC stock is trading at $115 on the NYSE and $114 on the Midwest Stock Exchange (MSE), an investor could guarantee a profit by purchasing the stock on the MSE and simultaneously selling it on the NYSE" [1, p. 407].

It is extremely rare that traders in the futures market take actual possession of the items being traded. They are simply betting on movements in prices. One glance at the commodity futures list explains why. No one wants 40,000 lbs of lean hogs or 15,000 lbs of orange juice delivered on their front porch. So it behooves them to settle their contracts in some other manner.

Currency Futures

We have discussed futures only in the context of Treasury bonds. Let us look at certain other examples. See the listing for Euros under Currency Futures. The CME lists units of 125,000 Euros for September and December settlement. December Euros range from 1.2245 to 1.2332. Let's say you buy a contract at the close of 1.2288 for settlement on December 21, 2012. You pay $153,600 for the contract, and you are betting the Euro will rise relative to other currencies. The seller of a similar contract is betting the Euro will fall. Euro futures quoted on July 19, 2012, the date of the table, reflect the economic difficulties that Europe was having during that year. A year earlier, for example, the Euro futures closed at 1.4320, indicating a much brighter outlook for the Euro than a year later. Suppose the price of the contract at closing is 1.2488. You have gained $2,500, and the seller of a similar contract has lost the same amount.

Index Futures

Both of these examples involve items that one could actually buy and possess. Suppose, however, we enter into a futures contract for something that is intangible, such as an index future. Look at the listing for the Dow Jones Industrial Average (DJIA) under Index Futures. Trading is offered on the CBT at $10 x the index value. The range on July 19 was 12,688–12,870. If you buy one unit at the close of 12,860, you are betting the DJIA will rise.

Even though you cannot take possession of an index, the futures contracts for them are useful in the sense that one can hedge against changes in the value of whatever the index represents by buying or selling them. There are numerous index futures, and the list provided in the table is only a small portion of the total. If you own a portfolio of stocks and you find an index that roughly tracks the values of your stocks, you can hedge against a decline in their value by selling an index future. Thus, if there is a decline in the value of your stocks, your profit on the futures market will roughly offset the loss on the actual stocks. This is sometimes referred to as a "macro-hedge," and banks and other institutional investors often use this approach.

Options

Options are among the most popular of derivative contracts because of the added flexibility they give the trader. An option allows the holder the *right* to buy or sell a financial instrument or commodity at some future date at a designated price. A "put" option is an option to sell an item in the future, while a "call" option is an option to buy an item in the future. The item involved may be a financial instrument, or it may be another derivative contract, such as a futures contract. We shall consider such an example. An option carries an up-front cost, which is a sunk cost, whether the holder chooses to exercise the option or not. The seller of an option contract is obligated to perform if the buyer exercises the option.

Let us look at a situation in which an investor is considering purchasing a futures contract on a financial instrument. But, rather than buying the futures contract, the investor decides to purchase a call option, which gives him or her the right to purchase the futures contract any time within the next six months at a given price, referred to as the "strike price." Say, the strike price is $100,000, and the option costs the investor $2,000. The investor can wait until the expiration date of the option six months hence before deciding whether to purchase the futures contract. If the price of the futures contract on that expiration date is $105,000, the holder of the option would obviously want to exercise it and purchase the futures contract, and he or she would have immediately made $5,000. The net, however, would be only $3,000 because of the cost of the option. If the price of the futures contract is at $102,000 or less, the option holder would decide to let the option expire without exercising it. The transaction would have cost the option holder the $2,000 price of the option and nothing more. The use of the option, therefore, assures investors against a loss, whereas if they had purchased the futures contract at the beginning date, they would be vulnerable to a loss.

Consider the other side of this picture. If the investor had been thinking of selling a futures contract in the expectation the underlying instrument would decline in value, he or she could assure against a loss by purchasing a put option, say, with the same strike price of $100,000. Then, if the futures contract has declined in value by the expiration date of the option, by more than the $2,000 cost, the holder could exercise the option and take the profit. If futures had gone up in value, the option holder would choose to let the option lapse, and the cost would have been capped at the $2,000 cost of the option.

Again, the pricing of options is a tricky business for the counterparty who is selling the option contract. If, in the first example, the holder of the call option finds that the price of the futures contract has risen by $10,000 by the expiration date of the option, the seller of the option would have to make good on the difference, which would more than wipe out the $2,000 earned on the sale of the option.

The examples we have considered of both futures and options suggest that the counterparties who are selling risk protection are vulnerable to great losses, and experience has shown, especially in recent years, how true this is. Banks and other financial institutions often play this role. It can be extremely profitable for those who are able to judge risk and price it properly, but it can be the death knell for institutions that do not have that skill, as in the case of Barings Bank. These are among the activities for which the proposed Volcker Rule would require greater scrutiny.

Credit Derivatives: Credit Default Swaps

Credit derivatives, also referred to as credit default swaps (CDSs), are of particular importance to banks because credit risk is the most pervasive of all risks that banks face. These instruments are, in effect, insurance policies against losses on bank loans.

The mechanism transfers the risk of default on loans from the bank to a third party who is willing and able to take the risk for a fee. The bank does not off-load the asset, but gets rid of the credit risk.

This market is of recent origin and has grown rapidly during the last two decades. The industry has been essentially unregulated, and as a result records were not kept on its size or growth. Deutsche Bank estimated the size of this market at $5.44 trillion in 2004. *The Wall Street Journal* estimated it at $17 trillion on December 31, 2005. *The Economist* estimated it on April 30, 2008, at $62 trillion.[6] Due to the losses experienced by the industry during and since 2008, however, it is thought that its size has receded somewhat.

Let's look at an example of one of the early uses of a credit default swap by Chase Bank, published in the financial press.[7] A group of investors forms a trust; the trust sells bonds of $50 million. The trust sells a CDS to Chase to cover $50 million of loans on Chase's books. The trust places the funds in Treasury securities paying 5.4 % and uses these securities as collateral for the guarantee that it is making to Chase. The trust and Chase then do a "total return swap," which means that Chase pays its total return on the loans to the trust. This return is Libor + 365 basis points. In return, Chase receives from the trust a negotiated return of Libor + 125 basis points. The difference of 240 basis points, or 2.4 % of the $50 million, is Chase's cost of credit protection. The return to the trust, which is taking the risk, is 2.4 % plus the 5.4 % earnings on its securities or a total of 7.8 %.

But the $50 million fund in the trust is adequate to insure against a considerably larger amount in loans. It is not necessary to have 100 % reserves against the loan risk, since the probability of total default would be very small. The fund could be leveraged to provide CDSs against two or three times its total value. In this specific case, the trust decided to insure an additional $100 million of Chase's loans with the same reserve. Now the return to the trust is 720 basis points plus the 5.4 % or a total return of 12.6 %.

This is a large return, even though trust investors have guaranteed $150 million in total loans. Such returns are adequate to entice investors who like to take risk into the market. Now, one begins to see where greed sets in, and this is exactly what happened in this market in recent years.

Little was known by the public at large about CDSs until the failure of the American International Group (AIG), then the largest insurance company in the world. It had engaged in the selling of CDSs to the point at which it had a half-trillion Dollars of coverage extended on them on a global basis [2]. Of course, the lion's share of the insurance it extended covered loan portfolios made up of mortgages that were headed into default, the result of which was the failure of AIG and the need for a bailout by the Federal Reserve under Section 13(3) in the amount of $182 billion. For insurance in the financial world, this episode turned out to be the equivalent of tornados and hurricanes in the property and casualty world and the AIDS epidemic for life insurance.

---

[6] *The Economist,* April 30, 2008. Vol. 399.

[7] *The Institutional Investor Magazine,* December, 1997.

There is one important distinction, however, between CDS-type insurance coverage and that of the traditional life or property and casualty insurance policies. In the traditional fields, there has to be an insurable interest on the part of the purchaser of insurance in whatever is being insured. For example, I cannot take out a fire insurance policy on my neighbor's house because I think it is a fire trap and I see an opportunity to make some money if it burns down. I do not have an insurable interest. The same is true with life insurance. But in the CDS field, I can buy a credit default swap on the XYZ Bank's loan portfolio with no questions asked. This is what many people did, which fueled the growth of this industry during the recent crisis. Michael Lewis points this out vividly in his book, *The Big Short* [2]. He notes that many investors expressed great surprise that firms were willing to issue CDSs in great quantities even after it was widely known what was happening to mortgages. Many investors took advantage of this opportunity.

While it seems that firms such as AIG are recovering and paying off their bailouts, it is unclear what the future of this industry holds. The lapse of judgment in recent years among insurers was striking. One weakness noted by many economists and policymakers was that the insurance industry is regulated by the states, and there is hardly any regulation at the federal level, but there are no specific proposals afloat to substantially modify the industry or its regulation.

Swaps

Another means of risk control is the use of swaps. The idea of currency swaps had their origin during the Bretton Woods era, when exchange controls were in place. Swaps replaced the earlier practice of "parallel loans." Under that system, a British firm wishing to invest in the United States had to find a US supplier of the funds because of the exchange controls preventing the movement of funds across borders. The US supplier loaned the funds to the British firm's US affiliate. The British firm loaned an equivalent amount to a British affiliate of the US firm [1, p. 78]. Obviously, affiliates had to be established beforehand to make this work, and banks were often asked to stand in the middle to work out adjustments if exchange rates fluctuated. It became very complex, and the invention of swaps simplified the whole process.

A typical use of swaps would be a swap of interest rate obligations on loans. For example, suppose an American company would have to pay Libor + 70 basis points for a five-year bond issue but would have to pay only Libor + 30 basis points for a five-year floating-rate bank loan. The company would prefer to have a fixed-rate obligation but takes the loan because it is less expensive. Meanwhile, a Japanese bank has incurred a fixed-rate obligation in Eurobonds at Libor + 0.

The Japanese bank swaps its fixed-rate obligation to the American company for the bank's cost of funds plus 50 basis points or Libor + 50. After the swap, the American company has acquired the fixed-rate obligation that it originally wanted at 20 basis points less than it would have cost in the United States. The Japanese bank assumes the floating-rate obligation to pay Libor + 30, but this is reduced by the 50 basis points it earned on the swap; its net cost then is Libor − 20 [1, p. 280]. This kind of swap of either payment obligations or income streams is called a "plain vanilla" swap.

See also the example below of a rate swap that involved the Beaver Country Day School in Boston and Lehman Brothers. The school issues debt at a floating rate, as shown in the graph. The school is persuaded by Lehman to swap its floating-rate obligation for a fixed rate, represented by the straight horizontal line in the graph. For a time, the school is better off because it is paying at a rate lower than its floating rate would have been. At a point, however, rates decline and become considerably lower than the fixed rate, but the school has to continue to pay the fixed rate. In the long run, the school had to pay much more than it would have if it had not tried the swap. This was a gamble on future conditions in the credit markets, and we can see that the school made a mistake in assuming in 2008 that rates would remain high.[8]

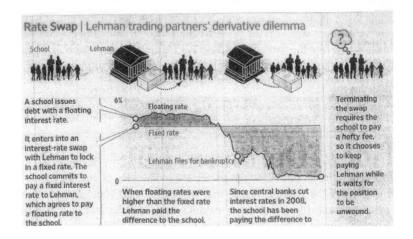

Summary on Risk and Derivatives

One fundamental fact should be remembered about risk in the financial system. Primary securities, such as equity and debt, represent the direct securitization of real business risk, and investors take that risk by buying those securities. Derivatives, on the other hand, are bilateral contracts that do not represent direct securitization of real risk. They are simply bets on future values. It is in this sense that they are likened to casinos and, some critics say, add an unnecessary risk to the economy. Alan Greenspan often defended the use of derivatives and remarked that derivatives serve the purpose of transferring risk to those most willing and able to take it.

---

[8] *The Wall Street Journal*, September 17, 2009, Section C.

While this statement is technically true, it ignores many of the unseen risks in this market in which people become entrapped.

Some critics say that derivatives encourage more highly leveraged trading strategies. There is some evidence that this is an accurate statement as well, and LTCM is an excellent example. I conclude that it is true that derivatives add nothing to the economy in terms of production or substance, but they do redistribute risk within the system, and in this sense, they serve a useful purpose.

In summary, in any economy, the banking and financial system is central to the efficient allocation of capital and to the management and allocation of risk. This is why it remains a continuing challenge to keep the financial system free of self-serving interests and corruption.

Payment System Risk

Finally, one other type of risk in the financial system is payment system risk. This is risk in the process of settlement, which refers to the discharge of obligations of buyers and sellers through the transfer of funds and/or securities. It is an operational risk, as opposed to those linked to lending, investing, or trading, as our earlier examples have been.

In the late 1960s, trading in securities was hindered by paperwork or the "back-office problem." Paper jams occurred, and delays in settlement were commonplace; it routinely took days to settle purchases and sales of stocks, bonds, and other securities. In the 1970s, however, a forward-looking development began to take place that enabled multiple increases in trading and new issue volume. These were the creation of the Depository Trust & Clearing Corporation, owned by the US banks, brokers, and dealers, and the creation of Euroclear and Cedel in Europe. They created depositories to enable securities transfers to be made through electronic book entry. These institutions provide custody and asset servicing for 3.6 million security issues, valued at $34 trillion. In 2009, they provided settlement for $1.48 quadrillion in securities transactions.[9] It should be clear from the staggering size of these numbers that it would be impossible to handle today's volume of financial transactions if they were still paper based. Since their beginning, these institutions have succeeded in automating virtually all tradable financial instruments, converting them from paper to electronic images. The only vestiges of paper-based transactions that remain in the financial system today are paper currency and checks, and both are declining rapidly in use.

At the same time these developments were taking place in the private financial sector, the Treasury was doing the same with marketable Treasury debt. It is also virtually all in electronic (book-entry) form. The Treasury, with the help of the Federal Reserve, created the "Treasury Direct" system in the late 1960s and early 1970s. Treasury Direct allows individuals, business firms, banks, and investors of any kind,

---

[9] One quadrillion is 10th to the 15th power or 1,000 trillion.

foreign or domestic, to hold accounts directly with the Treasury, accessible through the Federal Reserve Banks and branches, or online on a 24/7 basis.

Through these accounts, investors can purchase and hold Treasury bills, notes, bonds, TIPS, and savings bonds. The system allows persons to conduct purchases, reinvestments, sales, and other account maintenance tasks via computer anywhere. There is no fee for any of these services, regardless of account size. Despite the availability of these free services, many individuals still prefer to go through banks or brokers to buy or sell Treasury securities, for which they are charged a fee.

The Treasury sells all of its securities by auction at the time of original issue. The auctions are conducted for the Treasury by the Federal Reserve Banks, and for those with Treasury Direct accounts, the sales can be completed online without having to go to the Fed. Bids are entered by investors on either a competitive or noncompetitive basis. In competitive bids, investors specify the rates they will accept, whereas in noncompetitive bids the investor agrees to the rate that is set at the auction. At the close of the auction, Treasury accepts all noncompetitive bids. It then accepts competitive bids in ascending order of the yield bid until the overall quantity of accepted bids reaches the offering amount. Finally, all bidders, competitive and noncompetitive, whose bids are accepted, receive the same yield as the highest accepted bid.

Interest payments on coupon securities and principal payments at maturity are wire transferred to the bank accounts of investors. If the holder of a Treasury Direct account wishes to sell an instrument prior to maturity, it can be wire transferred to a private brokerage account and sold.

Support for these systems is provided by the backbone wire transfer network operated by the Federal Reserve System – Fedwire, established in the late 1960s. There are also other private electronic networks handling transfer of payments and securities and, in some cases, other business information. The largest private network in the United States is the Clearing House Interbank Payments System (CHIPS), owned and operated by the New York Clearing House, which is, in turn, owned by the New York banks. Another that is globally significant is the Society for Worldwide Interbank Financial Telecommunications (SWIFT). Both CHIPS and SWIFT handle large numbers of international transactions, and both interconnect with Fedwire. Within the European Union, the Trans-European Automated Real-time Gross Settlement System (TARGET) was created in the 1990s, similar to Fedwire, and also interconnected with the other networks. Therefore, virtually all the financial systems of the entire Western world are automated and interconnected so that paper hardly has to move at all anymore.

As a consequence of these developments and other means of automating payment processes, the volume of checks has declined from 85 % of the total of non-cash transactions in 1979 to about 32 % in 2006 and continues to decline at a rate of over 4 % per year. In value, debit card use has now surpassed the volume of actual cash usage, and by 2006 it had almost reached the physical volume of check payments. As further evidence of the shift to electronics and the decline in the use of cash, the production of new currency in 2010 by the US Treasury's Bureau of Engraving and Printing was the lowest in 30 years.

Over the years, the Federal Reserve has actively promoted conversion to electronic means of payment and lobbied for years for the passage of the Check Clearing for the 21st Century Act, in 2004, referred to as "Check 21." This Act has led to unimaginable efficiencies in the payments area. It eliminated an age-old law that the writer of a check could legally demand to have the cancelled paper check returned, once it had been charged to the writer's account. Check 21 allows substitute checks (electronic images) to be produced as legal proof of payment. Now, rather than shipping paper checks all over the country to get them back to the bank on which they were drawn, which the Fed had to do at great cost for many years, banks send electronic data from checks to the Fed, and entries are made to their reserve accounts. The paper checks are retained by the bank of first deposit, whose account is credited by the Fed, and they are destroyed after some retention period.

In addition to the backbone electronic networks that we have mentioned, other smaller electronic payment and clearing systems are operated by the central bank and by other private banking institutions. Among these are automated clearing houses (ACHs). They involve end-of-day net settlement, as opposed to instantaneous gross settlement as in Fedwire. These systems handle batched payments – preauthorized payments by individuals and businesses, automated payrolls, individual bank online systems, etc. Payments flow through these systems and are settled on a net basis at the end of the business day, similar to the settlement of paper checks through bank-owned clearing houses. A bank pays or receives the net of what it owes or is owed with only one payment, and this settling payment goes through Fedwire. Now, the ACHs pick up the added volume of electronic image processing under the Check 21 Act.

Consider, as an example, the following multilateral netting concept. Bank A owes Bank B $200; Bank B owes Bank A $100; Bank B owes Bank C $100. This would normally require three payments, but it can be netted by Bank A paying Bank C $100, and the system settles with one payment. Net settlements have had a major impact; they have reduced deliveries among participants across the country by an estimated 90 %. In 1994, CHIPS volume was running about $1 trillion per day. Net settlement reduced this to $10 billion, 1 % of gross.

On the operational side of the financial system, we have entered an era in which efficiencies have been created that were unthinkable only a few years ago. Laws as well as firmly entrenched practices and habits remained in the way for a long time. Now, time zones no longer matter, and round-the-clock trading and settlement at periodic intervals is being implemented. The Fed, for example, has gone to a 22½-hour trading day with the remaining 90 min reserved for settlement and reconcilement of accounts. Eventually, even this will go away, and in the future, we will begin each trading day one split second after the end of the last one.

References

1. Smith RC, Walter I (2003) Global banking, 2nd edn. Oxford University Press, New York
2. Lewis M (2010) The big short. WW Norton, New York

Part IV
Central Banking and Monetary Policy

Chapter 11
What Are the Purposes and Functions of the Federal Reserve System?

To understand the monetary policy process, we must take a more detailed look at the central bank itself, how it is structured, and why it is organized in the manner it is.

The Three Major Functions of the Federal Reserve

Monetary policy and the supervision and regulation of banks, which we discussed in Chap. 6, are two of the three major functions of the Federal Reserve System. The third is the provision of financial services to the banking system and to the US government. This includes the clearing and settlement of payments, paper and electronic; the issuance of currency and coin to banks and the destruction of unfit currency; the provision of banking services to the government, such as the processing and settlement of government payments through the Treasury's account that is maintained by the Federal Reserve Banks; the original issue and final redemption at maturity of Treasury securities; and any other functions that may be required by the Treasury as its fiscal agent. Among these fiscal agency functions are the collection of tax revenues, operation of the Treasury Direct system (in Chap. 10), freezing of foreign assets in the US banks when necessary, the processing of food stamps, and numerous others. Finally, in 2010, the Dodd-Frank bill added an expanded consumer protection function to the Fed's operational responsibilities.

These financial service functions have historically accounted for about 75–80 % of Fed system employees. The three major functions, taken together, are often referred to as a "three-legged stool," meaning that each of the three is necessary in order to do the total job assigned to the Fed. For example, information provided through the payment function and through the supervision and regulation function produces valuable data on the safety and soundness of the banking and financial system, which are important inputs to the monetary policy process.

Not all central banks have exactly the same mix of functions. Some governments, for example, assign the supervision and regulation function to other agencies,

W.H. Wallace, *The American Monetary System: An Insider's View of Financial Institutions, Markets and Monetary Policy*, DOI 10.1007/978-3-319-02907-8_11, © Springer International Publishing Switzerland 2013

and the US Congress has considered proposals a number of times to remove this activity from both the Fed and the FDIC and consolidate it under one super-regulatory agency. In some countries, the payment functions are handled by agencies other than the central bank or by the private sector. Again, similar proposals have been made in the United States, but Congress has not seen the necessity to make such changes.

Although operational and regulatory functions are important to the Fed and to the effectiveness with which it does its overall job, by far the most important and the most sensitive of its activities is that of monetary policy.

The Structure of the Federal Reserve System

The Fed was established by the Federal Reserve Act of December 23, 1913. It was quickly dubbed by the press as "a Christmas present for the president," because President Woodrow Wilson had been instrumental in expressing his preferences about what the central bank should turn out to be. Allan Meltzer, in his encyclopedic history of the Federal Reserve, notes that Congress had to choose between two extremes. "At one extreme were the proponents of a single central bank, owned by the commercial banks and run by bankers. The group favoring this alternative looked to the European central banks as models, particularly the Bank of England. At the opposite extreme were those who opposed a central bank of any kind on the assumption that it would be a monopoly and would be run for the benefit of the bankers" [1, p. 65].

The 1913 Act followed several years of research by the National Monetary Commission, appointed by Congress after the Panic of 1907, which published over 30 volumes of research results. The Act says little about the broader purposes of the legislation. It talks of furnishing an elastic currency, affording means of rediscounting commercial paper, and improving the supervision of banking; the Act speaks of setting discount rates "with a view of accommodating commerce and business" but mentions no other objectives [1]. Notably absent from these originally stated purposes was any mention of the central bank having anything to do with economic stability for the economy at large. As we shall see, these came later.

The Federal Reserve Act specified that the central bank would be a decentralized system with regional banks located in not less than eight nor more than 12 regions. An organizational committee was created by the Act that would decide what the boundaries of those regions would be and where the regional banks were to be located. The committee specified 12 districts, and the system still has those original districts. Only minor changes have been made in district boundaries since then, primarily for operational reasons. The operations of the districts were to be overseen and coordinated by the Board of Governors (BOG) in Washington, consisting of seven members, appointed by the president and confirmed by the senate for 14-year terms. (See chart on page 172).

The establishment of a decentralized central banking system, owned and controlled by the government, was different from other central banks and was the response to populist and agrarian views that feared a highly centralized bank that might be controlled by money center bankers.

The reserve banks were opened for business in November 1914, just after the beginning of World War I in Europe in August. At that time, it was thought that the 12 district banks would truly be the central banks for their respective regions. As time passed, however, innovations in technology and electronic telecommunications changed the nature of banking, which rendered the district boundaries almost meaningless.

As the chart on the following page shows, each of the district reserve banks has a board of directors partially elected by member banks and partially appointed by the BOG. In the beginning, each district bank issued stock to member banks equal to 3 % of the member bank's capital and surplus, with the provision that an additional 3 % could be "called" if needed. It has never been needed. The purpose of this plan was to raise capital for the operation of the banks. The amount of stock held by members is still fixed at the 3 % level, and the Dollar amount is adjusted each year as the members' capital and surplus either grows or shrinks.

The ownership of stock by member banks is sometimes misunderstood to imply private ownership of the Fed by the banking system. However, the stock does not convey any rights of ownership; it is like a tax on members. All they get in return is the privilege of voting for some of the directors and a 6 % statutory dividend on the amount of stock held, which has remained fixed at that level from the beginning.

Each reserve bank has nine directors. Three are Class A directors who represent lenders. They are bankers and are elected by the member banks in their respective districts – one by small banks, one by medium-sized banks, and one by large banks. The definition of the size classes is administered by the reserve bank. There are three Class B directors who represent borrowers. They cannot be bankers and are generally people from nonbanking business or industry or the professions. They are also elected by the member banks by size group. Finally, there are three Class C directors who represent the public interest. They are appointed by the BOG; they also cannot be bankers, nor have any financial interest in a bank, such as ownership of stock. They are usually business, professional, or academic persons. The BOG designates one of the Class C groups as Chair of the board and one as Deputy Chair. In this manner, the Federal Reserve System has been organized to prevent control by the banking industry. This separation has worked in the system's favor over the years, and there have been surprisingly few instances of conflicts of interest arising from the directors.

However, one highly publicized case of conflict of interest in recent years was the Fed of New York's Class C Director, Stephen Friedman, who was then Chairman of its board. Mr. Friedman was an executive of Goldman Sachs, which at the time of his appointment was not a bank. However, in 2008, the financial crisis forced Goldman to change its status from an investment bank to a financial holding company, which disqualified Mr. Friedman from continuing to hold the chair of the Fed of New York's board. He was forced to resign, but before the resignation took effect, he presided as Chairman in the selection of William Dudley, a former Goldman chief economist, as President of the New York reserve bank, to succeed

FEDERAL RESERVE SYSTEM

Board of Governors

(7 members, appointed by the President, confirmed by the Senate for 14-year terms)

Cannot be reappointed; President designates one of the 7 as Chair and one as Vice Chair for 4-year terms; subject to separate Senate confirmation in those roles; can be reappointed until expiration of their 14-term

Federal Reserve Banks

District:	1	2	3	4	5	6	7	8	9	10	11	12
Head Office:	Boston	New York	Philadelphia	Cleveland	Richmond	Atlanta	Chicago	St. Louis	Minneapolis	Kansas City	Dallas	San Francisco
Branches:		Buffalo		Cincinnati	Baltimore	Birmingham	Detroit	Little Rock	Helena MT	Denver	El Paso	Los Angeles
				Pittsburgh	Charlotte	Jacksonville		Louisville		Oklahoma City	Houston	Portland
						Miami		Memphis		Omaha	San Antonio	Salt Lake City
						Nashville						Seattle
						New Orleans						

Each District has 9-member board of directors:

3 class A directors; representing lenders; elected by member banks in the district (most are bankers)

3 class-B directors; representing borrowers; elected by member banks in the district (cannot be bankers)

3 class C-directors; representing the public interest; appointed by Board of Governors, which designates one of the three as Chair and one as Deputy-chair (cannot be bankers and cannot hold any financial interest in a bank, including stock)

All directors have 3-year terms and are limited to 2 terms

Members contribute initial capital:

Each member bank is required by the Federal Reserve Act to commit 3% of its capital and surplus to fund the capitalization of the Reserve Bank in its district. (i.e., they purchase stock in the Federal Reserve Bank in that amount. The stock carries no ownership rights and no control over the activities of the Reserve Banks, except for the right to vote for the Class A & B directors of each district)

Major Policy-making group is FOMC:

Federal Open Market Committee (FOMC)

7 members of the Board of Governors and 5 Reserve Bank Presidents

Chair of Board of Governors is Chair of FOMC

President of New York Reserve Bank is a permanent member, and is Vice Chair of FOMC

Other Reserve Banks rotate as follows:

Cleveland and Chicago, every other year

Boston, Philadelphia and Richmond, every third year

Atlanta, St. Louis and Dallas, every third year

Minneapolis, Kansas City and San Francisco, every third year

Timothy Geithner, who had been appointed Secretary of the Treasury. Mr. Dudley still holds the position. Also, Mr. Friedman influenced Fed policy regarding Goldman's bailout and profited from it by purchasing a large amount of additional Goldman stock, thus increasing his wealth. This was a clear conflict of interest and should not have been allowed to happen under existing rules. Mr. Friedman requested the BOG to waive the rule, to allow him to continue to serve for a period after his eligibility was no longer valid, to complete the work he had started. In one of the most egregious and probably illegal decisions the BOG ever made, it granted the waiver, allowing the incidents mentioned above to occur. This resulted in a severe blow to the credibility of the Fed, after many years in which it enjoyed a totally unblemished record.

In the early days, monetary policy was heavily influenced by Benjamin Strong, President of the New York reserve bank, because of his experience, expertise, and charisma. The New York reserve bank conducted open market operations unilaterally on Strong's directions. Each of the 12 reserve banks bought and sold Treasury securities for the purpose of generating income to operate the banks. The entire system, however, recognized that Strong was about the only person around who knew what he was doing in the Treasury markets. As a result, the other 11 banks delegated to New York the task of managing their accounts as well, so, by default, these nascent operations in the open market became centered in New York. This meant, in effect, that the New York reserve bank was dictating the nation's monetary policy, which, in turn, meant indirect but powerful influence by the New York money center banks who had Strong's ear.

This invited a power struggle between members of the BOG and the Reserve Bank presidents. After a few years, Congress, influenced by the populists and the financial world generally, realized that this was a departure from what they had bargained for in creating a decentralized system. Thus, Congress amended the Federal Reserve Act in 1935 to create the Federal Open Market Committee (FOMC) and specified that it would consist of the seven members of the BOG and five of the Reserve Bank presidents on a rotating basis. The impact of this change was profound. The amendment required that any decision on monetary policy involving the buying and selling of Treasury securities must be approved by the FOMC. This shifted the voting power on policy from New York to Washington, where the members of the BOG had seven of the 12 votes. It thus diluted the influence of New York bankers in the policy process [2].

It was not until 1942 that Congress agreed to a further change to allow the New York reserve bank president to be a permanent voting member of the FOMC. Since then, only the four remaining voting seats rotate on an annual basis. This change made sense because the New York reserve bank is the operational center for policy actions. Now, as the chart shows, the FOMC is regarded as the third major piece of the Federal Reserve System, in addition to the BOG and the reserve banks. The Chair of the BOG is also Chair of the FOMC, and the New York reserve bank president is Vice-Chair of the FOMC. See chart on page 172.

Monetary Policy

We have touched upon numerous aspects of central banking and monetary policy in earlier chapters. Because monetary policy is a pervasive influence on the financial system as a whole, its effects are felt in the way financial institutions operate, so we have attempted to highlight those in our earlier discussions of banking. Some examples are as follows:

– Reserve requirements, reserve accounts and the maintenance of reserves, excess reserves, and the recent transition to payment of interest on reserves
– The Federal Funds market, which operates through the reserve accounts that banks hold with the Federal Reserve System
– The Federal Funds rate as an important indicator of supply and demand conditions in the short-term money and credit markets and as an indicator of monetary policy changes
– The reserve requirement ratio as a powerful tool of monetary policy, although a seldom used one
– The fact that the Fed's buying and selling of securities in the private market affect the Federal Funds rate and the overall supply of money and credit
– The Fed's role in the supervision and regulation of banks and the regulations that bear on the operations of banks and are closely related to monetary policy
– The involvement of the Fed in crisis situations and, in particular, the details of the recent financial crisis of 2007–2012 and how it has stretched the usual limits of monetary policy

So what is left to discuss? In this chapter and the next, we shall dig more deeply into monetary policy – first, how the objectives of monetary policy are determined and by whom; and second, how a specific policy is decided upon and the analysis and decision-making procedures leading up to monetary policy actions. We shall consider all the economic information that has to be taken into account, such as the most current economic data on the US economy, financial data regarding the condition of markets, and economic and financial data on other countries whose policies can affect the American economy and whose economic conditions must be considered in setting the US policy.

Finally, we shall go into further depth on the mechanics of monetary policy operations – what actually is done each day to carry out monetary policy directives and the instruments or tools that are used to conduct monetary policy – and we shall discuss the targets, both long term and short term, of monetary policy.

Objectives and Targets of Monetary Policy: Short Term and Long Term

How does the monetary policy of the central bank affect the banking system, the financial markets, and ultimately the public at large – individuals, businesses, investors, savers, consumers, retirees, and so on? As we shall see, it is the system of financial institutions and markets that provides the "transmission mechanism" through which monetary policy affects the overall economy.

Although monetary policy works through the financial system, and the Fed relates closely to that system, overall public interest in the central bank focuses upon how it affects the economy as a whole. People often ask, for example, whether the Federal Reserve can affect the major macroeconomic variables, such as employment, economic growth, income, productivity, and GDP. The answer is yes, but not directly. The Fed has no tools – buttons it can push or levers it can pull – that will boost employment or raise GDP. It must work through the financial system to achieve these broader goals.

Therefore, the direct targets of monetary policy are always financial targets – either interest rates or money growth. This doesn't mean that monetary policy is not working toward broader objectives, but the mechanism is more indirect. For example, Congress passed the Employment Act of 1946, under which the Fed, for the first time, was given a mandate to pursue price stability, full employment, economic growth, and a stable exchange rate for the Dollar. These broad objectives have been underscored and reiterated by Congress over the years since, but this was the first time that Congress officially assigned to the Fed the task of economic stabilization.

Of course, the question on the minds of Congress and many others in 1946 was what would happen to the American economy in the postwar years. That is, were we in for more recession or for rampant inflation or some other destabilizing influences? Congress wanted to be sure in passing the Employment Act that it had gone on record as to what it expected of the Federal Reserve in this period.

Remember, originally, the major role of the central bank was to provide liquidity to the banking system through the discounting process – not overall economic stability. There was debate at the time of the Employment Act about whether the Fed should have, or whether it could even handle, this enlarged role. Many critics thought that the objectives that Congress had espoused were inherently incompatible. Economists were quick to point out that experience had shown that we could not achieve full employment and low inflation at the same time. An economic theory known as "the Phillips curve" had proved that it was impossible. (See graph on page 176.) It was not clear what Congress wanted because the Act was not specific about what was expected, that is, what is meant by full employment, what is a reasonable rate of economic growth, what does stability of prices or exchange rates mean? How stable is stable? Congress didn't quantify anything but left it to the Fed to decide what these variables meant.

Years later, in 1977, the Congress amended the Federal Reserve Act, to actually write into the Act its mandate for Fed policy. In this amendment, the Congress stated, "The Board of Governors of the Federal Reserve System and the Federal Open Market Committee shall maintain long-run growth of the monetary and credit aggregates so as to promote effectively the goals of maximum employment, stable prices and moderate long-term interest rates." These words have over time come to be known as "the dual mandate" and have been interpreted to mean simply low unemployment and low inflation. In both the 1946 Act and the 1977 amendment, however, Congress stopped short of quantifying these objectives.

In 2011, the senate considered another amendment, which would have narrowed the mandate to just low inflation and would have removed the mandate to the Fed to seek low unemployment. Members of Congress were reacting to what they considered the ineffectiveness of the stimulus programs that had been pursued since the onset of the recent recession. No action was taken on this proposal, and the dual mandate still stands [3].

The Phillips curve below illustrates a negative association between the inflation rate and the unemployment rate. At point A, inflation is low and unemployment is high. At point B, inflation is high, and unemployment is low. Thus, the theory suggests that policies aimed at reducing inflation tend to increase unemployment, and policies aimed at reducing unemployment tend to increase inflation. But in recent years, such as the 1990s, mainly because of technology and the resulting increases in productivity, we had low inflation and low unemployment simultaneously. This illustrated that the Phillips curve, as a two-dimensional construct, does not take productivity into account. Thus, while it is a theory that often holds true, it is not an immutable fact [4].

The Phillips curve

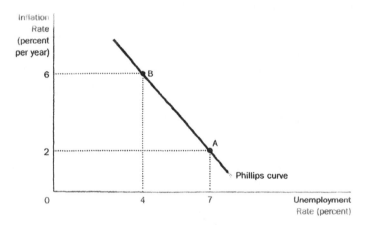

In recent years, public interest in monetary policy has grown because of people's greater awareness of how they are affected by it. The growth of credit and, thus, the increased sensitivity to movements of interest rates, account for much of this increased interest. The greater use of floating-rate or adjustable rate debts has made many people aware that unexpected increases in interest rates can suddenly raise the cost of their existing credit and, as we have observed in recent years, can lead to default on mortgages and to foreclosures. On the other side of the coin, reductions in rates can wipe out income from savings or investments and can substantially reduce pension income to retirees. These factors have made people in general more aware of their susceptibility to market volatility.

Increased coverage of monetary policy by the media and increased competence of the media to cover the subject have also added to public awareness. In addition, more openness on the part of the Fed itself means there is greater coverage than ever before about what the Fed is doing. Added to these reasons is the fact of globalization and the increased realization that one's well-being is influenced by the monetary policies of other nations as well as our own. Witness the impact we have felt in 2012 and 2013 of the economic problems of Europe through its effect on markets, levels of trade, etc. All of these developments mean that monetary policy looms larger in the public's mind than ever before.

As we have noted, financial markets, like other markets for goods and services, are private markets and are subject to the basic forces of supply and demand from the private sector, apart from any action taken by the central bank. When demand for money is strong or supply is short, the price (interest rate) rises, and, conversely, when demand is weak or supply is abundant, interest rates decline. Thus, a policy of ease increases supply and lowers rates, while a tightening policy decreases supply and raises rates. But the Fed must take whatever happens in the private markets as a given, and this influences its policy actions.

Central bank monetary policy generally "leans against the wind," which is to say that it is countercyclical in nature. For example, if inflation is a concern, the Fed will attempt to reduce the supply of money and credit available or to dampen the demand for it by raising its price or interest rate. If growth is slackening and the economy needs a boost, the Fed will increase the supply of money and lower its cost to entice investment and spending. All of these situations involve some element of judgment and discretion. The policy actions can be small or large, depending, respectively, upon whether the Fed is simply trying to fine-tune the economy or to make some major change in its direction.

This discretionary aspect of monetary policy has always been – and still is – controversial. The alternative would be a rule-based monetary policy, which would restrict the Fed's actions to a predetermined course set by Congress or some authority beyond the control of the central bank itself. We shall discuss some rule-based alternatives in Chap. 12.

In any case, however, the outcome of the Fed's actions is not always a certainty, despite commonly held perceptions to the contrary. The central bank can have difficulty offsetting overwhelming market forces in either direction. Generally speaking, actions to restrain the economy are usually much more effective than actions taken to boost it. The latter are often compared to trying to push on a string. The most recent period of attempting to recover from the severe recession that began in 2007 is a good example of this difficulty. Efforts to stimulate the economy have not had the effect that the Fed and the public had hoped they would have. One rule of thumb the Fed has always observed in its conduct of monetary policy is to try to maintain "orderly" markets, that is, not to take actions that would cause excessive volatility in markets upon which the entire financial world depends. We shall discuss, however, an instance in which a deliberate exception to this rule of thumb was implemented in order to achieve an overriding policy objective.

Therefore, despite the power that central banks have in most countries, they recognize the need to use that power carefully because volatile markets and financial disruptions are to be avoided, if possible. Today, financial markets are more complex because they are global. Achieving stability in one's own markets may contribute to instability elsewhere in the world. Or assisting other countries to achieve an objective that is desirable in a global sense – as the United States sometimes has to do – may make one's own markets more volatile. For example, in 1998, when the US economy was booming, the Fed eased monetary policy to help resolve the Southeast Asian and Russian financial crises, at some cost in terms of added inflation in our economy. Therefore, one of the by-products of globalization of markets is the interdependency of monetary policies of the major central banks of the world.

Global monetary policy is essentially made by four dominant central banks – the Federal Reserve System in the United States, the European Central Bank (ECB), the Bank of England, and the Bank of Japan. The ECB, in existence only since 1999, has supplanted the once-powerful central banks of Germany, France, Italy, and other members of the European Monetary Union (EMU). Those central banks are now mere branches of the ECB. At some point, the People's Bank of China may join the group of dominant central banks but hasn't so far because the Yuan is not a fully convertible currency, the currency is not allowed to float freely in international markets, the Yuan may not be held in other parts of the world without the consent of the Chinese government, and there are other political issues that keep China from operating as a fully open economy.

Many observers feel that the ECB has been too restrictive in recent years when the European economies have been badly in need of stimulus. They eased briefly in 2009, the year before they were hit by the Greek crisis, but in 2011, in the face of deteriorating economies throughout the EMU, they tightened again, to the dismay of policymakers elsewhere in the world. It could be honestly said that the ECB has been of little help in dealing with the pervasive European crisis that has since developed. There is an important difference in the ECB's mandate vis-a-vis that of the Federal Reserve that we discussed earlier. The ECB is given a hierarchical mandate under the terms of the Maastricht Treaty of 1992, which created it. The ECB mandate reads, "The primary objective of the European Central Bank shall be to maintain price stability. Without prejudice to the objective of price stability, the ECB shall support the general economic policies of the Community." The last part of the statement has been interpreted to refer to "a high level of employment and sustainable and non-inflationary growth," but they are clearly subsidiary to price stability. This contrasts to the Fed's dual mandate, where the two are of equal priority.

There is a cultural difference underlying the differences in monetary policy, which is evident in a study of European versus American monetary policies over time. Europeans are traditionally more concerned about the dangers of inflation than Americans. This is based on their experience with ruinous hyperinflation during the interwar years, particularly in Germany. The German mind-set on monetary policy has dominated European thinking on the subject, both before and after the creation of the ECB. The American mind-set has tended to lean toward more concern about the ravages of depression based on our experiences in the 1930s. To a great extent, these differences in philosophies still exist. This is a fundamental reason that European monetary policy is often criticized for being too tight and American policy for being too easy.

Most major central banks around the world would list as their long-range objectives for monetary policy the same as those of the United States, and, currently, it is typical that price stability occupies top priority. The usual interpretation of price stability means keeping inflation low, not necessarily the absence of it. Indeed, much recent attention has been given to the possibility of deflation – a sustained and pervasive decline in prices. Japan had major problems with deflation in the 1990s, and the United States experienced it in the 1930s. While the Fed considers deflation unlikely in the United States today, the subject has received attention in policy discussions, during the 2002–2003 period and, most recently, when interest rates have approached zero. The effects of deflation can be devastating to an economy, because production stops, jobs are lost, and recession generally follows.

In short, the Federal Reserve and most central banks desire to achieve price stability and high employment, neither of which they can control directly. But they must operate through the financial system using the short-term goals over which they do have control, such as interest rates and the supply of money. I would argue, as I have often had to do in the past when I am asked to explain Fed policy to individuals or groups, that the short- and long-term objectives are consistent and compatible, notwithstanding the Phillips curve and other arguments to the contrary. My reasoning is that price stability generally goes with interest rate stability, and interest rate stability means a stable investment climate. Because encouragement of business investment in the short run means higher employment and growth in the long run, we achieve our long-range objectives by focusing in the short term on price stability.

The Instruments (Tools) of Monetary Policy

The Fed must work with the tools it is given and within a framework that will achieve the objectives that are best for the economy. The traditional tools of monetary policy are discount rate policy, reserve requirement policy, and open market operations. The first two of these were discussed in some depth in Chap. 3, and we shall devote most of our attention in this chapter to the third, open market operations, which have become over the years the most important tool of monetary policy.

There are still other tools. One that we have mentioned earlier is moral suasion, which might be more appropriately described as a means of avoiding the use of overt policy actions by persuading someone else, such as the banking system or a consortium of individual banks, to do the job for the central bank. We illustrated this approach in the LTCM hedge fund example.

There is also a potential fifth tool – the decision by Congress in 2008 to require the Fed to pay interest on both required and excess reserve balances. This action gave the Fed another tool, if it chooses to use it, and Chairman Ben Bernanke has said that the Fed will use it at the right time. For example, if the Fed decides to raise the rate it pays on reserve balances, this would be a tightening move for policy because it would draw in reserves from the banking system, which is a reduction of the money supply. To lower the rate it pays on balances would be an easing move because it would encourage banks to withdraw funds from their Fed accounts, thus increasing the money supply. Bear in mind that money in the hands of the Fed is no longer money. To be part of the money supply, money must be in the hands of the private banking system or the public at large. Action that the Fed might take to change this rate has the effect of putting a floor under market rates because banks would not lend in the Federal Funds market at rates lower than they could receive from the Fed on reserve balances. Some advisers have urged the Fed to use this tool recently, to lower the rate it pays on reserve balances, perhaps even to zero, to flush out the funds into the banking system and encourage lending to private consumers and businesses. Instead, the Fed has pursued other means of increasing liquidity in the economy.

The tools of the central bank are blunt instruments in that they impact the entire economy, not just particular sectors or regions. The Fed has been criticized in years past for not directing assistance to industries, such as housing, energy, education, and agriculture. It argues, however, that it cannot do so with the blunt instruments that it has, and it could also be argued that it would be inappropriate to do so because other public policies and agencies have been set up by the government to do these jobs. Thus, the Fed says it does not, and should not, engage in credit allocation. It would be disingenuous not to observe, however, that this is no longer quite a true statement. Because of the extreme circumstances that developed after 2007 with the housing sector and the mortgage market, the Fed was forced to buy mortgages from banks and from Freddie and Fannie, thus pumping money into housing, in order to avoid a complete collapse of that industry. We shall see other instances in which the Fed has had to depart from this well-established rule because the banking crisis became the whole economy's crisis.

Discount Rate Policy

As we have noted, the discount rate is the rate the Fed charges on overnight loans – and, more recently, on longer-term loans – to banks.

Please note that this section is, to some degree, repetitive of the discussion in Chap. 3, on borrowing from the central bank. It is useful, however, to review certain facts. See also the table of money rates on pages 42–43 for the discount rate and the Federal Funds rate.

Raising or lowering the discount rate influences the willingness of banks to borrow and sends a highly visible signal from the Fed regarding the direction of monetary policy. Under the old discount window policy – before 2003 – the discount window was a closely administered process. The "lender-of-last-resort" philosophy prevailed, and banks were not necessarily welcome to borrow. These tight-fisted policies resulted in a period of several decades in which the discount window was used very little. The amount borrowed was minuscule, and banks instead turned to the Federal Funds market as a funding source. The discount window was dormant for an extended period.

Now, under the new "market-oriented" discount policy, changes in the discount rate are viewed as somewhat more sensitive signals of policy. The reductions in the discount rate beginning in August 2007, through December 2008, not only increased lending significantly but also sent a strong signal to the markets of an ease in monetary policy. These moves, combined with the temporary use of the Term Auction Facility that we discussed in Chap. 3, helped to dispel some of the crisis mentality associated with the subprime mortgage collapse.

Reserve Requirement Policy

The second policy instrument is the setting of reserve requirements. Again, this was discussed in Chap. 3, where we first raised the issue of required reserves. But let us review certain facts regarding how this requirement relates to monetary policy.

Changes in reserve requirements can have a powerful effect on bank reserves and on the potential multiple expansion of reserves throughout the banking system. But this tool is rarely used by the Fed. The last change was in April 1992, when the marginal rate was lowered from 12 % to its present 10 % level. This change was made when the Fed was trying to stimulate the economy, coming out of the "white collar" recession of the early 1990s.

The reserve requirement level was set by law in the early years of the Fed. It was not until the 1930s that Congress gave the Fed the ability to change it, and that is limited even today. The theory was that large money center banks should carry higher levels of reserves than smaller banks because they would have to provide the cushion in the case of runs on banks or massive bank failures – the pyramiding effect. This theory is still reflected, though to a lesser degree, in the three-tier breakdown that continues to exist.

Changes in reserve requirements are used more frequently by a number of foreign central banks than in the United States – for example, China. A reason is that financial markets are not as highly developed in many countries as they are in the United States and other highly industrialized nations. Therefore, open market operations are not as effective in those countries. Some countries, either by law or by central bank policy, have totally done away with reserve requirements on banks.

References

1. Meltzer AH (2003) A history of the federal reserve, volume I: 1913–1951. The University of Chicago Press, Chicago, p 65
2. Liaquat A (2009) Lords of finance: the bankers that broke the world. Penguin Books, New York, p 175
3. Alice M. Rivlin (2012) The case for preserving the federal reserve's dual mandate. Testimony before the House Financial Service Committee, 8 May 2012
4. Mankiw NG (2006) Macroeconomics, 6th edn. Worth, New York, p 391

Chapter 12
How Is American Monetary Policy Made, and How Does It Affect the Domestic and Global Economies?

Open Market Policy

The third and most powerful tool of monetary policy is open market operations. This involves the buying and selling of Treasury securities in the open market. As the Fed pays for securities that it buys, it puts funds into the banking system, which raises bank reserves and causes lower interest rates. Conversely, as the Fed is paid for securities that it sells, it draws funds from the banking system, which reduces reserves and causes an increase in interest rates.

It is important to remember that the central bank is prohibited by law from buying securities directly from the Treasury, nor can it lend directly to the Treasury. Its transactions must be conducted in the private markets, that is, the open market. Thus, it pays or receives the same prices for its trades that all other investors face. The logic behind this restriction is that the central bank is prevented from directly monetizing the government's debt, as happens in some other countries. Even though the purchase of Treasuries in the open market indirectly provides a market for the government debt, the restriction at least avoids any kind of collusion regarding pricing, and subjects the Fed to the same market conditions as other investors.

This procedure was not thought of as a monetary policy tool in the earliest days of the Fed. But, as the Federal Reserve Bank of New York bought and sold securities for its own account, notice was taken of the impact its actions were having on conditions in the market. Thus, open market operations as a tool of monetary policy were discovered, in effect, by accident. Over time, and through the efforts of Benjamin Strong, they became a major focus of monetary policy and, as we have noted, were officially recognized in 1935 with the creation of the Federal Open Market Committee. A number of other central banks today have functions that resemble the Fed's open market operations.

Open market operations have become the most flexible and most effective tool of monetary policy for several reasons. First, they are daily operations; a decision is made each and every business day on what the policy of the day shall be – easing,

W.H. Wallace, *The American Monetary System: An Insider's View of Financial Institutions, Markets and Monetary Policy*, DOI 10.1007/978-3-319-02907-8_12, © Springer International Publishing Switzerland 2013

tightening, or no action at all. Second, policy actions can be small or large, as need dictates. Third, they can respond quickly to changes in market conditions. Fourth, there are several techniques the Fed can use to achieve a particular result, such as the use of outright sales or purchases or the use of repurchase agreements that give the Fed the added flexibility of reviewing the effect of a decision the next day, and either reversing it, confirming it, or taking a different action. Finally, the Fed has a choice of whether to focus its actions in the short-term or the long-term end of the Treasury market, depending upon which particular part of the interest rate structure it is trying to affect.

Amounts of daily activity may range from no action at all to several billions. The Fed buys and sells from its portfolio of Treasury securities in the System Open Market Account (SOMA), of $1.8 trillion, owned outright as of March 20, 2013. See the Federal Reserve System balance sheet below.[1] In addition, the Fed holds $72.4 billion in government agency securities, a large share of which are mortgage-backed bonds issued by Fannie Mae and Freddie Mac.

Federal reserve system consolidated balance sheet

	$ Millions	
Assets	November 21, 2007	March 20, 2013
Gold certificate account	11,041	11,037
Special drawing rights account	2,200	5,200
Coin	1,178	2,120
US government and agency securities, repurchase agreements, term auction credit, and other loans		
Held outright		
Bills	267,019	0
Notes and bonds	470,984	1,694,972
Notes and bonds, inflation indexed	36.911	78,879
Inflation compensation	4,756	10,802
Federal agency debt securities	0	72,423
Mortgage-backed securities	0	1,085,507
Total securities held outright	779,670	2,942,583
Repurchase agreements	55,000	0
Loans	58	392
Special advances by FRBNY to bank and nonbank financial institutions	0	1,886
Items in process of collection	4,365	497
Bank premises	2,114	2,303
Central bank liquidity swaps	0	7,965
Other assets	38,848	234,572
Total assets	894,474	3,208,553
Liabilities		
Federal reserve notes outstanding, net of FR bank holdings	786,377	1,132,556
Reverse repurchase agreements	35,383	92,925

(continued)

---

[1] www.federalreserve.gov/releases/H-4.1/current.

(continued)

Assets	$ Millions	
	November 21, 2007	March 20, 2013
Deposits		
Term deposits held by depository institution	0	3,045
Other deposits held by depository institutions	20,967	1,756,224
US Treasury general account	5,324	71,131
Foreign official accounts	96	8,952
Other	306	74,562
Deferred availability cash items	3,088	1,138
Other liabilities and accrued dividends	5,896	12,925
Total liabilities	857,437	3,153,459
Capital accounts		
Capital, paid-in	18,089	27,547
Surplus	15,457	27,547
Other capital accounts	3,488	0
Total capital	37,034	55,094

It also holds $1.1 trillion in mortgage-backed securities that it bought from banks to support them during the recent crisis. While the Fed could use any of these categories of securities for open market operations, it traditionally uses only its holdings of Treasuries for this purpose. In recent years, normal open market operations have increasingly used repurchase agreements (repos), instead of outright purchases and sales. With repos, the Fed buys or sells a certain amount with the understanding that it will reverse the transaction the next day or a few days later.

Also, most activity in the open market has tended to focus on the short-term end of the spectrum of securities, such as Treasury bills. These actions are reflected in the left end of the yield curve. See the graph on page 134. The Fed can shift the focus, however, to the longer maturities, depending upon market conditions. For example, in 2011, after short-term rates had been driven virtually to zero, the Fed announced a policy of conducting open market operations in the medium range of maturities, such as 2- to 7-year notes. The press referred to this change of policy as quantitative easing (QE). The Fed bought securities in these longer ranges to bring down long-term rates.

The Fed at times has also pursued a policy called "Operation Twist," in which they will buy in one end of the range and sell in another. It tried this approach in 2012 by buying in the longer end of the spectrum and selling in the shorter end. The effect of this on the total money supply is netted out, but it has the effect of shifting rates, raising short-term rates and lowering longer-term rates, thus twisting the yield curve. The Fed's reasoning on this was that lower long-term rates would help to boost the lagging housing industry.

At the beginning of the recent financial crisis in 2007, the Fed injected liquidity heavily in the markets through open market operations. Two peak days occurred in November 2007, when on the 27th they injected $14.5 billion and on the next day, $26 billion, through purchases of securities. These were extraordinarily large amounts, and they were done in an effort to stem the impact of the forthcoming recession.

Operations of this size cause considerable volatility in the Federal Funds market, and in this instance, caused the Federal Funds rate to drop by 150 basis points below its target, then set at 4.5 %. Overall, the Fed was successful in keeping the banking system moving smoothly as credit markets were on the verge of freezing up. Other central banks were having the same problem, as the dumping of mortgage-backed bonds was taking place around the world. The ECB, for example, injected 50 billion Euros into the European markets in this period. It is interesting to speculate how high interest rates would have gone if the central banks had not taken these actions.

To put the Fed's holdings in perspective, and to see what its capacity for dealing with markets actually is, consider the size of the SOMA in relation to the overall US debt outstanding. See the two tables below.

The first table shows the Federal Reserve's holdings in SOMA to be $1.8 trillion, which is 10.7 % of total US debt. This part of the federal debt is virtually costless to the Treasury because the interest the Fed receives on it is paid back each year to the Treasury, net of the Fed's own operating expenses. In 2012, the Fed returned to the Treasury $88.9 billion from its total net income of $91 billion. The difference was the Fed's operating expenses for the year.

Structure of the US government debt, March 25, 2013[a]

Total treasury debt outstanding	$16.8 trillion
Intra-governmental holdings	$ 4.9 trillion
Owned by the public	$11.9 trillion
Total foreign holdings (see table below for details)	$5.6 trillion
Federal reserve system holdings	$1.8 trillion

[a]www.treasurydirect.gov/NP/BPD

Major foreign holders of US debt, March 25, 2013 ($ billions)[a]

China, Mainland	1,264.5
Japan	1,115.2
Oil exporters	262.0
Brazil	253.4
Caribbean Banking Centers	236.4
Taiwan	196.6
Switzerland	192.7
Russia	162.9
Luxembourg	144.7
Belgium	143.5
Hong Kong	142.9
United Kingdom	135.7
Ireland	107.4
Others, below $100 billion each	1,258.6
Total, foreign held 5,616.5 (33.4 % of outstanding US debt)	

[a]www.treasury.gov/resource-center/data-chart-center/tic/documents/mfh.txt

The second table clearly shows the popularity of US Treasury securities all over the world, as 33.4 % or \$5.6 trillion of our debt is held by foreign investors – governments, central banks, financial institutions, businesses, and individuals. One can be sure that these foreign investors would not be willing to continue to hold American debt if it were not considered safe and if it did not represent a reasonable return on their investments. It is important to note that foreign investors seek Dollar-denominated securities because of their safety and reliability – not because the United States asks them to do so, which is an impression often left by the press and by politicians.

It is also useful to compare the Treasury debt with other debt outstanding in the US economy. The table below gives an interesting comparison of US Treasury debt to other forms of both public and private debt, as of the end of the first quarter, 2010, when Treasury debt was only \$12.9 trillion.

Total US public and private debt, March 31, 2010

Federal government debt	\$12.9 trillion
State and local government debt	2.4 trillion
Household sector debt	13.5 trillion
Nonfinancial business sector debt	10.9 trillion
Financial sector debt	15.0 trillion
Total	\$54.7 trillion

After reviewing the above figures, it is difficult to believe that at the end of the decade of the 1990s, the United States ran three years of budget surpluses. Studies were done to consider alternatives to holding Treasury debt if there should be a total payoff. What would the Fed use for open market operations and for collateral for the currency? Consideration was given to corporate, municipal, and foreign debt. Later, however, this became a purely academic question – as recent tax reductions, two wars, and economic slowdown cast doubt on any possibility of debt elimination, although debate continues on how to reduce the Treasury's debt, and the political pressure to do so continues. For further explanation of items on the Federal Reserve's balance sheet, see the section beginning on page 206.

While it is important, as we have noted, for a central bank to hold Treasuries to conduct open market operations, let us consider one little-understood fact about central banking. Irrespective of its holdings of securities or anything else, a unique function of a central bank is that it can simply create money. The lending of funds through the discount window and the recent auction of funds are examples. The Fed simply credits the deposit accounts of banks and debits loans to banks, and money has been created – often referred to in the media as the use of the "printing press," which is, of course, a misnomer. And the banking system can further expand on this through its own lending; remember the discussion of the multiple expansions of bank deposits in Chap. 4.

Setting the Targets

To understand how decisions are made in the policy process, we must consider the targets of open market operations. The short-range targets, as we noted, are stated either as a rate of money supply growth or as a rate of interest. Obviously, the money supply and interest rates move inversely to each other, so that a target to lower money supply growth is tantamount to a target to raise interest rates, and vice versa. Interest rates have been the Fed's principal targets continuously for three decades. Traditionally, the rate targeted is the Federal Funds rate. However, since the financial downturn that began in 2007, monetary policy has forced the Federal Funds rate to near zero, in an attempt to boost the economy. Therefore, since 2011, longer-term rates have been used as targets for monetary policy.

Within recent years, increased attention has been given to other targets, such as an inflation target. Motivation to do this is varied, ranging from an attempt to make the Fed more credible by adopting a rule that the financial community and the public can more easily understand, to that of simply removing some of the Fed's discretion in setting monetary policy. If the target were mandated by law, it would be a "rule-based" monetary policy.

Chairman Ben Bernanke, in his career as an economist before becoming Fed Chair, was a strong advocate of inflation targeting [1]. He and others were able to show in studies of the United Kingdom, Canada, and New Zealand, that the adoption of inflation targeting by their central banks had resulted in lower and more stable rates of inflation over almost two decades in each case. Previous Chairman, Alan Greenspan, opposed the idea, because he wanted to retain as much flexibility as possible for the FOMC in its policy decisions.

After he became Chairman, however, Mr. Bernanke clarified his position and indicated that he was not for a rule that tied the Fed's hands, but favored a "flexible" inflation targeting approach. He explained this by saying that, if our inflation target were set at 2 %, and we approached that level, but unemployment were still unacceptably high, he would not tighten policy immediately in order to meet the 2 % target. This clarification seemed to satisfy others on the FOMC who had opposed the idea, and at its meeting in January 2012, the FOMC, for the first time, officially adopted a 2 % inflation target.

Among other rule-based approaches that have been advocated, one of the most seriously considered was that of Milton Friedman, a well-known 20th century economist whose contributions to monetary policy have been enormous. Friedman's view was that the Fed should follow a policy of money supply growth, which is roughly equivalent to the rate of real growth of the economy. He believed that this approach would assure non-inflationary economic growth. His views were supported by many, both within and outside the Fed, but were never implemented.

Another controversy regarding the targeting of monetary policy, which has developed in recent years, is that of using policy to burst bubbles in asset prices – first, equities, then real estate. Some critics of the Fed believe that it should have raised interest rates in the late 1990s to stop the sharp rises in stock prices. Chairman

Greenspan argued that to do so would erase real values, and that one cannot tell a bubble from a justified increase in asset prices or values. He felt that, since the Fed's tools are blunt instruments, a small increase might not be enough to accomplish the purpose and that a large increase could cause recession. He was saying, in effect, that the market should decide, and the Fed should not interfere.

This debate about attacking bubbles continues because of the mortgage crisis. As we noted earlier, one of the principal criticisms of the Fed in the most recent recession is that it failed to use its regulatory authority to stop the expansion of the bubble in housing prices. Again, Mr. Greenspan did not favor doing so. Critics say that letting the bubble grow makes the inevitable crash worse than if earlier action were taken. In view of the devastating impact of the recent recession on the economy, this debate is likely to continue about whether "bubble busting" is an appropriate target of monetary policy because other asset-price-based crises will undoubtedly occur. It is interesting to note that the ECB has recently argued that a central bank should attempt to control asset prices, but there is no evidence that the ECB has ever tried to do so. Despite its short life and limited experience, not to mention its disastrous performance in handling the current European financial crisis, the ECB, nevertheless, is usually quick to lecture other central banks about how they should do their jobs.

The Shift from Interest Rate to Money Supply Targeting

The Fed has moved at various times from one kind of targeting to another. In August 1979, Paul Volcker was named Chairman of the Federal Reserve Board. The decade of the 1970s had been the worst period of inflation in the United States in the postwar period and remains the worst on record. Many things had been tried. President Richard Nixon had attempted price controls, which failed. President Gerald Ford came up with the idea of a new program called "Whip Inflation Now." It was a voluntary program, and virtually everyone in Washington, including me, had to wear a 5-inch-wide "WIN" button. This failed. President Jimmy Carter came in with the appeal to all Americans to tear up their credit cards – another voluntary program that failed.

Chairman Volcker knew that voluntary programs would never work in killing inflation, which was then at an annual rate of nearly 17 %. He also knew that the correct prescription was to tighten monetary policy. He came home from an international meeting in October 1979 in which he had been besieged by central bankers and finance ministers in other countries who complained that the United States was exporting inflation to them. They made it clear that they looked to him to do something about America's inflation problem. Volcker called the FOMC to a special meeting on Saturday, October 6. He explained his timing of the meeting by stating that he wanted to make a public announcement of a change in monetary policy before the markets opened the following Monday.

He persuaded the FOMC to support him unanimously in a move to change the target for monetary policy from interest rates to the money supply. He announced that the Fed would "cut back sharply on the rate of growth of the money supply" in order to get inflation under control. He could just as well have said the Fed will increase interest rates, but he thought that to couch it in terms of the money supply would be more politically acceptable. He was counting on the fact that people would not recognize that this move meant the same thing as increasing interest rates. He was right. This is the action that I referenced earlier, as one that was taken despite the knowledge that it would be disruptive to the markets. But, in Volcker's mind, and in those of the other FOMC members, it was necessary and worth the cost to rid the economy of inflation.

The tightening action that was taken drove the Federal Funds rate to 20 %; the prime rate exceeded 21.5 %. The economy went into recession. But inflation was killed. The effect of these actions can be seen in the graph of the Federal Funds rate below.[2]

Shortly after the period of tight money began, in late 1979, Chairman Volcker was invited to speak to a group of business people in the Washington area. During the Q&A session after his speech, he was asked, "Why are you doing this? Why do interest rates have to be so high? You're killing the housing industry, and you're killing the auto industry! Nobody can buy anything on credit anymore." Volcker's response was, "Well, it's like the story of the farmer who was seen out in the field beating his mule over the head with a 2×4. An irate passerby stopped and asked the farmer, 'Why are you beating that poor mule?' The farmer said, 'If I expect to get any work out of him, I have to get his attention first.'" Then, Volcker went on to say, "That's what we're trying to do, is to get peoples' attention focused on the dangers of inflation."

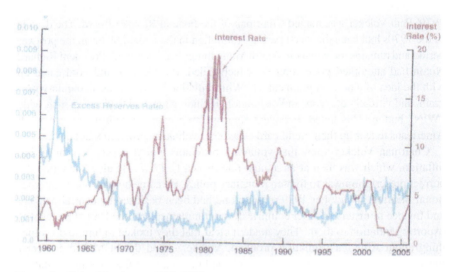

The market Federal Funds rate, 1960–2005

[2] www.federalreserve.gov/releases/h3/hist/.

The press picked up on this story, and Volcker's answer was read all over the country. After that, he began to receive 2×4s in the mail, usually about 8–10 in. in length, and in total, he received over 7,000 of them. Some people sent bricks; auto dealers mailed in boxes of car keys with the message, "You might as well have the keys! We can't sell the cars at these interest rates." I stopped into Volcker's office and asked him if I could keep one of the 2×4s as a memento. I told him I thought we were at a historic moment for monetary policy – one that probably would be talked about for years to come. And so it has!

So I keep this 2×4 in my office, and I take it to my money and banking class when we get into the discussion of Fed policy, and explain to the students that it is an instrument of monetary policy. It was an effective form of protest, but it did not cause Volcker to vary for one minute from the course of action that he believed was best for the country.

A few months later, I was waiting for a flight at National Airport in Washington, when I ran into my first economics professor, who at that time was the Secretary of Labor. He walked up to me and said, "I'm holding you personally responsible for this disaster we have on our hands. You guys have cost the American economy a half-trillion Dollars in real output, and it's all your fault." I responded, "Well, professor, I would be happy to take credit for the Volcker policy because I think it was the right thing to do. But you have to remember that I'm only the Staff Director. I'm not a voting member of the Board." He replied, "Yeah, I know that, but as Staff Director, you're the one who tells them what to do." So, while I knew this whole conversation was "tongue-in-cheek," I felt good about getting a little of the "blame" for it.

Now, some 30 years after the fact, Volcker is given credit for having killed inflation and having thus set the stage for the prosperity of the decades that followed. Both of his successors, Greenspan and Bernanke, have praised him for his stubbornness in pursuing an anti-inflation policy when it was so unpopular. In fact, I was pleased to note that Chairman Bernanke, in a recent lecture to students at George Washington University, said he still proudly displays his 2×4 that Volcker had given him. While inflation is still there, of course, and it has had its ups and downs, it has moved in a fairly narrow band, and it has never again approached the levels we experienced in the 1970s.

The Return to Interest Rates

After this unusual period of tight policy, the Fed went back to interest rate targeting. William Greider describes this move as an abandonment of monetarism. He errs in saying this because the Fed never adopted monetarism. They simply set a money supply target as a mechanism for raising interest rates, knowing that it would be temporary [2].

The recession was soon over, and expansion began again in the fall of 1982.[3] Had the Fed been less independent, or more subject to political control, it would not have

_____

[3] For a more detailed discussion of Volcker's fight against inflation, see William L. Silber [3], pp. 125, 180, 237.

been allowed to get by with these actions. One prominent economist noted at the time that "…central banks around the world seem to have ganged up on inflation, fought the fight, and won." It is true that governments and central banks began to realize in the 1990s that if they were to be active participants in a globalizing world economy, to trade with other nations, and especially, to become members of free trade zones or monetary unions, they would have to come to grips with the problem of inflation which they had ignored for generations.

The IMF's consumer price index for industrial countries showed an annual rate of inflation over 12 % in 1980, but by 2002 the rate had dropped to just 1.4 %. In the United States, consumer price inflation – excluding food and energy, or the core rate – fell from 12.4 % in 1980 to 2.4 % in 2002. This transition to a world of lower inflation and less frequent occurrences of recession was referred to as the "Great Moderation." This lasted until mid-2007, when the bottom dropped out.

The Federal Open Market Committee

In discussing what is involved in deciding the policy to pursue at any given time, let's consider the preparation for the FOMC meeting at which these decisions are made. The Committee meets eight times a year (twice per quarter) in Washington, usually convening on a Tuesday. Participants in the meetings are the seven members of the BOG, the 12 reserve bank presidents and certain key staff members. Though all participate in the discussions, only the 12 voting members actually vote.

There are three books prepared prior to each meeting. First, the *Beige Book* is distributed to all participants two weeks in advance of the meeting. It contains a summary of economic conditions by district, obtained by survey within each district, and a national summary. This is "grass-roots" information based on questionnaires and discussions conducted in each of the 12 districts of key business people, academics, consumer groups, union leaders, etc. Thus, it is often fresher information than published statistics, which usually lag changes in actual conditions. The *Beige Book* could be considered a leading indicator of economic conditions overall. The information is released to the public and usually gets considerable press coverage, especially if it contains any hint of a change of direction in the economy.

The second book is the *Green Book*, prepared by the BOG staff, and is released to the FOMC participants on the Thursday prior to each meeting. It contains an up-to-date summary of the economy, global and domestic, as well as the staff's projections about the future – assuming no change in policy. The book is kept confidential because of the staff forecasts.

The third book is the *Blue Book*, released to the participants the day before the meeting. It contains current financial market conditions, and draws heavily upon information supplied by the BOG staff and by the New York reserve bank staff. The book contains policy options for the Committee to consider, but does not contain a policy recommendation. This book is also kept confidential.

The policy options are always couched in terms of three choices, options A, B and C. Option A is a move toward greater ease; option B means staying the present course, and option C is a move toward more restrictive conditions. And there might be variations within each, for example, from moderately stimulative to very stimulative. There are periods of time, of course, when certain of the options might not be relevant. During the recent period of economic recession, Option C has not been considered because it would be totally inappropriate under the circumstances. However, at turning points, all the options come under serious consideration. There will be a time, for example, when a robust recovery of the American economy begins, that debate will begin to focus on moving from option A to option B, and perhaps even further to option C, if inflation threats become more pronounced. In any event, the staff is always prepared to discuss with the participants the consequences of a particular course of action.

The meeting agenda will consist of a staff presentation of the key information in the *Green* and *Blue Books,* a special presentation on international financial conditions, and a discussion led by the "Manager of the Open Market Desk" as to how he or she sees the financial market situation at that time.

The Manager of the Desk is a senior official of the Federal Reserve Bank of New York, whose responsibility it will be to implement and put into effect whatever action the FOMC decides upon. The trading department at the New York Fed is commonly referred to as "the Desk."

After the presentations, there will be considerable discussion by all participants, during which a consensus might emerge as to the direction and the degree of any policy move to be taken. The outputs of various econometric models will be considered, including the Fed's own FRB/US Model and its FRB/Global Model, as well as the judgmental forecasts of various members who draw on the research efforts of the staffs at the reserve banks and at the BOG. The Chairman's role in this process is interesting because it tends to shift with each successive chairman. William McChesney Martin, who was Chairman when I joined the Fed in the mid-1960s, and his successor Arthur F. Burns, who had been a retired Columbia University economics professor before he became Chairman in 1970, were always consensus seekers. They tended to hold back at the meetings until they had heard the views of the others around the table. Chairman Paul Volcker[4] was somewhat more forward with his views and would often state them up front. One never had any difficulty knowing where Volcker stood on policy issues. Alan Greenspan then returned to a more consensus-seeking approach, and, today, Chairman Ben Bernanke tends to follow the same pattern.

If a consensus emerges in the discussion, the Chairman will usually state how he reads that consensus. If one has not emerged, the Chairman will state his preference; then others will react. A vote is finally taken. It may or may not be unanimous, and those who do not agree will submit a statement as to the reason for their dissent.

---

[4] Paul A. Volcker succeeded Arthur F. Burns in 1979, after the brief 18-month chairmanship of G. William Miller, who was appointed to the Fed in 1978 by President Carter and subsequently moved to the position of Secretary of the Treasury in 1979. Miller was a businessman who had been CEO of Textron and was the only non-economist to serve as Chairman since William McChesney Martin, who served 1951–1970.

Then a public announcement is made of the outcome of the meeting. Most meetings are one-day only, but often, two-day meetings will be held to hear additional presentations or the results of research that has been completed. In any event, the announcement is typically made, in the form of a press release, at 2:15 p.m., Eastern Time, on the final day of the meeting. This release explains the action that was taken and the reasoning behind it, who voted for it, and who dissented from it, and their reasons. The release will often also express the way the Committee is leaning on policy issues – sometimes called "the bias" – whether a change in policy has been made or not. Before the next meeting, a further release is made of the actual minutes of the previous meeting. A recent development, under Chairman Bernanke's leadership, is that he holds a full, detailed press conference just after the meeting, once per quarter, and he patiently answers questions from the press.

The practice of releasing the actions of the FOMC is of recent origin. Chairman Greenspan felt strongly that this needed to be done to make the Fed more open to the public and to increase public understanding of what the Fed was trying to accomplish. The process of issuing press releases after each meeting started in 1994, but was done only when a change in policy had been made. Then, in 2000, it was changed to a process of issuing press releases whether or not a change in policy was made. Greenspan's view was that often the decision not to make a change in policy is of as much significance as that of making a change.

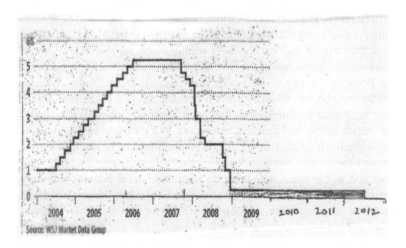

The target Federal Funds rate, 2003–2012

The wording of press releases is sometimes enigmatic. Compare the following excerpts from announcements of the FOMC of November 1, 2005, and later (italics are mine). This was a period in which the FOMC was gradually raising rates. Beginning in June 2004, when rates had reached their lowest level in history – a 1 % Federal Funds rate – the FOMC began raising rates 25 basis points at a time at each meeting for 17 successive meetings, increasing the Federal Funds target rate from 1 % to 5.25 %. See the graph of the target rate above.

The FOMC decided on November 1, 2005, to raise the target rate by 25 basis points to 4 %. Its press release read as follows:

> The Committee perceives that, with appropriate monetary policy action, the upside and downside risks to the attainment of both sustainable growth and price stability should be kept roughly equal. With underlying inflation expected to be contained, the Committee believes that policy *accommodation* can be removed at a pace that is likely to be *measured*. Nonetheless, the Committee will respond to changes in economic prospects as needed to fulfill its obligation to maintain price stability.

Then, after its next meeting, of December 12, 2005, it said:

> The Committee judges that some further *measured* policy firming *is likely to be needed* to keep the risks to the attainment of both sustainable economic growth and price stability roughly in balance. In any event, the Committee will respond to changes in economic prospects as needed to foster these objectives.

To translate the language of these releases from "Fed-speak," the term *accommodation* means ease. After the November 1 meeting, the Committee was saying that it is removing accommodation, or that it is tightening. But, it was saying that it will do this in a *measured* way, which means gradually. After the December 12th meeting, the Committee was saying that it will be very likely to continue to tighten but will do so gradually. Then, after the meeting of June 29, 2006, when the target Federal Funds rate reached 5.25 %, or the point at which the Committee planned to stop tightening, it said the following:

> Although the moderation in the growth of aggregate demand should help to limit inflationary pressures over time, the Committee judges that some inflation risks remain. The extent and timing of any additional firming that *may* be needed to address these risks will depend on the *evolution of the outlook* for both inflation and economic growth…etc.[5]

Here, the Committee was not saying that it will not tighten further, but that it does not seem necessary. If the outlook should change, however, and the threat of inflation recurs, the Committee will consider tightening again.

By the time of the third quote, it was perceived that the FOMC believed it was out of the period of accommodation and had possibly reached the "neutral rate." While the Fed itself does not usually use the term *neutral rate*, analysts of monetary policy use it to mean a rate that is not so low as to stimulate inflation, and not so high as to suppress real growth. In any event, it can be seen in the graph on page 194 that the FOMC regarded the Federal Funds rate of 5.25 % as satisfactory for an extended period, until the onset of the recession in late 2007. It can also be seen how rapidly the FOMC brought the target rate down in response to the recession. It had reached its current level of 0.25 % by December 2008.

In the press release after the more recent FOMC meeting of October 24, 2012, the Committee said,

> To support continued progress toward maximum employment and price stability, the Committee expects that a highly *accommodative* stance of monetary policy will remain appropriate for a considerable time after the economic recovery strengthens. In particular,

---

[5] www.federalreserve.gov/releases, Nov. 1, 2005; Dec. 12, 2005; June 29, 2006.

the Committee also decided today to keep the target range for the federal funds rate at
0–1/4 % and currently anticipates that exceptionally low levels for the federal funds rate are
likely to be warranted at least through mid-2015.[6]

In this press release, the FOMC also stated that it intended to continue buying
Treasury securities in the longer-term end of the maturity spectrum to try to keep
long-terms rates low to benefit the housing sector, which is a strong engine of overall economic recovery. Also, in his remarks to the press following that meeting, and
after being pressed by reporters as to what circumstances might cause a shift in
monetary policy to a more tightening mode, Chairman Bernanke stated that he
would not consider departing from the accommodative policy until the unemployment rate reached 6.5 %. In mid-2013, the policy of accommodation is still in
place, but evidence is increasing that the Fed is contemplating a tightening of
policy sooner than the 2015 estimated date, in light of growing improvement in the
economic recovery.

Before the FOMC adjourns, a "directive" is prepared stating the action of the
Committee and directing the Manager of the Desk to carry out whatever operations
he or she feels are needed to meet the FOMC's objectives until the next meeting.
While voting members agree at the meeting on the wording of the directive, it actually states essentially the same information as the press release, but on some occasions may provide some further detail, for example, on the assumptions that underlie
the decisions that were made. In truth, the Manager, currently Brian P. Sack,
Executive Vice President of the New York reserve bank, does not need the directive,
because he has participated in the meeting and knows in detail what the Committee
expects. But it has become a formality. The Manager sticks the directive in his
pocket, takes the train back to New York, and begins the next day to take actions to
carry out his instructions.

Open Market Operations

Open market operations are the day-to-day activities to implement the FOMC directive. The Manager works with a group of 18 "primary dealers." Membership in this
group rotates each year from among the total population of government securities
dealers who have been previously "qualified" to trade directly with the Federal
Reserve. To qualify requires that the dealer maintain at least $150 million in capital,
agree to participate in all purchases and sales conducted by the Desk, and be willing
to buy or sell the quantities needed to meet the Desk's requirements on any given day.

For example, say the Desk is selling $500 million in 90-day Treasury bills on
overnight repurchase agreements. The dealer firm bidding the highest price will be
given as large a quantity as it wants or can handle, and the Desk then parcels out the
remainder to the next highest bidder, and so on. The reverse applies if the Desk is
buying; dealer firms would have to come up with the needed quantity, and the Desk

---

[6] www.federalreserve.gov/newsevents/press/monetary/, October 24, 2012.

begins with the lowest offer. There are no quotas involved, as there are in the Treasury's sales of new issues of securities, such as the situation we discussed regarding Salomon Brothers in Chap. 8. The Desk's objective is to get the best deal for the Federal Reserve–that is, the highest price in the case of sales, and the lowest price in the case of purchases. Despite the responsibilities they take on, firms scramble to be selected as primary dealers because doing so is prestigious and profitable and opens doors for other business.

The primary dealers maintain accounts with the large-money-center banks, or as we have noted, may be banks themselves. When they buy, or when the Desk sells, they draw down their accounts in these banks, and bank reserves are immediately lowered. When they sell, or when the Desk buys, they deposit funds in the banks and bank reserves are immediately increased. The availability of credit to the primary dealers is therefore critical to the operation of monetary policy because the dealers often have to turn to the banks for added credit to fund the purchase of securities the Desk is selling. The money center banks therefore stand ready to lend to the primary dealers for the purpose of carrying their inventories of securities as the need arises.

If all these conditions are met, open market operations run smoothly. But recall the stock market crash of October 19, 1987, the largest percentage decline in the market's history to that point. Banks were loaned up to dealers on stocks, bonds, and government securities. Since the collateral they were holding had suddenly declined in value, banks refused to lend further to dealers. Liquidity in the market immediately dried up.

I remember the date of October 19 because I was then Chief Operating Officer of the Federal Reserve Bank of Dallas. Chairman Greenspan was coming to Dallas to address the opening session of the annual meeting of the American Bankers Association the next day. I had asked one of our senior vice presidents to go to DFW airport to pick up Mr. Greenspan and take him to his hotel. I told this driver that I knew the Chairman would want to know what happened in the market, which was already on a downward slide, so he should be prepared. (This was before cell phones.) When he arrived, Greenspan asked our driver what the market did. The driver told him it was down five-0-eight. Greenspan said, "Good! It recovered." Our driver said, "No, Mr. Chairman, that's five hundred and eight points."

When Greenspan arrived at his hotel, he received a call from President Reagan asking him to return to Washington to advise him on what to do about this crisis. This meant he would have to forego the speech he was to give the next day. On the next day, Chairman Greenspan issued a press release, containing the very simple announcement that the Fed would lend in whatever amounts necessary to the banks in order to allow them to lend the needed amounts to dealers to carry their securities. He thus guaranteed the liquidity of those markets, and this was communicated to banks all over the country. This was a use of moral suasion that worked, the markets cleared up, the logjam was broken, and within a matter of days the market had virtually recovered its losses.

While there was risk in this action, it kept the economy from going into the ditch, as it had done in 1929.

A Day at the Desk

Having reviewed the role of the primary dealers, let's go back to the Manager of the Desk. A day at the Desk is an interesting experience. During my career with the Federal Reserve, I was invited several times to spend a week at the Desk, participating in all the meetings and discussions.

The Manager begins each day with a breakfast meeting at 8:30 with invited guests from dealer firms – not only from primary dealer firms but others as well. The purpose of this meeting is to get input from the guests on their perceptions of conditions in the financial markets. If the Manager already has in mind a plan of action for the day, he or she is careful not to let the guests know what he or she is thinking. The participants understand that the Manager is not going to give away any secrets, but is strictly seeking input from them, and they are usually happy to provide information.

For example, if he or she is under a directive to lower the Federal Funds rate, or some other longer-term interest rate, the Manager will want to know whether the guests think that the market is easing of its own accord or whether it might be moving in a tightening direction. The guests are likely to know what the FOMC has directed the Manager to do because the press release is public information, but they will not know how much and when he or she is likely to take action. If the participants knew, for example, that the Manager intended to buy securities on that day, they could go into the market before the Fed action occurs and buy securities in anticipation of the price rise that will result from the Fed's action. Conversely, if they knew he or she planned to sell securities, they could go into the market and sell securities short before the Fed acts and profit from the decline in price the Fed's action would cause. Consequently, the Manager is careful not to put these advisers in a conflict-of-interest situation.

After gleaning whatever intelligence he or she can from the "street people," as they are sometimes called, the Manager will then convene a meeting of the staff, some of whom have been up all night talking with foreign central banks about any actions they may be planning in the New York markets on that day. For example, suppose the Manager is alerted to the fact that another central bank – say Korea – is coming into the New York market to buy securities on that day, and he or she had in mind a buying move also, the Manager might decide to wait another day to see how much easing results from the other central bank's action before taking action. Foreign central banks are usually willing to share such information with the New York Fed.

As another example, say that the Treasury has scheduled a new security offering on that day. This selling action will tighten the markets and put upward pressure on rates. The Manager may decide that the plan for the day needs to be an even greater easing action than originally planned to neutralize the Treasury's action and keep the markets orderly. One can easily see how complicated this decision process can get, and the need for timely and accurate information.

At any rate, from this staff meeting, a tentative course of action will have been decided. At 11:00 a.m. the Manager will make a conference call that will include two voting members of the FOMC – one member of the BOG and one reserve bank president, who rotate weekly in this role. The purpose of the call is to advise them what his or her plan is for the day and to get their concurrence. It is rare that these individuals will disagree with the Manager's plan because they know that the Manager is the most knowledgeable person in the System regarding what is happening in the markets. It is important to note also that, even if conferees disagree with the Manager, he or she can still go ahead with his plan. The only exception would be if the Chairman stops the action. As far as I know, this has never happened.

I remember sitting in on one of these 11:00 a.m. calls when Chairman Volcker, who at one time had been Manager of the Desk, decided to sit in on the call. Much discussion took place because the action being planned that day was somewhat unusual. Volcker decided to leave the call after a few minutes, and when he did, he said to the Manager, "Well, I sure hope you know what you're doing!" I thought to myself that such a comment, especially from someone like Volcker, could undermine the Manager's confidence. I asked the Manager later if that remark bothered him. He said, "No, I always get this from Volcker." And that Manager was one who definitely knew what he was doing.

Let's suppose that from these meetings the Manager has decided that the Federal Funds market is not easing sufficiently to maintain a 50-basis point reduction the FOMC has directed him or her to achieve and maintain. The Manager has therefore decided that to achieve this, the Desk should buy $500 million in 90-day Treasury bills in the open market, thus putting additional reserves into the banking system. He or she decides to do this with an overnight repurchase agreement, which provides the flexibility to watch market developments for another day. The next day the Manager can close out the repo and do no more if markets are moving in the direction desired; he or she can sustain it with another move if they are not; or, if markets are stubbornly moving in the opposite direction, the Manager can take a stronger move, perhaps through an outright purchase, and in a larger amount.

After the decision is made, the Manager enters the trading room and announces to the traders what the action will be. Each trader will contact one of the primary dealers. Nowadays, they are already online with the dealer firms. It is interesting to note that on the AP news ticker in the trading room, it takes no more than 20–25 s for the media to pick up what the Fed is doing. They get the information from the Dealers. The cable news channels, such as CNBC and Bloomberg, instantly pick it up as well. Then, the world knows that the Fed is entering the market to buy $500 million in 90-day Treasury bills on overnight repurchase agreements, and they will put whatever interpretation on this that they wish. I have timed this several times.

The traders stand by their screens to receive the return bids or offers from the dealers. The offers, as in this example, are received in a matter of minutes. They go into the computer and are displayed on a large screen overhead. A decision is quickly made on where to cut off the purchases; the transactions are implemented by wire transfer to the primary dealers' bank accounts; and the action is finished. From the time the Manager announces the plan, the action is complete within 30 min. Such is the efficiency of open market operations. I think it is easy to see why this has become the most effective way to conduct monetary policy.

We have previously mentioned the transmission mechanism, or the process by which a monetary policy decision ultimately impacts the economy at large.

After the actions that we have just reviewed are finished, the impact of these transactions feeds out to other banks and financial institutions around the country, causing the banking system as a whole to have more or less money to lend, and putting upward or downward pressure on rates. In our example, banks have more funds to lend, and interest rates are lowered.

Then, in the real, or nonfinancial, sector of the economy, businesses adjust investment plans, and consumers adjust spending plans accordingly. These increases or decreases in spending result in more or fewer jobs and more or less income. The economy as a whole either shrinks or expands. The public at large feels the impact. It is important to keep this transmission mechanism in mind because it is what makes sense out of monetary policy.

Remember that for monetary policy, the goals or mandates are set by Congress, the targets are set by the FOMC, and the Desk carries out the operations to hit the targets and achieve the goals.

Global Monetary Policy and the European Crisis

Consider what the Federal Reserve's role is in the context of global monetary policy. We have previously commented on the interdependence of monetary policies, which has been enhanced by the continuing process of globalization in the past three or more decades.

A change in American monetary policy will have an effect upon other countries, particularly our major trading partners, in several ways – exchange rates, interest rates, income, and employment. Therefore, to conduct effective monetary policy, a central bank must know what other central banks are doing. They may be required to intervene on behalf of each other to support currencies. Also, they may lend to each other to help relieve pressures in certain parts of the world. These loans are called "currency swap agreements." You will notice in the Federal Reserve System balance sheet on pages 184–185 that the Fed had $8 billion outstanding on March 20, 2013, in loans to foreign central banks. This figure reached a peak of $325 billion in the depths of the recent recession and was mainly due to the European financial crisis.

Most major industrial nations today are characterized by liberalization or elimination of capital controls, deregulation of industry and finance, and floating exchange rates. These factors have led to a globalization of asset markets. US holdings of foreign securities have increased by a factor of ten since 1980. Foreigners hold 33.4 % of US government debt, as we have noted. Ten percent of American citizens hold foreign equities, and ten percent hold foreign bonds. Foreign exchange (Forex) transaction volume surpassed $4.0 trillion per day in mid-2010 – 2.5 times the volume of a decade earlier – and it is still growing. The lion's share of this trading is in Dollars.

All of these developments have made it impossible for us to act independently of one another in financial matters, particularly in monetary policy. We have become painfully aware of this necessity since the beginning of the Greek crisis in 2010.

Then, as months passed, we observed this crisis spread to Ireland and threaten Portugal, Spain and Italy, all causing successive pressures on the Euro.

As the process of globalization has picked up speed over the last couple of decades, we have seen how the contagion effect has taken over. For example, foreigners bought heavily into mortgage-backed securities, invented in the United States, and we thus exported our financial crisis to Europe, Asia, and elsewhere. We are now importing the financial problems of Europe. This is inescapable, for as long as we have trading and financial relationships with other nations, we will feel the impact of their problems. And, currently, the European situation is a significant drag on the American economy.

When Greece's problems were first brought to the surface in mid-2010, Europeans, in their usual self-congratulatory style, were saying, "We were smart. We adopted a common currency. The Euro will save Greece." What actually happened, however, is Greece almost sank the Euro.

The irony of Europe's dilemma, especially to students of American history, is that Europe today is struggling with the same issues Americans struggled with in the 1780 and 1790 s – when we were trying to decide what the powers of our new national government would be, versus that of the states.

We settled that issue. We established a monetary union; the Constitution gave the power to issue money only to the US Congress and prohibited the states from issuing money. But, at the same time, we also set up a fiscal union. Alexander Hamilton argued, and President George Washington agreed, that the debt of the colonies would be consolidated and become the debt of the United States. This gave us a fiscal unity, in that the federal government had the power to tax and spend on behalf of the nation as a whole. The presumption was that this was in the best interests of all the states.

The act of consolidating the debt of the colonies was opposed initially by Virginia and Maryland, which were the wealthier colonies and were essentially debt-free. They, therefore, did not want to take on responsibility for the debts of the profligate colonies of Massachusetts and Connecticut. But, in the compromise of 1790, Virginia and Maryland agreed to the consolidation of the debt, if Massachusetts and Connecticut agreed to the location of the national capital on the falls of the Potomac – now Washington [4]. The similarity of those events to the European crisis of today is striking and unmistakable.

The Europeans have not yet established a fiscal union. They established only the monetary union in 1999, and this worked reasonably well for a while – the Euro became a strong currency – until problems developed with Greece in 2010. Today, they are debating the notion of authorizing the issue of Euro-zone bonds that would be collective obligations of all the 19 nations that comprise the union. They have begun to take minor steps in that direction, and these are their first moves toward a fiscal union. To complete the process, they will have to follow these initial steps with a coordination of taxing and spending policies, and a control mechanism of some kind on their overall debt. Germany has opposed this, because, while weaker countries would benefit, the strong ones, like Germany, would bear the lion's share of the cost of it.

But Germany, in July 2012, indicated that its condition for agreeing to a fiscal union would be that every member country agree to transfer control of its budget to the European Commission. This would be a very significant move in that it means each country would give up a degree of sovereignty. These developments, taken together, suggest a movement toward the United States of Europe.

A consensus seems to be building that the European Monetary Union will have to take these next steps, because Greece cannot save itself. Yet, if Greece is allowed to drop out of the Euro-zone and goes back to the Drachma, it will suffer even greater consequences. The currency will be immediately devalued by the markets, and then Greece would not be able to get credit from anyone – it would have no lifeline left to the European Community. And the other countries will suffer as well because this would set a precedent.

The Austerity Versus Stimulus Debate

A significant anomaly developed in the arena of global monetary as well as fiscal policy as a result of the recent worldwide recession. Contrary to the traditional views espoused in economic theory for generations, that nations should pursue stimulative policies – that is, lower interest rates, lower taxes, and increased government spending – in the face of serious economic recession, the exact opposite has been advocated and actually implemented by the European Union. Despite the fact that, in 2013, European countries remain deeply mired in a devastating recession, with double-digit rates of unemployment and sharp reductions in real output, they have pursued strong policies of debt reduction, decreased public spending, and higher taxes. The belief was that austerity will increase "confidence" in the future of the economy and lift it out of recession. The result has been that pursuit of austerity has made matters far worse for all economies involved. The ECB has done virtually nothing to relieve this disaster in terms of either increased lending or reduced interest rates.

Similar policies have been advocated by some members of Congress and others in the United States. Adding fuel to the fire was a study by Carmen Reinhart and Kenneth Rogoff of Harvard, which argued that rising debt causes declines in real output and production, and specifically showed that, when public debt rises above 90 % of GDP, the economy slows significantly [5]. This was all that was needed to vindicate the views of those politicians and members of Congress who advocated immediate debt reduction and other austerity measures. The only problem was that the Reinhart-Rogoff views were challenged by a group of economists at the University of Massachusetts at Amherst, who showed that Reinhart and Rogoff were wrong in their analysis and in their conclusions [6]. The data simply did not support their allegations.

It was fortunate that, due to the independence of the Federal Reserve, US monetary policy pursued stimulative measures that have kept the American economy from experiencing a repeat of the 1930s, and the same has been true of US fiscal policies, notwithstanding the views of some members of Congress. It is widely believed that as of mid-2013, the US economy is finally on a path of sustained recovery. More recently, Japan has switched to an aggressive policy of stimulus, which appears to be lifting that economy out of a long-term slump.

As of early 2013, it seemed that sentiment in favor of continued austerity in Europe is waning in light of the overwhelming evidence of the disaster it has brought those countries. Christine Lagarde, director of the IMF, to her credit, blew the whistle and pointed to the damage that austerity had caused in Europe.

In an article addressing this conundrum, Princeton economist and Nobel laureate Paul Krugman has been highly critical of the overall policy of austerity and of the work of Reinhart and Rogoff. He notes that officials and policymakers will seize upon anything that supports their point of view, and he states, "To the extent that policymakers and elite opinion in general have made use of economic analysis at all, they have done so in the way a drunk uses a lamp post: for support, not illumination" [7].

The Value of the Dollar: A Policy Question

Foreign exchange markets are sensitive to the monetary policies of all major nations. An easing of monetary policy lowers the value of the nation's currency relative to other currencies. A tightening of policy raises its relative value. Efforts to affect the value of the Dollar are monetary policy actions, carried out by the Federal Reserve intervening in the foreign exchange markets to buy or sell Dollars. While, in the American system, the Treasury decides what the overall policy on the Dollar should be, it is up to the Fed to take the actions to implement that policy.[7] But it is also true that monetary policy decisions made independently by the Fed affect the value of the Dollar, as we have just noted. Therefore, this is an area in which it is possible that the Treasury's international economic policy and the Fed's monetary policy could conflict. Surprisingly, however, they rarely do; there is unusually close cooperation in this area.

One of the ironies in this field is that the Treasury usually professes belief in a "strong Dollar." It is the politically correct thing to say, and it sounds good. But at the same time, the Fed may be pursuing policies that keep the Dollar low for various reasons – to boost US exports or to improve the trade deficit. However, there are limits as to how high or how low the Dollar should go. We have been testing these limits on the low side in recent years.

Recent US policy has been to hold the value of the Dollar down, relative to key currencies such as the Yen and the Euro. Such a policy stimulates exports, retards imports, and assists the US economic recovery. However, the risk is that such a policy at some point cuts back on foreign investment in the United States. Interest rates become no longer attractive to foreigners, who worry about the declining value

---

[7] Such trades are conducted by "The Foreign Desk," also located at the Federal Reserve Bank of New York. It is the currency trading department for the Federal Reserve and the Treasury.

of their investments. This has been the case in the past decade, as expressed by China, Japan, and Korea. The risk is a negative long-run effect of reducing the inflow of needed capital upon which the United States has depended heavily in recent decades. The inflow of foreign capital has offset America's low savings rate and has kept US interest rates much lower than they would have been otherwise. One can see from these illustrations that swings in the value of a nation's currency can have serious impacts upon the stability of its entire economy.

Many economists would argue that the level of the Dollar, or any currency, is not so much the issue as is its stability. Volatility of exchange rates hampers trade. Stability promotes trade. But, as we have said before, there is a kind of perversity in the markets that works in our favor. Despite the economic theory mentioned, the fact is that investors still seek Dollar-denominated investments, almost regardless of the Dollar's level, mainly because of the safe-haven argument. We still see this today, even as the Dollar is under great pressure, and the safe-haven argument rests on the assumption of continued stability.

Nations must make choices as to which variables they wish to control and which they will let the free market determine for them. In macroeconomic theory, there is what is called "the impossible trinity," in which the three variables are an independent monetary policy, free capital flows, and a fixed exchange rate. The theory is that a nation can have any two, but not all three [8]. See the diagram below.

The Impossible Trinity

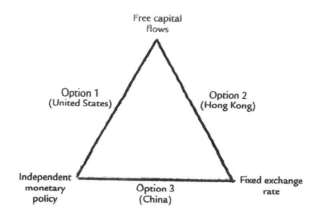

The examples used are Hong Kong, China, and the United States. Hong Kong, with a fixed exchange rate and free capital flows, does not have an independent monetary policy. China, with an independent monetary policy and a fixed exchange rate, does not have free capital flows. The United States, with an independent monetary policy and free capital flows, does not have a fixed exchange rate.

Consider the possibility, for example, that the United States were to decide to fix the exchange rate for the Dollar relative to the Euro at parity. That is, make the

Dollar equal in value to the Euro in the foreign exchange markets. We could do this by intervening in the markets to buy Dollars and perhaps selling Euros. We could force the two currencies to parity, but we would have violated the impossible trinity by attempting to achieve all three objectives at once. What would we have to give up in order to achieve this? The answer is that we would have to give up an independent monetary policy. We would have to use monetary policy to support the fixed exchange rate and would not be able to use it for other purposes, such as economic stabilization.

A Note on the Legal Status of the Federal Reserve System Within the Government of the United States

There have been questions about the legal status of the central bank since the beginning of our nation. The Bank of the United States, established in 1791, and the Second Bank of the United States, established in 1816, were intended to be central banks, in that they were given powers to perform certain activities for government under their charters granted by Congress.

The fact that they were organized as private institutions with private shareholders, and enabled to do business in the private sector in competition with other banks, was intended to strengthen them and assure their viability. Those private functions, however, were the issues that caused trouble for these banks and ultimately resulted in their demise because of charges of profiteering and corruption.

The Federal Reserve System was our third attempt at central banking in the United States, and it has also been subject to question and debate since its establishment in 1913. Some have argued that the Federal Reserve is unconstitutional because of the exclusive power granted–under Article I, Section 8, Paragraph 5, of the US Constitution–to Congress to, "coin money and regulate the value thereof" [9]. It is argued that in the Federal Reserve Act, Congress did not actually delegate those constitutional powers to the Federal Reserve System, and, therefore, some people have argued that Federal Reserve Notes issued by the Federal Reserve are not legal and that our monetary system is therefore unconstitutional.

There have been at least three US Supreme Court decisions that have assured the legal status of the Federal Reserve. The first of these pre-dates the Federal Reserve System by almost a century, but it nevertheless established a legal foundation for it. This was the case of McCulloch versus Maryland, decided in 1819, just three years into the term of the Second Bank of the United States. The circumstances of this situation were that the state of Maryland attempted to tax notes issued by the Second Bank, which were circulating in Maryland. James William McCulloch, who was in charge of the Baltimore Branch of the Second Bank, argued that the state could not tax notes issued by an agency of the Federal Government, which he contended was the status of the Second Bank. In the opinion, written by Chief Justice John Marshall, the court ruled that the state could not tax notes issued by the Second Bank, and it was further stated as part of that decision that Congress's power to establish a bank that could issue paper notes was constitutional.[8]

Subsequently, Congress passed the National Banking Act of 1863, in which it authorized the Treasury to issue paper notes in the form of fiat currency, and it established national banks, which in turn were authorized to issue paper currency (i.e., National Bank Notes) backed by Treasury securities.[9] McCulloch versus Maryland had established the constitutional foundation for these notes.

In 1917, four years after the passage of the Federal Reserve Act, another Supreme Court case was heard, challenging the constitutional status of the Federal Reserve and the notes which it had begun to issue (i.e., Federal Reserve Notes). The Supreme Court upheld the power of Congress to establish the Federal Reserve System for the purpose of controlling currency and the money supply. Thus, by default, it did delegate some of its Article I powers to the newly created Federal Reserve System.[10]

Another case, in 1935, also underscored the legal status of the Federal Reserve's currency-issuing powers. In this case, Norman versus the Baltimore and Ohio Railroad, the court ruled that Congress had constitutional authority to ban the payment of US government debts in the form of gold. This was shortly after the passage of the Gold Reserve Act in 1933, which had eliminated the private ownership of gold for monetary purposes, and it had abrogated the gold payment clauses in Treasury bonds and other securities. Even private contracts, which required payment in gold, could not be enforced. The effect of the Supreme Court's decision was to redefine paper currency as legal tender, since at that point, paper currency and checks were the only forms of money available.[11]

This decision by the court appeared to settle the question of the constitutionality of paper money and of the agency issuing it, namely, the Federal Reserve System.

An Explanation of the Balance Sheet of the Central Bank

An analysis over time of the balance sheets of the central bank provides considerable information on the course of monetary policy. In addition, it offers insight into the condition of the economy, which leads to monetary policy actions.

The two dates shown for the balance sheets of the Federal Reserve System on Pages 184–185 are selected to show the financial condition of the central bank at the beginning of the great recession (November 21, 2007),and the most current at the time of this writing (March 20, 2013). Changes in the accounts between these two dates show the impact of the downturn on the Federal Reserve as a result of the policies that it pursued between November 2007 and March 2013.

---

[8] McCulloch v. Maryland, 17 U.S. (4 Wheat) 316 (1819). For discussion, see J. K. Lieberman [10].
[9] See Chap. 1, p. 9.
[10] First National Bank v. Fellows, 244 U.S. 416 (1917).
[11] Norman v. Baltimore & Ohio Railroad Co., 294 U.S. 240 (1935).

According to the National Bureau of Economic Research (NBER), which tracks business cycles, the economy began its recovery phase from the recent recession in late 2009. But the recovery has been agonizingly slow and has proceeded in fits and starts, so that many observers, including myself, feel that we are not yet out of the woods. The fragility of the recovery has, in the view of the Fed, made it necessary to continue to pursue accommodative policies to stimulate the economy, and the worry has been that a premature start of tightening policies could sidetrack the recovery and, if strong enough, could send it back into recession. This was the major concern of the "fiscal cliff debate" at the end of 2012 and, to a lesser extent, remains a concern today.

The most striking change between the two dates on pages 184–185 is the growth in total assets from $894.5 billion in November 2007 to $3.2 trillion in March 2013, an increase of 3.6 times. This is the largest increase in the 100-year history of the Federal Reserve, and has gained national attention. In effect, it has resulted from the purchase of securities to stimulate the economy. The increase in the total securities held outright represents $2.1 trillion of the $2.3 trillion overall increase in total assets. Roughly half of this increase is in mortgage-backed securities.

It is also interesting to note that, as of March 2013 the Fed has sold its entire holding of Treasury bills, that is, those with maturities of one year or less. This resulted from the policy of Operation Twist, in which the Fed sold securities in the short-term end of the yield curve while buying equivalent amounts in the middle and longer-term end.

The increase in other assets largely accounts for the remainder of the overall increase in assets, and this would represent holdings of foreign currencies, foreign securities, and some loans made under special arrangements during the recession to nonbank financial institutions. There has also been an increase in Central Bank Liquidity Swaps, which represents Federal Reserve loans of Dollars to other central banks, primarily in Europe, to help them deal with their financial crisis.

One other item worthy of note in reviewing the financial statements is the increase in the Special Drawing Rights Account from $2.2 billion to $5.2 billion. While insignificant in relation to the totals, it is important in that it represents an increase in America's contribution to the International Monetary Fund (IMF). Remember our discussion of the role of the IMF in Chap. 2. As a result of the recent global financial crisis, the G-20 group of nations has urged an expansion of the IMF's role to become more active in assisting countries having economic difficulties, that is, to become more like a world central bank. To meet these enlarged responsibilities, the 188-member nations agreed to an expansion of the IMF's capital to $755 billion.

The Special Drawing Rights Account represents the members' shares of the capital of the IMF, and they can draw on the account to settle transactions with other central banks. The $3.0 billion increase in the account show's America's increased contribution to the capital of the IMF.

Other items of interest in the financial statements are the asset account labeled *Items in the Process of Collection* ($497 million), and its companion account under liabilities, *Deferred Availability Cash Items* ($1,138 million). The net of these two items represents the float in the banking system. The first is a receivable to the Fed.

It represents credit that the Fed has passed to banks, for which it has not collected. The other is the opposite, where the Fed has collected on transactions but has not passed the credit to the institution to which it is due. Thus, it is a liability to the Fed. Two to three decades ago, the balances in these accounts were much higher, on the order to $20 billion or more. This was due to the widespread use of paper checks and other paper-based means of payment that took much longer to collect. Their reduction indicates the improvement in the efficiency of the payment system, largely due to the growth of electronic means of payment, under which there is virtually no float.

Finally, one other item should be noted in the capital accounts. The paid-in capital account ($27.5 billion) represents the 3 % of member-bank capital and surplus that is required under the Federal Reserve Act to capitalize the Federal Reserve Banks. The other capital accounts are kept equivalent to paid-in capital to represent the other 3 % that the act authorized the Fed to call for if needed. As we noted in our discussion of this issue in Chap. 11, the additional 3 % has never been needed.

References

1. Bernanke B, Laubach T, Mishkin FS, Posen AS (1999) Inflation targeting: lessons from international experience. Princeton University Press, Princeton
2. Greider W (1987) Secrets of the temple: how the Federal Reserve runs the country. Simon & Schuster, New York, p 539
3. Silber WL (2012) Volcker: the triumph of persistence. Bloomsbury Press, New York, pp 125, 180, 237
4. Wood GS (2009) Empire of liberty: a history of the early republic, 1789–1815. Oxford University Press, Oxford, p 162
5. Reinhart C, Rogoff K (2010) Growth in a time of debt. The American Economic Review: Papers & Proceedings 100, May 2010, pp 573–578
6. Polin R, Herndon T, Ash M (2013) Does high public debt consistently stifle economic growth? A critique of Reinhard and Rogoff. Political Economy Research Institute, University of Massachusetts, Amherst, 15 Apr 2013
7. Krugman P (2013) How the case for austerity has crumbled. The New York Review of Books, 6 June 2013, pp 67–73
8. Mankiw NG (2006) Macroeconomics, 6th edn. Worth, New York
9. Corwin ES (1978) The constitution and what it means today 1978 edn, Fifth Printing, Revised by H.W. Chase and C.R. Ducat. (Princeton NJ, Princeton University Press, 1990), p 95
10. Lieberman JK (1992) The evolving constitution. Random House, New York, p 147

Chapter 13
A Career with the Federal Reserve: Some Personal Reminiscences

In earlier chapters, I have related some of my personal experiences in the Federal Reserve as they relate to monetary policy, bank supervision, relations with Congress, and other federal agencies. In this final chapter, I have collected some remembrances of other events and circumstances that were of special interest to me at the time. I hope the reader will find them of interest as well.

During my career with the Federal Reserve System, I had the unique opportunity to be involved in a variety of aspects of both Fed operations and policy. Starting out as a research economist at the Richmond reserve bank, I participated in the monetary policy process and attended several meetings of the FOMC with the President of that bank. In this role, I met and observed the style of William McChesney Martin, formerly the Fed Chairman.

While at Richmond, I found that I particularly enjoyed the opportunity to meet and speak to groups about the role of the Federal Reserve. This included invitations to meet and talk to students in colleges and universities as a guest lecturer. I found, to my surprise, that in those days of the 1960s, there was little knowledge about the Federal Reserve and little interest in it except in the banking industry itself where they were subject to its regulations, or in a narrow subset of the academic world.

All that has changed radically in recent decades as the Fed has taken on a much more visible role in the economy, and that has occurred for a wide variety of reasons, which I have discussed in earlier chapters.

But I was fascinated with both the Fed's history and its growing significance in the economy of the country. I believed from the beginning that it would be to our advantage for the public to have a better understanding of what we do and why we do it. That is why, then as well as now, I have welcomed the opportunity to explain the Fed to others. As we approach the 100th anniversary of the passage of the Federal Reserve Act, on December 23, 1913, I believe the need for that understanding is greater than ever!

W.H. Wallace, *The American Monetary System: An Insider's View of Financial Institutions, Markets and Monetary Policy*, DOI 10.1007/978-3-319-02907-8_13,

My Relationship with Arthur F. Burns

As a result of my initiation at Richmond, I became interested in other aspects of Federal Reserve operations, and after about six years at Richmond, I was made aware of the fact that the Board of Governors was searching for a person to take on a new position entitled Budget Director. I didn't know what this might entail, but I let it be known that I was interested. I was invited to the Board in Washington and was interviewed by several senior staff persons regarding the job. Then, I was advised that the Chairman would like to see me. I was surprised, but pleased, because I had not met Dr. Arthur Burns, who had become Chairman. My relationship with him ultimately turned out to be one of the highlights of my years with the Fed.

I was told that the reason the Chairman was personally interested in this position was that he was required to testify routinely before both the House and Senate Banking Committees, and these committees were headed by critics of the Fed, such as Congressman Wright Patman of Texas and Senator William Proxmire of Wisconsin. Both of these individuals and other members of the committees liked to pick at the Fed over details of the Fed's budget, and particularly its discretionary expenditures, which in many instances they thought were wasteful uses of the public's funds. Burns did not know about these expenditures and was embarrassed to have them brought out during his testimony, and then to be picked up by the press. Therefore, his plan was to set up an internal budget control office, which he likened to a mini version of the OMB. I was told that he was looking for a tough guy to run it who would not only exercise control over all discretionary expenditures but would also shield him from having to deal with what he thought was a trivial problem. All he wanted to discuss with the Congress was monetary policy.

Arthur Burns was an intimidating individual, and he did not put new acquaintances at ease very quickly. We nevertheless had a relatively cordial conversation, and when it became time for me to leave, he walked to the door with me and said, "Now, Mr. Wallace, you are a mild-mannered individual, and I am not sure you are quite right for this job. What I want is a seven-foot son-of-a-bitch, who can stand in the doorway and say no to Reserve Bank presidents and other officials if you believe they are spending the Fed's money inappropriately."

I went home thinking I had probably blown that opportunity. So you can imagine my surprise when, about a week later, I received a letter from the Board offering me the job. I had passed muster with Chairman Burns.

I sank into the job pretty quickly and began to establish cordial working relationships with all 12 Reserve bank presidents and their staffs regarding budgeting processes and the handling of sensitive expenditures. But I had no feedback from the Chairman himself and always wondered whether I was satisfying him with my performance in the job. That changed one day when I was called into his office just after he had returned from a trip to Cincinnati, where he was asked to make a few remarks at the dedication of the newly completed Cincinnati branch of the Fed. He said to me, "Mr. Wallace, I have just discovered the Cincinnati Branch! I want to know why you let them build such an extravagant building. I'm sure I will have to explain it to the Congress when and if they discover it."

I thought, "Wow! The scope of my job has just changed, and I didn't know it." I tried to explain to him that the Board, of which he is chair, approved the budget for that building, and I had no involvement in it. He countered with, "Yes, but you're supposed to be watching these things!" So, I took it upon myself to expand my role in watching more closely all aspects of the budget and expenditures process, including capital expenditures, and as a result, we were able to keep the Chairman off the hot seat. The Cincinnati Branch never became an issue with the Congress.

During the next few years, several opportunities arose for me to return to one of the Reserve banks in a senior-level position, which I ultimately wanted to do because of the opportunities that exist in those locations for more community involvement, which I enjoyed, plus the fact that pay was better by far than at the Washington level, where we were stuck in the equivalent of the federal government pay scale.

That opportunity arose after I had been at the Board for about three years. I was offered the position of First Vice President and Chief Operating Officer of the Federal Reserve Bank of Philadelphia. I knew and admired the President of that Reserve bank, David Eastburn, also an economist, and I knew that I would enjoy working with him. I went to Philadelphia, met with their Board, and told Dave Eastburn that I would accept the job.

The next day, I was back at my office in Washington when I received a phone call from Burns' secretary. She said, "The Chairman wants to see you!" I asked if she knew what he wanted to see me about, and she said, "I think it's the Philadelphia thing." I knew then that I had a problem on my hands.

I went to the Chairman's office, and he said, "Now, I want you to sit down here and explain to me why you want to go to Philadelphia." I tried to explain that it represented job advancement, that I had gone as far as I could at the Board without being appointed to the Board itself, and that, of course, is a political thing. Burns took a few puffs on his pipe and said, "Well, just let me tell you that what you do here is far more important than anything you will ever do in Philadelphia. What's more, you have not gone as far as you can here. I am prepared to create a special position of Staff Director for you, which will advance you over the rest of the Board's staff."

I was in a dilemma. I went back to my office and called Dave Eastburn and said, "You'll never guess what just happened." He said, "Yes, I think I can. You've been to see the Chairman. I had guessed that we weren't going to be able to get you away from him."

Finally, I knew where I stood with Arthur Burns, and it made me feel good, but I always wondered whether I made the right decision by staying at the Board as Staff Director rather than going to Philadelphia.

Relations with Other Agencies and Foreign Central Banks

During the time that I was on the Board's staff, I maintained close working relationships with a number of other federal agencies. These included, within the Treasury Department, the Bureau of Public Debt, the Bureau of Government Financial

Operations, The Bureau of Engraving and Printing, The Bureau of the Mint, and the Secret Service (which was then in the Treasury). In addition, I had liaisons with the Department of Agriculture, because the Federal Reserve processes food stamps, the FBI on bank-related security issues, and the National Security Agency (NSA) on the protection of sensitive economic data.

The concern about counterfeiting of the currency reached a high level during this time because of the proliferation of color copiers. Central banks around the world became alarmed on the suspicion that these copiers would bring the art of counterfeiting into everyone's homes. Experience had shown that, particularly in the United States, virtually anything that even looks like money will pass. There are advantages and disadvantages to this fact. On the one hand, it indicates a high level of confidence in the currency, in that users do not have to question its legitimacy every time they use it. But, the downside is that counterfeiters can get by with even the most rudimentary forgeries that are easy to produce.

Two distinct efforts began within the Federal Reserve and the Treasury as a result of this concern: (1) the proposal to produce a Dollar coin that could eliminate a substantial portion of the paper currency in circulation, and thereby reduce counterfeiting, and (2) a variety of proposals to make the circulating paper currency more difficult to reproduce by counterfeiters.

A Dollar Coin

The first attempt at the Dollar coin since the old original cartwheels–or Eisenhower Dollars, which didn't circulate–was the Susan B. Anthony Dollar. The Mint seized upon the idea of the Anthony Dollar and pushed hard in Congress to get it approved. The Fed was not enthusiastic about it because in our view, nothing would make a Dollar coin circulate (even a small one) unless action was taken to remove the one-dollar note from circulation.

The Board was asked to testify on this situation before the congressional committees on government operations, which had supervisory authority over the Mint. Normally, when the Board is asked to testify on any issue before Congress, the Chairman will testify, or will designate another member of the Board to do so. In the case of the Anthony Dollar, none of the Board members was willing to testify, so I, as Staff Director, was assigned the task. This was the first time in many years that a staff person had been asked to testify on behalf of the Federal Reserve before a congressional committee.

In my official statement, I testified that the Fed's position was that we did not favor the issuance of the coin because we did not believe it would circulate, and that, while it would save millions of the public's money, we were not prepared to recommend the elimination of the one-dollar note. We felt that, if that recommendation were made, it should come from the Treasury, which has the ultimate overall responsibility for the nation's currency and coin. (I was expecting to be kicked under the table by Stella Hackel, the Director of the Mint, who was sitting next to me, and who was a strong advocate of the Anthony Dollar. But we were good friends, and she did not kick me.)

In the questioning that followed, notwithstanding the fact that I thought I had made the Fed's position perfectly clear in my prepared remarks, I was asked by committee Chairman Frank Annunzio, "Mr. Wallace, why are you trying to shove this coin down peoples' throats?" This was just another of many examples I had observed that members of Congress pay no attention to what is going on. So I repeated my remarks. But, despite my position, my name will forever be associated with the Susan B. Anthony Dollar. I was even invited to the White House for President Jimmy Carter's official introduction of the coin.

It was on that occasion that I met Susan B. Anthony, the great-niece of the original. She told me that we had made her aunt look too pretty on the coin. She remembered her aunt as "a hard looking woman," not at all as pretty as the one on the coin.

As we expected, the Anthony Dollar did not circulate, and the whole episode is looked upon by the public as an ill-conceived notion in the first place and a total disaster. A little known fact, however, is that the Treasury made a handsome profit on it. About 850 million of the coins were minted at a cost of about $0.03 each. Around 250 million went into circulation immediately, never to be seen again. The remaining 600 million sat for years in bags on the floors of the Federal Reserve Bank vaults, until the Treasury finally retrieved most of them and melted them down in their assay offices. But, if you do the arithmetic, it is obvious that as banks pay the face value of the coins, $250 million in revenue was received by the Treasury, while the cost of production for the entire 850 million was $25.5 million, earning the Treasury a net profit of about $224.5 million.

Currency Counterfeiting

The other effort, that of protecting the currency from counterfeiting, turned out to be one of the most interesting projects in which I was involved during my entire Fed career. I attended a meeting on this subject at the New York reserve bank, at which the directors of currency printing from the Bank of England and the Bank of Canada were present. They both approached me and advised me that the governors of their central banks had been talking with Chairman Burns about forming a committee made up of the central banks of the English-speaking countries to address the issue of protecting the currency against forgeries, particularly those that might be produced by color copiers.

When I returned to Washington from that meeting, Chairman Burns told me that the committee was being formed, and that they would also be asking Australia and New Zealand to join with the United States, Britain, and Canada in the effort. He said that it would be given a high priority among the five central banks involved and that he wanted me to be on the committee. I was asked to contact the Bureau of Engraving and Printing (BEP) and the Secret Service (which has the legal responsibility for enforcing the anticounterfeit laws) and ask them to participate. They both agreed that their respective directors should be members of the committee.

Much to my surprise, a couple of days later, I was asked to come to the Chairman's office to discuss the committee. I didn't know what was up but when I got there, Burns told me that the heads of the central banks had agreed that an American would chair the committee. He then said, "Therefore, you're going to chair it." I protested, "But, Mr. Chairman, I'm not familiar with all the technical aspects of currency production, and we're going to have the Directors of the BEP and the Secret Service on the committee, both of whom are more qualified than I am on this subject." He said, "That doesn't matter. I'm told that both of those individuals have particular axes to grind, and you're a neutral party. So you're going to chair it! Any questions?" I said, "No, sir, I'll be happy to do it."

As soon as I returned to my office, I received a call from the Director of the Bank of England's currency printing works, Michael Cubbage. He said, "I have just heard that you're our chairman. I am delighted with this and look forward to working with you. And, by the way, don't worry about the fact that you don't have a background in this area. We'll bring you along with whatever you need to know." Michael and I became fast friends during the project and remain so today. I received similar messages from the other central banks and, to my surprise, from the directors of both the BEP and the Secret Service. I wasn't quite sure what I had gotten myself in for because here I was chairing an international committee on which virtually everyone else knew more about the subject than I did.

The committee immediately went to work, and, over the next couple of years, we examined every conceivable aspect of the ink, the paper (or other substance) on which the currency is printed, the design and color of the notes, etc. We even hired a consumer research firm to test public reaction to certain changes in design and color of the notes, etc.

We knew that the recommendations our committee would make might not necessarily be uniform among the countries, but as far as protective features were concerned, they would ultimately turn out to be quite similar. We also knew that the recommendations would have to go to the Secretary of the Treasury in the United States because the Secretary has ultimate decision authority over any changes in design, color, denomination, or any other features regarding all US currency and coin. We therefore expected that there would be political issues to consider when we got to that point.

While the other countries also faced similar approval hurdles, the central banks in all of the other nations have considerably more delegated authority to implement changes than we do in the United States. For example, in all the other countries involved in this effort, the decision was made early on to eliminate the lowest denomination of paper currency – the Dollar in Canada and Australia and the Pound in the United Kingdom – and to substitute a coin of those denominations. These changes were made essentially under the authority of the central banks. To have made this change in the United States would have required an act of Congress and would have invited a firestorm of opposition. While we were able to show that such a change would have saved American taxpayers millions, and that it probably would also have resulted in increased circulation of the two-dollar note, as it did in Canada, we never had a Secretary of the Treasury who was willing to step up and face that task.

For all these reasons, the other countries were able to implement their changes much earlier than we were. In the United States, it was not until almost 15 years after the start of this project that we were able to implement some of the most important changes that we recommended. These included enlarging the portrait on the notes, and moving it off-center, the implementation of a moldmade watermark in the paper (which cannot be picked up by copiers), the use of microprinting around the portrait on some denominations, the use of a reflective seal on the note, which changes color in a various angles of light, the implementation of additional colors in the note, and the implementation of certain covert changes involving ingredients in both the ink and the paper that will cause copies of the notes to be visibly impaired and recognized as counterfeits.

Interestingly, the use of colors in the notes turned out to be one of the most controversial of our proposed changes, and we were not able to get approval for some of the more highly visible color changes we proposed. Also, the proposal to change the sizes of notes for different denominations was rejected. And, finally, one of the more important changes we recommended, to change the substrate on which the note is printed from paper to another substance, was rejected. In this regard, a material developed for us by DuPont (now known as Tyvek, which is now popularly used in sealing buildings under construction) was tested. This material was virtually indestructible, and we thought highly of it for the heavily used denominations. In fact, the Australians adopted this material in certain denominations of their currency, and it has worked out well.

Of course, many of these proposed changes invited the comments as well as the objections of various interest groups and lobbyists. The paper manufacturers, such as Crane, which has had the US currency paper business since the BEP was established, wanted us to continue to use paper. Organizations representing the vision-impaired were concerned because their constituency depends upon the tactile feel of the currency to detect authenticity as well as denomination.

On one occasion, our committee was discussing the depth of the engraving of the currency. The depth is measured in microns, and I did not know a micron from a country mile. We had engaged in what I thought was an interminable discussion of what depth would be most effective in deterring forgeries, that is, whether it should be 20, 30, or 40 µm in depth. After listening to this discussion for hours, I finally blurted out during a break in the discussion, "I think we should go with 30 µm!" There was dead silence around the table as everyone looked at me. Then my friend Michael Cubbage, said, "Well! Our chairman says 30 µm. Let's go with it and make it our standard." I thought to myself, "My gosh! What have I done? I don't know anything about this." But we went with 30 µm, and to my knowledge, the depth of engraving on the currencies of these nations is still at 30 µm.

End of the Burns Era

Notwithstanding what I believe were the outstanding contributions that Arthur Burns made to the Federal Reserve System, his tenure with the Fed ended on a down note. Many observers look back upon his years as Chairman as the years in which the central bank lost control of inflation. Also, because of his close association with President Richard Nixon, he will forever be viewed as having presided over an easing of monetary policy to assure the reelection of Nixon in 1972.

While I have never attached credibility to this latter allegation, it is not possible to prove that it was not part of his motivation at the time. Knowing the integrity of the man and his never-ending determination not to allow the central bank to be involved in politics, or even the appearance of political favoritism, I find it very difficult to believe that he consciously allowed monetary policy to be determined by any motivation other than that which he perceived as best for the American economy.

On the broader allegation that Burns allowed inflation to get out of hand, it is hard to say that there is no truth to the charge. We discussed in detail in Chap. 12 the difficulties that three presidential administrations in succession (Nixon, Ford, and Carter) had in understanding how to control inflation. Burns certainly had the commanding control over the FOMC during his entire tenure that he could have initiated the same draconian policies that Paul Volcker later did. It can only be concluded that he did not see the need to do so, perhaps out of concern for the volatility of the markets that it would create, or perhaps because he thought the Fed could not get by with it during the Democratic administration of Jimmy Carter, although Volcker later proved this latter assumption to be incorrect. In Burns's own personal views, he abhorred inflation, and it is unfortunate that he is remembered as having not been able to control it.

The Interregnum of G. William Miller

When President Carter declined to reappoint Burns as chairman in 1978, he resigned his seat on the Board and went to the American Enterprise Institute for a brief period before being appointed as Ambassador to West Germany in 1981.

G. William Miller, a Democrat who had supported Carter, was in line for some position in the administration. He had been a successful CEO of Textron and had served a term as class C director of the Federal Reserve Bank of Boston. Carter appointed him as Fed Chairman, which came as a surprise to many in the Federal Reserve System. As I noted in Chap. 12, Miller was the only noneconomist to serve as chair since William McChesney Martin.

Miller knew that he was not an expert on monetary policy, as well as many other things for which the Fed had responsibility, and he was open about it from the beginning. As a result, he leaned heavily on the staff for their input. Most of the senior staff appreciated that fact and respected him for it. We all recognized that he was a quick learner.

One episode occurred that caused me to think of him as a brilliant individual. He was invited to go to Richmond to give the dedication speech for the opening of that Reserve Bank's new building. He invited me to go with him on that trip because he knew that I knew many people there. As we rode the short 110 miles from Washington to Richmond, Miller and his wife were sitting in the back seat and I was on the front seat with the driver. He was working on papers, which I assumed to be the speech he was to give. I figured that if he needed any input from me, he would ask. As we drove into Richmond, and were literally five min from the bank, Miller folded his papers away. Then, he turned to me and asked, "Bill, what should I talk to these people about?" I thought, "My gosh! He hasn't written a speech!" I knew and he knew that there would be hundreds of people there, and there would be press coverage.

I sputtered a few thoughts like tell them how beautiful the building is and congratulate them on it, remind them that buildings are for people, and then compliment the people who work there. When he got to the podium, he did follow my advice but that took only about two minutes. Then he launched into one of the most beautiful speeches I had ever heard, totally off the cuff. He addressed monetary policy, the economic problems we faced with rampant inflation, which was true at that time, and other issues, which made him come across as a seasoned and well-informed leader of the Federal Reserve.

Bill Miller was like that in everything he did during his brief tenure as Chairman, which lasted only 18 months. By the time he left, he had impressed a large number of people. The end of his tenure came about because President Carter decided to purge his cabinet in mid-summer 1979. He was besieged by the economic problems of the time, not the least of which was inflation. So one of the cabinet officials he fired was Michael Blumenthal, the Secretary of the Treasury. He immediately appointed Miller as Treasury Secretary.

I was in London at the time these purges were announced, and I was in the hotel bar with my friends from England and Canada as we heard the news on TV. This was the evening before we were due to return home. I was asked who I thought Carter would appoint to replace Blumenthal. I said that, in view of Miller's close relationship with the President, it would not surprise me at all to see him appoint Miller. So I was asked, "Well, then, who would replace Miller at the Fed?" I remember saying that, in my mind, there is only one person who makes sense, especially at this time, and that is Paul Volcker. I didn't know until I got back to Washington the next afternoon, and saw the headlines in the newsstands in the airport that both of my predictions had been correct. I thought, "Gee, I wish I had put some money on that." It would have been the first time I was right on two counts.

The Courage of Paul Volcker

Despite my affection and respect for Arthur Burns, and my brief but rewarding relationship with Bill Miller, the highlight of my experience in the Fed focuses on the chairmanship of Paul Volcker. To this day, I believe that Paul Volcker was the best Chairman the Federal Reserve ever had, including the two who have followed him. He accomplished more for the country than any other central bank Chairman, and as anyone who follows the news is aware, he is still actively involved, at age 86, in trying to bring about improvements in the financial system and in the economy at large.

There are two major accomplishments that Volcker is remembered for in earlier years. The first is his role in assisting countries to make the transition away from the Bretton Woods agreements and the establishment of a floating exchange rate system in the late 1960s and early 1970s. This was while he was Under Secretary of the Treasury in the Nixon administration. The second is his leadership in attacking and conquering the problem of inflation in the United States in the early 1980s, just after having been named as Chairman of the Fed.

Both of these episodes are covered extensively in earlier chapters – the first in Chap. 2 and the second in Chap. 12. Also, Volcker himself discusses his involvement in these events in his book *Changing Fortunes*, which is referenced in the text. Further detailed discussion is found in William Silber's book *Volcker*, which is also referenced. I have discussed my own involvement with the Chairman and with the Board during the tight money period of the early 1980s when the attack on inflation took place. Therefore, it seems unnecessary to repeat those details here.

Paul Volcker is commonly accorded hero status because of what he accomplished in the fight against inflation. Both of his successors, Alan Greenspan and Ben Bernanke, have given him credit for this. This accolade is justified in my opinion because inflation has truthfully been under control since his actions were taken in the 1980s.

This is why I have designated Volcker as the best Chairman the Fed has had because he knew what needed to be done, he did it, and he could not be persuaded to alter his course regardless of the political pressure and criticism that was heaped upon him at the time. I have observed this trait of stubbornness in my personal relationships with him. Once Volcker has made up his mind that a given course of action is proper, it is virtually impossible to get him to change his mind. This trait has served him well. He knew on several occasions that actions he was taking could put him in jeopardy with the Congress and the President. But he did what he believed was best for the country in the long run and was proved right.

Since leaving the Fed chairmanship, Volcker has actively participated in advising presidents and congressional committees on matters related to banking, bank regulation, and economic policy in general. He is responsible for first articulating what has become known as the "Volcker Rule" and caused it to be written into the Dodd-Frank bill in 2010. In this rule, he advocates that banks not be allowed to gamble with customers' money, or what is more politely called "proprietary trading." He believes that if institutions wish to engage in such high-risk trading, those activities must be sealed off from mainline banking activities through tight corporate structures or firewalls that will protect depositors' money from any losses that such trading might cause. Even though regulators are having difficulty defining the distinction between proprietary trading and ordinary market-making, which banks must do to properly invest customer funds, the clarification will have to come soon because the Volcker Rule in now law, and the deadline is looming for its implementation and enforcement.

In the years I have known Paul Volcker, I have always perceived him as being on a mission to save the world from itself. That world is mostly the financial world, but in recent years, he has branched out even further. He has founded "The Volcker Alliance" and placed on its Board the top thinkers in the business and financial worlds. His objective is to improve the quality of public service. He has always had a deep-seated conviction that public agencies don't work very well because the people who run them are not the best. That may be attributable to poor compensation, low standards for employment, unclear missions, lack of ability to get rid of nonperformers, etc. He intends to attack all these causes and to bring about change. I have recently had some correspondence with him about this, and he is as enthusiastic about this new mission at age 86 as he has ever been in his lifelong dedication to the American economy and the public. He will be successful, I predict, as in everything else he has done.

Postscript

Part Federal Reserve history, part Money and Banking textbook, and part personal memoir, this book details the observations and experiences of Dr. William Wallace over his lengthy career influencing US and world monetary policy. Unfortunately, Dr. Wallace did not live to see publication, as he passed away unexpectedly in his sleep just prior to the final proofing process (and just a few weeks after his 80th birthday). In editing and proofing his book, we have attempted to keep to Bill's voice whenever possible. We intentionally did not update any of the tables or data herein, instead preferring to preserve the manuscript in the form it was presented to us. To our knowledge, the factual statements made in the text are correct as of December 1, 2013. We sincerely hope that Dr. Wallace is pleased with the published version of his work, and we hope that you will find the same pleasure in reading it that we do.

This book is an outgrowth of Dr. Wallace's teaching at the University of North Texas, where he taught in the Economics Department for over a decade. The book began as his notes for a graduate course in Monetary Policy and grew to manuscript-length based on his interactions with students, faculty, friends, and colleagues, as well as his continued work as a consultant. Undoubtedly, Bill would have thanked many people for their critical input in the writing process, but, sadly, we do not have access to a list of those who assisted him. If you are one of those lucky few who had the opportunity to communicate with Dr. Wallace on the subject of his career, his life, and/or this manuscript, please accept our genuine thanks; you all had a part in the writing of Dr. Wallace's final published work. As humble as Bill was, he would have given you all the credit.

W.H. Wallace, *The American Monetary System: An Insider's View of Financial Institutions, Markets and Monetary Policy*, DOI 10.1007/978-3-319-02907-8, © Springer International Publishing Switzerland 2013

About the Author

William H. Wallace received bachelors and masters degrees from the University of Mississippi and the Ph.D. in economics from the University of Illinois. He served on the faculties of the University of Illinois and Duke University prior to joining the Federal Reserve System.

At the Federal Reserve he was Vice President in Research at the Federal Reserve Bank of Richmond, later Staff Director at the Board of Governors of the Federal Reserve System in Washington DC, and finally, First Vice President and Chief Operating Officer of the Federal Reserve Bank of Dallas.

Since retirement from the Federal Reserve, he has taught at New England College in Henniker NH, Israel College in Tel Aviv, the Institute of Economics of the Russian Academy of Sciences in Moscow, and Old Dominion University in Norfolk VA, where he was also Dean of the College of Business and Public Administration.

He has been a consultant to foreign central banks under the sponsorship of the U.S. Agency for International Development, in Serbia, Kenya and Ukraine, and has consulted on banking and regulatory issues with several U.S. law firms representing American financial institutions.

He has published a number of articles in economic journals and in Federal Reserve publications, and a book, *Measuring Price Changes*, published by the Federal Reserve Bank of Richmond. In addition, he has published op-ed pieces in area newspapers and speaks frequently to business and professional groups in the DFW area. He is Adjunct Professor of Economics at the University of North Texas.

W.H. Wallace, *The American Monetary System: An Insider's View of Financial Institutions, Markets and Monetary Policy*, DOI 10.1007/978-3-319-02907-8, © Springer International Publishing Switzerland 2013

Bibliography

Books

1. Ahamed L (2009) Lords of finance: the bankers that broke the world. Penguin, New York
2. Bagehot W (1873) Lombard Street: a description of the money market. Scribner-Armstrong; reprinted by Richard D. Irwin, Inc., Homewood, IL, 1962, with new introduction by Frank C. Genovese
3. Bair S (2013) Bull by the Horns. The Free Press, New York
4. Bernanke BS (2000) Essays on the great depression. Princeton University Press, Princeton
5. Bernanke BS, Laubach T, Mishkin FS, Posen AS (1999) Inflation targeting: lessons from international experience. Princeton University Press, Princeton
6. Bernstein PL (2000) The power of gold: the history of an obsession. Wiley, New York
7. Board of Governors of the Federal Reserve System (2005) Purposes and functions of the Federal Reserve System, 9th edn. Board of Governors of the Federal Reserve System, Washington, DC
8. Bordo MD (ed) (1998) Money, history and international finance: essays in honor of Anna Jacobson Schwartz. University of Chicago Press, Chicago
9. Bruner RF, Carr SD (2007) The Panic of 1907. Wiley, New York
10. Burrough B, Helyar J (1989) Barbarians at the gate: the fall of RJR-Nabisco. Harper & Row, New York
11. Chandler LV (1958) Benjamin strong, central banker. The Brookings Institution, Washington, DC
12. Chernow R (2004) Alexander Hamilton. The Penguin Press, New York
13. Corwin ES (1978) The constitution and what it means today 1978 edn, Fifth Printing, Revised by H. W. Chase and C. R. Ducat. (Princeton NJ, Princeton University Press, 1990)
14. Ferguson N (2008) The ascent of money: a financial history of the world. The Penguin Press, New York
15. Friedman M, Schwartz AJ (1963) A monetary history of the United States, 1867–1960. Princeton University Press, Princeton
16. Greider W (1987) Secrets of the temple: how the federal reserve runs the country. Simon & Schuster, New York
17. Greenspan A (2007) The age of turbulence: adventures in a new world. The Penguin Press, New York
18. Hubbard RG, O'Brien AP (2012) Money, banking, and the financial system. Prentice-Hall, Boston
19. Kaufman H (2000) On money and markets: a Wall Street memoir. McGraw-Hill, New York

W.H. Wallace, *The American Monetary System: An Insider's View of Financial Institutions, Markets and Monetary Policy*, DOI 10.1007/978-3-319-02907-8, © Springer International Publishing Switzerland 2013

20. Keynes JM (1936) The general theory of employment, interest and money. Harcourt, Brace, New York
21. Kindleberger CP (2000) Manias, panics and crashes: a history of financial crises, 4th edn. Wiley Investment Classics, New York
22. Lewis M (2010) The big short. W.W. Norton, New York
23. Lieberman JK (1992) The evolving constitution. Random House, New York
24. Lind M (2012) Land of promise: an economic history of the United States. Harper Collins, New York
25. Lowenstein R (2000) When genius failed: the rise and fall of long-term capital management. Random House, New York
26. Mankiw NG (2006) Macroeconomics, 6th edn. Worth Publishers, New York
27. Mayer M (1993) Nightmare on Wall Street: Salomon Brothers and the corruption of the marketplace. Simon and Shuster, New York
28. McKinley V (2011) Financing failure: a century of bailouts. The Independent Institute, Oakland
29. Meacham J (2008) American lion: Andrew Jackson in the White House. Random House, New York
30. Meltzer AH (2003) A history of the federal reserve, volume I: 1913–1951. The University of Chicago Press, Chicago
31. Meltzer AH (2009) A history of the federal reserve, volume II, book 1: 1951–1969. The University of Chicago Press, Chicago
32. Meltzer AH (2009) A history of the federal reserve, volume II, book 2: 1970–1986. The University of Chicago Press, Chicago
33. Meulendyke A-M (1998) Purposes and functions of the Federal Reserve System. Board of Governors of the Federal Reserve System, Washington, DC
34. Mishkin FS (2010) The economics of money, banking and financial markets, 9th edn. Addison-Wesley, Boston
35. Paul R (2009) End the fed. Grand Central Publishing, New York
36. Paulson HM (2010) On the brink: inside the race to stop the collapse of the global financial system. The Hachette Book Group, New York
37. Rand A (1957) Atlas shrugged. Penguin, New York
38. Schumpeter JA (1959) History of economic analysis. Oxford University Press, New York
39. Siedman LW (1993) Full faith and credit: the great S&L debacle and other Washington sagas. Times Books, New York
40. Silber WL (2012) Volcker: the triumph of persistence. Bloomsbury Press, New York
41. Smith RC, Walter I (2003) Global banking, 2nd edn. Oxford University Press, New York
42. Sorkin AR (2009) Too big to fail: the inside story of how Wall Street and Washington fought to save the financial system – and themselves. The Penguin Group, New York
43. Steil B (2013) The battle of Bretton Woods: John Maynard Keynes, Harry Dexter White, and the making of a new world order. Princeton University Press, Princeton
44. Stewart JB (1991) Den of thieves. Simon & Shuster, New York
45. Stiglitz JE (2012) The price of inequality: how today's divided society endangers our future. W. W. Norton, New York
46. Thornton H (1802) An inquiry into the nature and effects of the paper credit of Great Britain. Reprinted by Augustus Kelly, 1962 New York, NY, USA
47. U. S. Central Intelligence Agency (2010) World Factbook, Langley, VA, USA
48. Volcker P, Gyohten T (1992) Changing fortunes: the world's money and the threat to American leadership. Times Books, New York
49. Wolman D (2012) The end of money: counterfeiters, preachers, techies, dreamers – and the coming cashless society. DaCapo Press, Boston
50. Wolff EN (2004) Recent trends in living standards in the United States. Edward Elgar Publishing, London
51. Wood GS (2009) Empire of liberty: a history of the early republic, 1789–1815. Oxford University Press, Oxford

Papers and Articles

Ackerman A (2012) SEC arms itself to better track trades. The Wall Street Journal, 12 July 2012

Bank for International Settlements, Basel Committee on Banking Supervision, Basel III (2010) International framework for liquidity risk measurement, Basel, Dec 2010

Eaglesham J, Justin B (2010) SEC to target bank 'Window Dressing'. Financial Times, London, 17 Sept 2010

Hackenthal A, Reinhard HS (2004) Financing patterns: measurement concepts and empirical results. J.W. Goethe-Universitat working paper No. 125, Jan 2004

Krugman P (2013) How the case for austerity has crumbled. The New York Review of Books, 6 June 2013

Polin R, Herndon T, Ash M (2013) Does high public debt consistently stifle economic growth? A critique of Reinhard and Rogoff. Political Economy Research Institute, University of Massachusetts, Amherst, 15 April 2013

Reinhart C, Rogoff K (2010) Growth in a time of debt. The American Economic Review: Papers & Proceedings 100, May 2010

Newspapers

Barron's. Dow Jones, Inc., 16 July 2012

The Economist, vol 397, Mar 11, 2005; vol 399, Apr 30, 2008; vol 400, July 29, 2008; vol 401, 16 Oct 2009

The Institutional Investor Magazine. Dec 1997

The New York Times. Risk builds as junk bonds boom, 16 Aug 2012

The Richmond Times Dispatch, 22–24 Jan 1998

The Wall Street Journal. Treasury decides to offer floating-rate notes, 2 Aug 2012

The Wall Street Journal. Taking stock, 12 July 2012

The Wall Street Journal. Century bonds: 100-yr tax-exempt municipals, 3 Feb 2011

The Wall Street Journal. Libor – an important Benchmark, 5 Sept 2007

The Wall Street Journal. Barclays pays $451.6 million settlement, 17 July 2012

The Wall Street Journal. Estimated notional value of derivative contracts: $583 trillion, 13 Apr 2011

The Wall Street Journal. New York Reserve Bank Director, Stephen Friedman, 4 May 2009

Testimony

Bernanke BS (2007) Testimony before the joint economic committee of congress http://www.Federalreserve.gov/boarddocs/speeches/2004

Rivlin AM (2012) The case for preserving the federal reserve's dual mandate. Testimony before the House Financial Services Committee, 8 May 2012

Statistical Releases

Board of Governors of the Federal Reserve System, Statistical Release H.6. Money stock measures, 24 May 2012. www.federalreserve.gov/releases/H.6

Board of Governors of the Federal Reserve System, Statistical Release H.4.1. Factors affecting reserve balances, 24 May 2012. www.federalreserve.gov/releases/H.4.1

Board of Governors of the Federal Reserve System, Statistical Release H.8. Assets and liabilities of commercial banks in the United States, 25 May 2012. www.federalreserve.gov/releases/H.8

Board of Governors of the Federal Reserve System. Annual adjustments for reserve calculations and deposit reporting, regulation D, 26 Oct 2011. www.federalreserve.gov/newsevents/press/bcreg/20111026a.htm

Other Web Sites

www.federalreserve.gov/releases/Z1
www.federalreserve.gov/releases/H.3/hist
www.federalreserve.gov/newsevents/press/monetary
www.treasurydirect.gov
www.treasury.gov/resource-center/data-chart-center/tic/documents mnfh.txt

Supreme Court Cases

First National Bank vs. Fellows, 244 U.S. 416 (1917)
McCulloch vs. Maryland, 4 Wheat 316 (1819)
Norman vs. Baltimore & Ohio Railroad Co., 294 U.S. 240 (1935)

CPSIA information can be obtained at www.ICGtesting.com
Printed in the USA
LVOW05*0302200115

423531LV00003B/7/P